COOKING UP HISTORY

To my greatly missed mother, Elizabeth Ann Clarke and grandmother, 'Madge' Hitchings. Two unique women and fantastic cooks in very different ways. They were the first people in my life to really make me think about food, the food that traversed several generations; from the post-war legacy to the excess and diversity of the 1980s.

COOKING UP HISTORY
Chefs of the Past

by Emma Kay

Agnes Bertha Marshall

PROSPECT BOOKS

2017

This edition published in 2017 by Prospect Books at 26 Parke Road, London, SW13 9NG

© 2017 Emma Kay

The author, Emma Kay, asserts her right to be identified as author of this work in accordance with the Copyright, Designs & Patents Act 1988.

British Library Cataloguing in Publication Data:
A catalogue entry for this book is available from the British Library.

No part of this publication may be reproduced, stored in a retrieval system or transmitted in any form or by any means, electronic, mechanical, photocopying, recording or otherwise, without the prior permission of the copyright holders.

ISBN 978-1-909248-53-3

Set in Adobe Garamond Pro and Cochin by Catheryn Kilgarriff and Rebecca Gillieron.

Printed by the Gutenberg Press Ltd., Malta.

Contents

Acknowledgements 6

Preface 7

Introduction 9

Chapter One
Early Modernist and New World Culinarians 19

Chapter Two
Women Cooks of the Enlightenment and Empire 68

Chapter Three
Eminent Gastronomes 112

Chapter Four
The Overlooked and Uncredited 170

Notes 213

Notes on Illustrations 226

List of Illustrations 228

Bibliography 230

Index 244

Acknowledgements

This is the part of the book where I usually wax lyrical about everyone, including the dog next door, for helping me achieve my writing goals.

Very simply, I am extremely grateful to Catheryn Kilgarriff of Prospect Books, for encouraging me and giving me the opportunity to realise the potential for this book.

Special thanks to my fantastic husband, for all his endless support and tireless childcare, in my absence. Also, to my wonderful little boy, Ben. Without him to provide endless hugs, or his happy ability to entertain himself while I sneak away to write each day, I'm not sure I could have done it. My super female friends and family – you know who you are – also deserve a special mention. Your constant offers of help, words of inspiration and countless cups of coffee (and the odd glass of wine), all of which propelled me forwards, have never been overlooked.

Lastly, I want to thank the millions of talented cooks, cookery writers and cookery teachers worldwide, for contributing such joy to such a diverse and fascinating subject. I look forward to what the culinary future holds.

Preface

Throughout history, as a society we have eaten an extraordinary amount of meals. In fact, we cannot survive without food. Yet, in the United Kingdom anyway, we continue to largely regard it as a non-academic subject. The role of food and the cooking of it has for centuries played a significant, if not vital, role in society. Everywhere we go there are cooks – school dinner ladies preparing lunches for our children, canteen staff serving hungry office workers, street sellers providing on-the-go snacks as we shop, restaurants for us to enjoy family events, romantic meals, work do's and get-togethers with our friends, road-side catering vans and service stations to break the tedium of long car journeys, soup kitchens for the needy, prison kitchens for convicts, hospital kitchens for the sick, railway food carriages, airline meals, bar food to soak up the excess alcohol, cafés to catch-up and chat, bakeries to fill the morning gap on the way to work, convenience stores for the way back, military kitchens to fuel our soldiers, sailors and air crew in times of conflict, food festivals, market stalls, expos…and on and on it goes. Someone, somewhere has had to prepare that food, provide the recipes for the menu, calculate the costs of that food and sell it. Our entire lives are governed by our next meal, often meals that have been shaped and imagined by others.

The culinary historical evidence is vast and we have archives which are rich in material, just waiting for a consolidated narrative. Cooks and their recipe books represent just one small aspect of this. Famous, ground-breaking and noteworthy cooks are an even smaller area of study within this genre. Our celebrity fuelled society, which embraces celebrity chefs, recipe books, flagship restaurants, all engineered by these gastronomic superstars, is not a new phenomenon. It has existed for centuries. I wrote about this subject in my last two books, notably a whole chapter in *The Georgian Kitchen*. What I hadn't anticipated when researching this current book was coming across such a vast field of possibilities. I had thought myself quite knowledgeable about the key influential cooks in society, when actually I had no idea how enormous a subject it was. I mention in the Introduction how my research largely focuses on the Americas and Europe, with a few other countries outside of this referenced. I state my reasons for this, but also strongly believe that there is a wealth of information on other nations to be had, from Asia in particular.

This book pays homage to a culinary past which continues to influence the present, revealing a collection of genuine culinary nuggets (and I don't just mean the chicken variety). It honours all those wonderfully talented men and women, who have contributed to one of life's most fascinating and essential subjects.

Introduction

The *Encyclopedia of Consumption and Consumer Studies* defines individual celebrity as three types: 'Ascribed', which is associated with bloodline or status, such as kings, queens, ladies, emperors etc. – those who automatically command respect by way of heritage. Then there is celebrity that is 'Achieved' through accomplishment and genuine talent – actors, musicians, sports stars and so forth. Finally, 'Celetoids' are people who experience intense though often short-lived moments of fame, as a consequence of their sudden elevation via the media.[1] As any kind of mass media only started to emerge in the eighteenth century, the latter definition has become more of a contemporary phenomenon. It would be easy to say that the majority of the cooks and cookery writers in this book achieved their success through hard work and aptitude, although many early professionals in this field certainly had royal or noble connections that elevated their social status by association. There are numerous examples of dynasties of cooks, family apprenticeships, learning their trade as a consequence of being born into wealthy households where their parents were employed. Or confectioners and pastry cooks with successful businesses that were passed down to their children. As printed material became more widespread and accessible, so too did the potential to achieve fame. Early globalization and advancements across all divisions of science, technology, the arts and education contributed to a boom in new opportunities for cooks, cookery writers, tutors, philosophers and critics on the subject. By the late nineteenth and early twentieth century, recognition through recipe writing alone was not as fruitful. Many culinary experts either owned or headed up restaurants, ran cookery schools and retailed patented merchandise. Writing became more a means to promote all the other aspects of the job and to capitalise on the lucrative market in both educational manuals and high-end cuisine. A smaller group, in a less crowded multimedia landscape and with greater opportunities to stand out, made becoming well-known in a field of study somewhat easier, even a hundred years ago. It reminds me of interviews you listen to by former stars of stage and screen, recalling how a photograph and simple letter addressed to the BBC, with a promise of hard work and dedication, could once open doors for talented struggling performers. These are the same principles that enabled so many cooks and cookery writers to achieve success in the past. There was also scope to invent, explore, develop. Nowadays we have seemingly done it all and either reinvent the past or reshape it to look as if it is something new.

In the twenty-first century celebrity chefs continue to be a globally growing phenomenon. They have become influential leaders in the field of personal branding. The large-scale consumer interest that they generate has enabled them to embed themselves into modern culture, even politics, in order to significantly raise their overall social status. Wind back two hundred years and we still know limited amounts about the way in which people of the nineteenth century consumed and purchased food – an interesting notion when you consider that some two-thirds of all working-class budgets in urban environments was allocated to food during this period. The main contributors to the development of gastronomy are critical to the study of food history. Society still does not lend credit to the hundreds of culinary masters in their fields who were around long before figures such as Gordon Ramsay, Jamie Oliver or even Isabella Beeton. Much can be learned from cooks and cookery writing, in terms of elements of historical daily life, concepts, class cultures, festivities and lifestyles. In this modern age of television, social media and the uncompromising press it is easy to take for granted the notion of celebrity, with its short-lived stardom and undeserving attention, often misguidedly rewarding the most unsuitable members of society.

The cooks included in this book span the later medieval period, from around the sixteenth century, with the very latest of these culinary heroes and heroines living into the first few years of the twentieth century. Chapter one focuses on those early pioneering cooks and cookery writers, made famous in part due to their association with whichever nobleman they were working for at the time, or as a consequence of their own well-educated and informed backgrounds. Trained, competent, skilled and literate, the principal cooks of the early modern age needed to be creative, scientific and knowledgeable of their patron's diet as well as appetite. The relationship between physiology, medication and food was still a critical factor during this period.

Known levels of literacy in late medieval England are still debatable. One of the most cited studies, from John Feather's *A History of British Publishing,* suggests that at least half the population of England could read and write by the middle of the sixteenth century, with around sixty percent of this figure including London and South-East regions. In more rural areas, this is believed to have been some fifty percent by the end of the seventeenth century. It is not hard to quantify why more populated urban areas had higher rates of literacy. Similarly, more men were literate than women, in particular tradesmen or clergymen, with all high class members of society, men and women, able to read and write. These figures are however contentious and difficult to legitimise. Undoubtedly though, there was a significant literate community of leisure readers by the end of the 1400s.[2] Many of the extraordinary cooks included in the first chapter would have been a part of this select group, as novice, innovative authors in their field, which in my mind entitles them to the recognition they deserve. Some of the very earliest publications, like Hugh Plat's *The Jewell House of Art and Nature,* first published in 1594, dealt with cookery as a collective secret, promising tantalising disclosures and recipes treated a bit like classified experiments. Medieval methods of cooking continued right up until the 1800s in front of an open fire; with the use of spits, pans and Dutch ovens; smoking, salting, frying, boiling and baking. Cooks had their work cut out for them, with punishing schedules and complicated, time-consuming processes to manage. Standards and measures of best practice for professional cooks were established early on, distinguishing their unique skills from other practitioners, such as tavern owners, bakers and butchers. The Worshipful Company of Cooks remains the smallest of the livery companies in London, with its origins reaching as far back as the twelfth century. William Fitz-Stephen is allegedly the first writer to mention cooking as a trade (even if it is somewhat disparaging), in his description of London around 1170:

> Those engaged in business of various kinds, sellers of merchandise, hirers of labour, are distributed every morning into their several localities according to their trade. Besides, there is in London on the river bank among the wines for sale in ships and in the cellars

of the vintners a public cook-shop. There daily you may find food according to the season, dishes of meat, roast, fried and boiled, large and small fish, coarser meats for the poor and more delicate for the rich, such as venison and big and small birds. If any of the citizens should unexpectedly receive visitors, weary from their journey, who would fain not wait until fresh food is bought and cooked, or until the servants have brought bread or water for washing, they hasten to the river bank and there find all they need. However great the multitude of soldiers and travellers entering the city, or preparing to go out of it, at any hour of the day or night – that these may not fast too long, and those may not go out supper-less – they turn aside thither, if they please, where every man can refresh himself in his own way. Those who would not cater for themselves fastidiously need not search to find sturgeon or the bird of Africa or the Ionian godwit. For this is a public kitchen, very convenient to the city, and part of its amenities. Hence the dictum in the Gorgias of Plato that the art of cookery is an imitation of medicine and flatters a quarter of civic life.[3]

Plato, as mentioned here by Fitz-Stephen, warned against people taking an interest in the occupation of cooks. Perhaps he foresaw the commercialization to come, a sort of mercenary attempt to prevent people from producing and sourcing their own naturally occurring sustenance.

Having studied Geoffrey Chaucer's *Canterbury Tales* at school many, many moons ago, I vividly remember the caricatured personalities, including the Cook, albeit an unfinished tale by the author. I was astounded by the caustic wit and sarcasm delivered by Chaucer, along with the level of detail and perception presented in his parade of colourful fourteenth century characters. Said to be based on Roger de Ware, a well-known cook in London at the time, Chaucer's character is a little overfond of drinking and fighting. The gaping, open sore on his leg is obviously designed to discourage us from ever liking the type of food he was likely to conjure up, with his pus-oozing appendage in tow. In particular, his cook-shop is described as flyspecked. More importantly, the very presence of a cook in Chaucer's tales is also testament to their importance. They were burgeoning middle class medieval professionals who would embark on apprenticeships, become skilled workers and then master cooks, either with their own business or as principal cook in a wealthy household. Roger de Ware is in fact recorded in the Memoranda Rolls of the City of London between 1364 and 1381, when he was presented in front of a jury of twelve and accused of being a 'common nightwalker'. Essentially this would have meant that he broke the King's curfew, which was maintained after a certain time of the night, forbidding people to go walking the streets. Bells were rung out signifying the curfew times and anyone caught out and about after the alarm would be escorted to Newgate Prison. The phrase 'common nightwalker' was also loaded with numerous connotations, including that of someone who unlawfully frequented ale houses of disrepute, engaged with prostitutes and fought in street brawls.[4]

By the seventeenth century, scientific progress meant that there was less of an integral relationship between cooking and diet, allowing cookery to evolve into its own creative art form. Commercial cooks in the kitchens of the nobility and royalty were the most likely to be revered and their work published during the later medieval period. As the 1700s advanced, Western Europe and North America began to enjoy a broad range of accessible, printed material and the Renaissance movement of the 1500-1600s was able to flourish through food and recipe writing. In France, spicy sauces were replaced by fat-based sauces – natural tastes favoured above disguised flavours. Smaller quantities and a fusion of ingredients from other regions and distant countries influenced French and then other culinary palates, motivated by an agreed consensus that French cuisine remained in the vanguard. By 1730, Europe as a whole was importing some 75,000 tons of sugar, which became the principal ingredient in many new dishes.[5]

Unusually, in the London Metropolitan Archives, there is a reference to an Elizabeth Saunders requesting wages from the court owed to her as her time as cook to Sir Charles Hazah in 1698, at a period when most chefs to the nobility were men. Whilst traditionally it was men who dominated the first few centuries of this culinary transformation, by the late eighteenth and nineteenth centuries, women were at the forefront of recipe writing and cookery tuition. Chapter two provides an overview of some of the great female names in cookery from this period. Many women made a name for themselves and prospered financially, as they were essentially writing for a large audience of like-minded readers, who spent significant amounts of time planning, preparing and organising meals in their homes. It is important to reiterate that this market was generally the high-end of society, alongside the burgeoning middle classes. Most of the poorer classes were more concerned with sourcing food to survive, than deliberating on how to cook and present it. It saddens me that in a world familiar with the names of men such as Carême, Escoffier and Ranhofer, the only recognisable female cooks prior to the twentieth century are Isabella Beeton and Hannah Glasse. But these two women, although commercially successful, frankly achieved very little in comparison to many of their accomplished peers. In chapter two I hope to rectify this by narrating some of the fantastic stories of hugely pioneering women in the field of culinary excellence, from Agnes Bertha Marshall, to Abby Fisher and Margaret Pearson.

Eighteenth century society was obsessed with fashion and gossip. It was a time of image-making and intrigue. Food and cookery had never been so interesting and key characters like Beauvilliers, Louis Eustache Ude, Nicolas Appert, the Gunter family and Grimod de La Reynière to name a few, began to emerge, helping to sustain interest in this new trend. Chapter three explores the developing era of gastronomic cooking and haute cuisine. Recipes became permanent records that transmitted knowledge, as opposed to scribbled down notes and bequeathed documents. The art of cooking was now a science, a technical process, a marrying of flavours to be mastered and devoured.

Philanthropic, innovative, analytical, draconian, cruel, poor and rich in extremes are all words you could associate with the eighteenth and nineteenth centuries. A prospering Industrial Revolution and widespread Empire, alongside a thriving consumer culture, coupled with the insurmountable issues that poverty afforded, makes this period in history one of the most written about and discussed. The Georgian age included some social and economic progress, against a background of food riots and protests by the poor, and legislation for social political reform, including the fight to abolish the slave trade. Nonetheless it was an era epitomised by debauchery and excess; promiscuity, gluttony and drunkenness, vices that were characteristic of the monarchy of the time. In contrast Queen Victoria's dignified, sober and puritanical approach generated an age of enormous cultural change; from an eclectic mix of Romanticism, Gothic revival and a chaste and controlled attitude towards everyday tasks. All of this is reflected in the way in which attitudes towards food and dining changed. The disparity between a country experiencing abject hunger and the relentless struggle to produce food, alongside the new middle class aspirations for more of everything, fuelled a complex mix of influences in society.

With a backdrop of endless wars raging across Europe and the Atlantic, this was also an age of sea power and the mass transportation of lives and goods. Not unlike today, thousands of migrants sought refuge in Britain from persecution and conflict. They brought with them a rich mix of skills and talents, none more so than the French, whose influence remains evident today with the numerous culinary terms that have remained integral to our own everyday language: omelette, aperitif, croquette, crêpe, mange tout, mousse and pâté, even the words restaurant and menu. The Italians, too, once provided Britain with confectioners and ice cream parlours on every street corner and introduced macaroni cheese, one of Britain's best loved dishes, thanks to the early 'grand tour' travellers. They returned with crates of macaroni pasta, which was served with melting parmesan at the dining tables of the hugely be-wigged 'macaronis', the fashionable young men of the 1700s. Britain has not pioneered these things; it has merely inherited them from others throughout history. It is no coincidence today that French food is still revered and judged the highest level of excellence in restaurants throughout the United Kingdom, because this is how it has been since the early nineteenth century. There was a time in Britain when every household of any financial and social merit required a French or Italian chef of the highest standard. Not only did they have to create the very best in French cuisine, they also had to be male. They were frequently paid huge sums of money and provided with as many perks as they could get away with asking for. These cooks were like prized possessions, a must-have in a society obsessed with French cooking and dining.

Purveyors of fine dining during the nineteenth century offered real celebrity potential. From the cooks to the new restaurant and hotel owners, the retailers and confectioners, recipe writers and tutors.

food and gastronomy were well-established, woven into the fabric of the cultural identities of many countries. It was big business and the prospering media, with its newspapers and periodicals of the time, flaunted this snowballing culinary entity.

The final chapter in this book resonates strongly for me. Growing up in a very middle class environment with all the trappings, yet attending a school that wasn't a grammar or private one, or anywhere close to outstanding, always made me appreciate different aspects of life and society. Since a young age, I have connected with the underdogs, the hard workers and survivors. I have always appreciated, and been frequently inspired by, the extent to which some work colleagues have dedicated huge amounts of their time and energy to a job, often carrying out countless thankless tasks, responding cooperatively to managers with less experience, integrity and fewer qualifications. I have listened to friends and family communicate their brilliant concepts, ideas for inventions and ingenious political solutions. And I have met and read about numerous people, with so much potential in all walks of life, potential which is rarely recognised or fully acknowledged. This last chapter is dedicated to them and the rest of life's heroes who have become forgotten, nudged aside, disregarded. During my golden years of museum management, I would be made to feel like the underdog myself on occasions and having worked in catering to support my education and career for a number of years – also toying with the idea of becoming a restaurateur for some of that time – I appreciate the level of real physical labour involved, as well as the need to continuously re-invent and conform.

After leaving school, my first taste of solo living was in Stratford-upon-Avon. As a very young exile in a temporary jungle of actors, directors and aspiring creative types, I watched the players on stage in my spare time and pulled pints to serve those same performers during working hours. Having spent my even younger years working in the kitchens, waitressing and occasionally cooking for one of Dartmouth's finest eateries, this is the time I first became aware of competition in the catering industry. The late eighties and early nineties were absurdly competitive in terms of small town restaurant and bar rivalry. I witnessed bullying, political tactics and poisonous gossip on a scale I have rarely experienced since. As for my own aspirations, perhaps due to these experiences, I learnt from a youthful age to work hard, but to remain humbled by those around me and not to compete with those intent on maintaining their egos.

Whilst we can marvel at the great gastronomic giants of the past and present, perhaps we can also benefit from taking some time to consider their mentors; those people that inspired them, funded them and encouraged them to become the celebrities they are. We must also take into account their circumstances and environments and where publicity and popularity has been gainful.

If you are looking for a cook in this book and cannot find him or her, the simple answer to this is that it was not possible to mention every noteworthy culinarian from the sixteenth century onwards. Some have been disregarded due to the fact that, despite being named authors or cooks, there is either little information available with which to tell their story, or I have simply made the decision not to include them. If you are also wondering why most of the cooks written about in this book are either European or American, this is simply because the early records of larger kitchens, such as those in Asia, were mostly made up of statistical data. Many historical sources just have not survived. Language is also a barrier, when faced with archive material that is simply inaccessible due to translation issues. In addition, little is known about cooking in Ireland during the sixteenth century, with few surviving recipe books or household accounts. In Wales, most of the wealthy aristocracy had a fashion for following English gastronomic influences, as opposed to traditional Welsh styles. Few historic recipes have survived from Wales, with the exception of a compendium of original manuscripts reproduced in *Welsh Culinary Recipes* by Mati Thomas during the early part of the twentieth century. That does not mean to say there is no potential for further research to be done in this area.

The majority of the best cooks today have been taught in the manner of the original masters from the late eighteenth and nineteenth centuries. Their techniques, systems and recipes remain integral to the profession. Of course, food trends come and go. A few years ago, 'Artisan' was the buzz theme. At the time of writing, it's now all

'Hipster', with breakfast cereal eateries, crisp and dip and cheese toasty emporiums, but the classical methods continue to form the foundation of what most restaurants create for their diners daily. Think about it. The basis of a macaroni cheese is just a béchamel sauce with cheddar. Now, if you read the rest of this book, you can find out just who it was that first created it.

Chapter One

Early Modernist and New World Culinarians

The period between 1600 and 1700 was a time when Britain was emerging out of the dark years of medieval discord. Restoration and a re-distribution of wealth brought with it the beginnings of economic growth, exploration and transition. America was being colonized by a new wave of European settlers who overcame great adversity, faced rival power struggles and conflicts with Native American inhabitants, resulting in one of history's most controversial genocides. Strong and influential mixed communities were founded, after bloody usurpations. Explorers, pirates and privateers treated indigenous communities like chattel. The world was a sinister, primitive place, whilst being on the cusp of social, spiritual, economic and technological revolution.

The 1500s witnessed the very start of the wider publication of books on cookery and household management, commonly aimed at the more literate market of noble men and women. Thomas Dawson who wrote *The Good Huswifes Jewell* (1585), *The good Hus-wifes handmaid for the kitchen* (1594), and *The Booke of Carving and Sewing* (1597) was among the most prolific. On the whole, books of this period would generally have been small and pocket-sized, with pretty borders and embellishments. Early recipe writing was devoid of basic information relating to cooking times, specific weights and measures and so on, as the writers were often addressing skilled cooks, rather than novices. You are unlikely to find recipes providing basic instructions on the fundamentals of cooking, such as boiling, frying and roasting etc., as it was understood these techniques were simply known from memory.[1] It wasn't until the eighteenth century that instructional recipe writing began to include that level of detail, and only then by a handful of writers. It must also be said that the medieval age was one in which an ability to disguise food was often talent enough to make a standard chef.

Cooks like Robert May, considered to be the first English writer to compile recipes in a format we are all familiar with today, alongside Hugh Plat, John Murrell and Edward Kidder, were all primitive protagonists in the late medieval culinary discourse. There were also a number of writers at this time scripting early general domestic guides that included advice on cooking, like Hannah Woolley's *The Gentlewoman's Companion* and the writer and poet Gervase Markham who encapsulates the seventeenth century's close relationship between cookery, medicine and perfumery in his book *The English Huswife*. The mysterious W. M, author of *The Queens Closet Opened* – a compendium of three separate books, allegedly based on the activities recorded in the kitchens of the wife of Charles I, Henrietta Maria – only adds to the fascination for secrecy and the customs of aristocracy during this arcane age, at the cusp of the Renaissance, where food and physiology were still so essentially interconnected. Typically, late medieval English cooking was fairly frugal and whilst some spices were available as a consequence of early exploration, these would have been at a considerable cost. Meals served at the royal court would of course have been more complex and extravagant. Breakfast remained as it did largely until the nineteenth century, a minimal meal consisting of cold meats or fish, bread and ale. Supper, which was consumed quite late in the evening, was generally also light, often made up of the leftovers from dinner. Dried, smoked and pickled fish were commonly eaten as an alternative to meat during designated meat-free days, while almond milk was a substitute for dairy products during Lent.

Cooking and recipes slowly shifted away from archaic associations with mysticism, herbalism and the apothecary during the seventeenth century. They became subtly redefined as experimental and scientific processes that lent themselves to new skills, to be developed in the kitchen. Transferring from the ownership of men, into the hands of women, recipe books of the sixteenth and seventeenth centuries were largely concerned with dietaries – on the basis that food nourished health in a myriad of ways, or they emerged out of generic manuals relating to household management and housewifery. Recipe books also became a merging point for art and nature, so that the act of cooking became an art form that could transform nature. Perhaps this is why so much emphasis is placed on moulding sugar pastes into flowers, birds and insects, on instructions as to how pastries could be fashioned into animal shapes, and on how to stuff carcasses with other parts of animals or fish. In his *Delightes for Ladies*, Hugh Plat concludes, 'so by art you may make many little fishes out of one great and natural fish.'

In a lot of ways during the seventeenth century, cooking becomes a great deal about controlling nature.[2] It wasn't only the English who were pioneering the way forward in cooking and culinary writing. The Renaissance impacted across Europe and spread into the wider new developing worlds. The American colonists were also facing a challenging time with establishing a system of cooking, both domestic and commercial, in a new world with unexplored terrains, hostile environments and unfamiliar resources. The seventeenth century rebel, and senseless crusader of death to all Native Americans, Nathaniel Bacon, was a wealthy, young English settler in Virginia. The diverse remains unearthed at his home included the bones of chickens, cattle, pigs, sheep, deer, rabbit, duck, geese, quail and pigeon, alongside the remains of turtles, catfish, sturgeon, bear, frogs and eagles, providing an interesting insight into the diet of the colonists.[3] The staple diet of early settlers did not transcend class, and everyday meals consisted of very similar dishes. People ate what they could get their hands on.

In Europe generally, the way people could access food by this time was changing in relation to steady improvements in transportation. The use of strong spices on meat to disguise the unpleasantries of the medieval age, gave way to the innovative notion that herbs and spices could actually enhance and complement the flavours of different food groups if used intelligently. New vegetables were emerging, having been introduced to Europe from the Middle East and Africa, like asparagus, peas and cauliflower. It is very easy to assume that all early influential cooks were French, English or Italian. There were a range of late medieval gastronomes throughout Europe, across the Atlantic and further afield, who have left a legacy which contributes to a much wider discourse on the evolution of cooking as it evolved from the dark ages to the Renaissance.

Since the beginning of recorded time, food has been equated with hospitality and friendship, and the higher your social status, the more food you would consume. As the Renaissance dawned, this tradition began to move away from quantity and more towards the quality of food consumed. By the eighteenth century, eating better mattered more than eating to excess.

The British

Markham, Murrell and Plat

Hugh Plat, Gervase Markham and John Murrell were all writers of the early seventeenth century. And it is perhaps to them we owe thanks, for their emphasis on the importance of women and recipe writing. Up until this time, food and cooking was very much the property of men. Although Plat, Markham and Murrell were not what we would identify as celebrities individually, as a trio emerging from the Elizabethan era, cavalier, courtly and aristocratic, they represent an interesting collective during a productive period in English cookery book writing. Interestingly Plat's *Delightes for Ladies* (first published in 1602) and Gervase Markham's *English Huswife* (1615) contain the earliest references to the use of corks in bottling.[4] It would be another century at least before the storage of liquids and corking for carbonation became recognised and applied in practice.

Hugh Plat was not a cook. He was a Cambridge graduate and his interests were varied, from horticulture to medicines, preserves, drinks and cooking. He was a courtier and inventor, a gardener and farmer, a self-made man who wrote a number of 'how to' books, including several that involved food and nutrition. *Delightes for Ladies* saw him move from gardening to indoor domesticity – to both the kitchen and the stillroom or distillery room, at a time when most houses of the wealthy contained both. He wrote about food and cooking in *Delightes for Ladies,* but it is understood that Plat acquired a great deal of his practical knowledge, such as how to remove stains from clothes and basic treatments for ailments including colic, gout and so on. from the German painter known simply as Mr. English.

Early Modernist and New World Culinarians

Figure 1. Design for a 'boulting hutch'. Illustration from Hugh Plat's *The Jewell House of Art and Nature*.

However, he was primarily an innovator and amongst other culinary discoveries, Plat is believed to be the first person to suggest pickling cooked meat in vinegar to preserve it. He was also an advocate on the benefits of macaroni for sailors. His pamphlet on *Certaine philosophical preparations of foode and beverage for sea-men*, recommended this dried, floury luxury. In accordance with his theories, he owned one of, if not the first, macaroni presses in London. I've read frequently that an illustration for this device can be found in his book *The Jewell House of Art and Nature*, but having searched through a 1653 version housed in the archives of the University of California, I have found no such image or even reference to the press. More about his pasta-promoting antics can be found in Malcolm Thick's *Sir Hugh Plat: The Search for Useful Knowledge in Early Modern London*. Plat was 'a great believer in the efficiency of soap', which despite being an expensive luxury item in the sixteenth century, was gradually becoming a popular necessity for those who could afford it.[5]

He invented many items in his lifetime, including those for the kitchen like his 1594 'vessell made of wood, to brew or boile in'. In particular, Plat's invention for a 'Boulting Hutch' was published in *The Jewell House of Art and Nature*, and a picture of it can be found in the accompanying illustrations (Figure 1 on P. 23), demonstrating a useful grain sifter, designed to make the whole process easier, more hygienic and less labour intensive.

Writing in the early to middle years of the 1600s, Murrell was, in contrast to Plat, a trained professional cook, native to London but well-travelled throughout France, Italy and the Low Countries. His experiences improved Murrell's wider knowledge of the craft of cooking, and he was inspired by continental influences. He wrote a number of books including A *Delightful Daily Exercise for Ladies and Gentlewomen*, published in 1621, and *A New Booke of Cookerie* which was, as he put it on the title page, 'All set forth according to the now, new, English and French fashion', exemplified here in his recipe for capon:

> To boyle a Capon Larded with Lemons,
> on the French fashion.
> Scald your Capon, and
> take a little dusty Oatmeale
> to make it boile
> white. Then take two
> or three ladlefuls of
> Mutton broth, a Fagot
> of sweet Hearbes, two or three
> Dates, cut in long pieces, a few parboyld
> Currins, a little whole Pepper, a
> piece of whole Mace, and one Nutmeg.
> Thicken it with Almonds. Season it
> with Uergis, Sugar, and a little sweet
> Butter. Then take vp your Capon,
> and larde it very thicke with a preserued
> Lemmon. Then lay your Capon
> in a deepe Meat-dish for boyld meates,
> and poure the broth vpon it. Garnish
> your Dish with Suckets and preserued
> Barberries.[6]

Early Modernist and New World Culinarians 25

Sugar pastes moulded and coloured were a bit of a speciality of Murrell's, and in accordance with the fashions of the time he particularly liked creating flower designs. To ensure authenticity he would dry roses, violets, marigolds, primroses etc. and then grind them down to a fine powder to extract their colours, sometimes enhancing these colours further by adding other natural dyes, like saffron.[7] Thomas Dewe, Murrell's original publisher, was keen to advertise and sell the sugar moulds made of tin described by Murrell in his books. These came in the shape of snakes, snails, frogs, roses, shoes, keys, letters and gloves, among other things.[8]

Murrell's nod to women as cooks, who were previously discounted before the Plat, Markham and Murrell feminist revolution of sorts, is

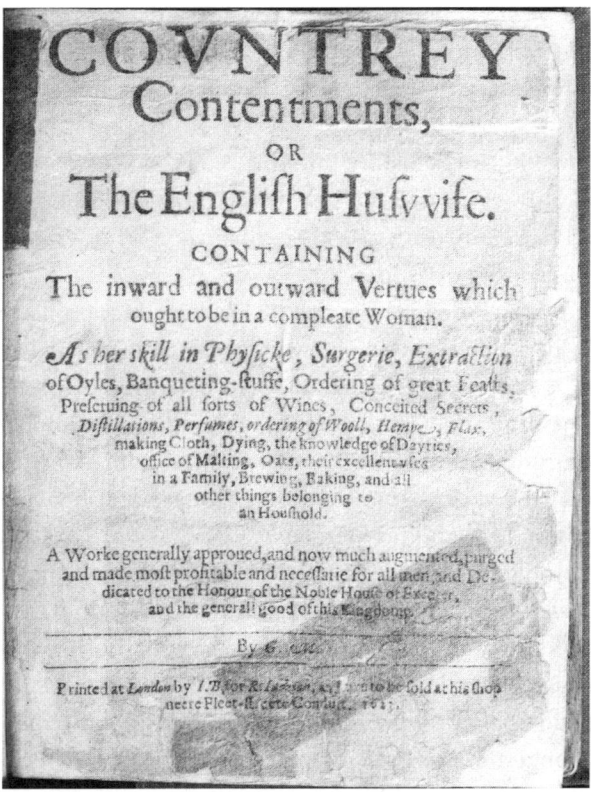

Figure 2. Title page from Gervase Markham's *The English Huswife*.

apparent in *A New Booke of Cookerie*. Here he advocates that women – or more specifically women from aspiring 'gentle' households – should be encouraged to carve the meat at table.[9]

The third of these advocates for female-friendly works, Gervase Markham, focused on the usual social class with which to promote his discourse – the elite large rural estate dwellers, who were both literate and receptive to household advice. His writing was more documented evidence, based on thorough and comprehensive observations, rather than fictional plagiarism, the latter often being the case in the seventeenth and eighteenth centuries. Refreshingly, Markham also cited every single person who contributed to and advised him about the content of his work along the way. Whilst his knowledge and career spanned fiction, prose and poetry, his most renowned works were based on husbandry and domestic Renaissance practices. Most notably *The English Huswife* contains chapters on cookery and recipes which are undoubtedly to be credited to some extent to the unknown countess he mentions.

Born in Nottinghamshire around 1568, an educated, military man who also circulated at the fringes of the Elizabethan royal court, Markham ended up a farmer, albeit one who wrote prolifically alongside his husbandry duties.

The recipes included in *The English Huswife*, first published in 1615, are heavily dependent on sugar, which was counteracted with citrus or vinegar, as well as on a broad variety of herbs and spices. This was typical of the time and a reflection of the popularity of imported luxury goods. Alongside these extravagant dishes, Markham is sure to reference instructions for cooking simple and traditional English fayre – roasting meat, poaching eggs and boiling oats.[10]

Markham is referenced in a popular journal of the nineteenth century, *Notes and Queries,* in an argument denoting the merits of fortified wine, notably sherry, debating which brand is considered the best and which is of a lower standard. Markham is quoted as reiterating that mainland Spain produces the highest quality, followed by Portugal, with the strongest of this 'sack' to be found in the Canary Islands. These opinions are jointly shared by the writer of the article.[11]

The very fact that Markham's opinions are being recognised and cited over 200 years after his death, is perhaps some testament to his legacy.

He is remembered still in a 1948 edition of the *Ballymena Observer*, which noted: 'Some of the clearest descriptions of arable farming in the seventeenth century have been left by Gervase Markham. Not much is known of him as a farmer, but the way he wrote marks him as a man of understanding and a good farmer.'[12]

In *The English Huswife*, Markham presents a glorious account of how one should serve and prepare for a feast on a grand scale. He outlines the precise order of activities on the day: that the Clerk of the Kitchen always ordered the meat from the Dresser, which was then delivered to the Sewer, who passed it onto the Yeoman-waiters ready to take to the table. Sallets and more sallets would dominate the first courses (that's various prepared vegetables or boiled salads from a contemporary perspective), and these were to be followed by fricassees, boiled meats, various broths and finally a mixture of fowl. But this was only the entrée. What followed was a procession of elegantly roasted fine meats, from the best beef sirloins to legs of mutton, goose, swan, veal, pork capons and pies, from deer in pastry to calves-foot pie and an array of cold pheasants, turkeys and partridges. Not content with roasted, boiled and baked victuals, the proceedings would often end with ornately cut and presented broiled meats. Known simply as 'carbonados', each dish was positioned on the table in such a way as to alternate the content visually. This practice of placing every dish on the table all at once lasted right through until the end of the Georgian period, when good sense began to prevail, with the knowledge that food tasted much better fresh and hot, rather than cold and congealed. But during the seventeenth century, when Markham was writing, this type of fit-to-burst table would have represented a visual homage to extravagance and affluence.[13] Both Markham's *English Huswife* and *English Husbandman* were 'bound together' and sold in one volume to the American market as early as 1620, which suggests that his work was popular both sides of the Atlantic.[14]

Although archival material on the life of Gervase Markham is scarce, one of his older brothers, Francis, fortuitously left behind a slim autobiography, which paints the picture of an educated young man who lived hand-to-mouth, moving into the military following a career in law and a position in the royal court. It seems Francis's fortunes remained unstable, as he wrote:

> I grew acquainted with a widow, Mrs Dorothy Lovell, whose daughter Mary I married January 3, 1608…I raffled with 10 ladies… each venturing £20 for a jewel worth £100. I won and got that help. I was poor.

Gervase similarly moved between a career in the military, to being a scholar and then to farming. It is likely he may also have had a life as insecure as his brothers from time to time. Perhaps the family fortunes were not sufficient enough to support them all. Certainly, there is some evidence to suggest ongoing feuds, with a family member once referring to Gervase as a 'poetical lying knave'.[15]

The following recipe is taken from *The English Huswife* and to me epitomises the essence of what constitutes the popular image of medieval cooking:

Puddings of a Hog's Liver

Take the liver of a fat hog and parboil it, then shred it small, and after, beat it in a mortar very fine; then mix it with the thickest and sweetest cream, and strain it very well through an ordinary strainer; then put thereto six yolks of eggs, and two whites, and the grated crumbs of near hand a penny white loaf, with good store of currants, dates, cloves, mace, sugar, saffron, salt, and the best swine suet, or beef suet, but beef suet is the more wholesome, and less loosening; then after it hath stood a while, fill it into the farmes, and boil them, as before showed; and when you serve them to the table, first boil them, then lay them on a gridiron over the coals, and boil them gently, but scorch them not, nor in any wise break their skins, which is to be prevented by oft turning and tossing them on the gridiron, and keeping a slow fire.[16]

Robert May

At the height of his fame, Robert May was a professional cook of the highest reputation and in the greatest demand. Born in

Early Modernist and New World Culinarians

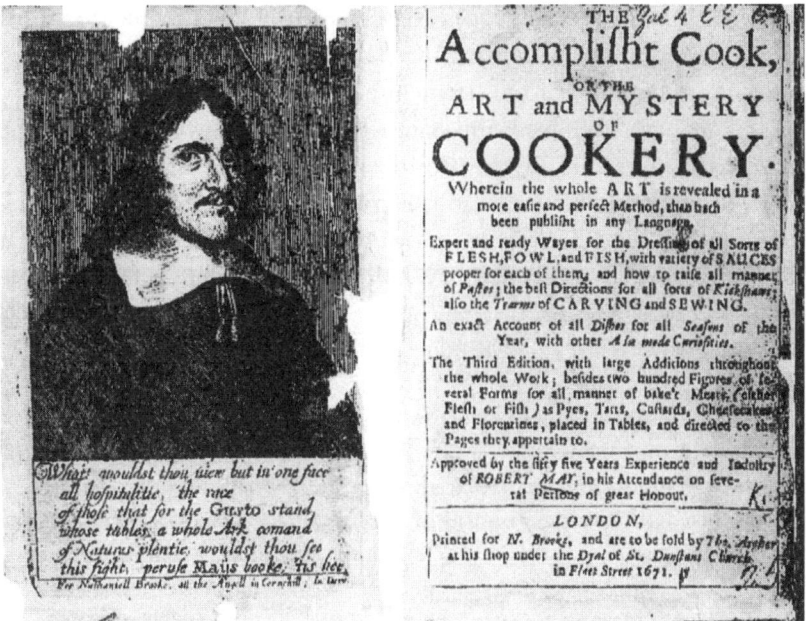

Figure 3. Frontispiece and title page of Robert May's *The Accomplisht Cook*.

Buckinghamshire in 1588. Robert May's father, Edwarde Mayes, was the chief cook to the Dormer family of Ascott Park, therefore exposing Robert to the early influences of cooking. Lady Dormer, recognising the potential in young Robert, sent him to train in France for five years. When he returned, he worked as an apprentice to Arthur Hollinsworth in London, renowned cook to the Grocer's Hall and the Star Chamber, before returning for a stint at Ascott Hall working alongside his father. What followed was a vast and varied number of culinary posts working for British nobility, including Lord Castlehaven, Lord Lumley, Lord Montague in Sussex, the Countess of Kent (who also wrote a successful medical and cookery book in 1653), Lord Rivers, Mr. John Ashburnham of the Bed-Chamber, Dr. Steed, Sir Thomas Stiles in Drury Lane, London, Marmaduke Constable in Yorkshire, Sir Charles Lucas and finally Lady Englefield. By 1660, at the age of seventy-two, he had acquired enough experience to feel inspired to write the acclaimed *The Accomplisht Cook, Or The Art & Mystery of Cookery* 'wherein the whole ART is revealed in a more easie and perfect Method than hath been publisht in any language'. May graciously gives thanks to all his previous employers, attributing the experience he gained from working for them as testament to his tremendous success.[17]

If you have ever read any Samuel Pepys, you will have seen the many references one of the world's most famous diarists makes to food, dining and cooking – and in particular his love of a good cake. Of course, a 'cake' back in the 1600s would have resembled more of a fruity luxury loaf, and Pepys may very well have indulged in one made by Robert May himself, or from one of his recipes at least, such as this one, which is for 'an extraordinary good cake':

> Take half a bushel of the best flour you can get very finely searsed [sieved], and lay it upon a large Pastry board, make a hole in the midst thereof, and put to it three pound of the best butter you can get; with fourteen pound of currans finely picked and rubbed, three quarts of good new thick cream warm'd, two pound of fine sugar beaten, three pints of good new ale, barm or yeast, four ounces of cinamon fine beaten and searsed, also an ounce of beaten ginger, two ounces of nutmegs fine beaten and searsed; put in all these materials together, and work them up into an indifferent stiff paste, keep it warm till the oven be hot, then make it up and bake it, being baked an hour and a half ice it, then take four pound of double refined sugar, beat it, and searse it, and put it in a deep clean scowred skillet the quantity of a gallon, boil it to a candy height with a little rose-water, then draw the cake, run it all over, and set it into the oven, till it be candied.[18]

Incidentally, *The Accomplisht Cook* contains a significant number of recipes around venison and sturgeon – a river fish now rare in the United Kingdom – exemplifying both the once age-old necessity for hunting, and the extent to which our everyday available food has altered over the centuries.

Edward Kidder

Edward's career was a little bit later, born as he was sometime in the mid-1660s. His portrait is held in the collections of the National

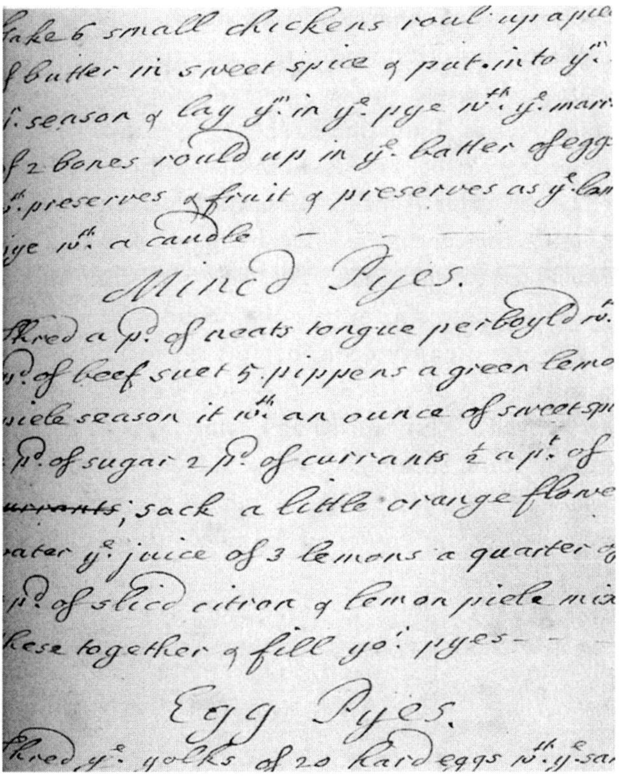

Early Modernist and New World Culinarians 31

Figure 4. Extract from Edward Kidder's *Receipts of Pastry and Cooking*.

Portrait Gallery in London, which depicts him as a very slight small-framed man, with an engaging face. This celebrated cook advertised his training school on the following dates and locations, in his book *Receipts of Pastry and Cooking*:

On Mondays, Tuesdays, and Wednesdays,
in the Afternoon, in St Martin's Le Grand.

And on Thursdays, Fridays, and Saturdays,
in the Afternoon, at his School next to Furnival's Inn in Holborn.
And Ladies may be taught at their own Houses.

Printed entirely using copper plates, Kidder's book is considered to be an important historical source of food images, particularly his decorative pastry work. He also wrote a collection of recipes with a woman named only as 'Katherine Kidder', the manuscript of which dates from 1699 and can be accessed from the Wellcome Library.

Kidder died in 1739. A brief obituary, which appeared in the *Newcastle Courant* that day, stated that he taught some six thousand ladies and was aged seventy-three. His wife was Mary and his two daughters were Elizabeth and Susan. His nephew George Kidder of Canterbury was also a pastry cook, but moved to London, possibly transferring to the role of silversmith. Kidder's will denotes he died a man of some wealth.[19] Edward Kidder came from an old respected family, originally from Sussex and a descendant of Richard Kidder, one time Bishop of Bath and Wells. He ran his business from Queen Street, Cheapside, at the corner of Furnival's Inn, operating two

Figure 5. Illustration of a 'Lamb Pastey' from Edward Kidder's *Receipts of Pastry and Cooking*.

Early Modernist and New World Culinarians

schools, one from his home in Cheapside and one in Holborn. He also offered private tuition, visiting ladies at home to teach them in their own kitchens. In death, he left his wife Mary a gold watch, a diamond ring, other trinkets and furniture. He bequeathed all his money and other personal belongings to both his daughters. Susan acknowledged Edward's nephew George by providing him with £150 in cash, together with the copper plates for the book *Nooks and Corners of English Life*.[20] John Timbs published a book of the same name. Whether the initial manuscript or just the copper plates were originally Kidder's own work is debatable, but Timbs writes a page or two about Kidder and his work midway through the book, noting that 'the copper-plates for the receipt-book' were given to George, via Edward's daughter Susan. Trying to trace the future success of the only other family member, George Kidder, to have entered into the trade also proved futile. One wonders whether the £150.00 (a small fortune in the 1750s) he received was used to fund his pastry-cook career, or rather set him up in an alternative business, such as the suggested silversmith trade. It may even have been squandered on a frivolous lifestyle. Certainly, we know that he did not use the copper plates he inherited to write his own recipe book. He may have simply sold them on, perhaps to John Timbs. This we will never know.[21] Here is one of the few recipes included in *Nooks and Corners* (which Timb's gives credit to as being from Plat's *Delightes for Ladies*) for March-pane (marzipan), a homage to the England of old, where March-pane was once eaten by Queen Elizabeth I, quoted in literary references and used to fortify large-scale medieval decorative desserts in the shape of castles or figurines:

To make a March-pane

Take two pounds of almonds, being blanched, and dryed in a sieve over the fire, beat them in a stone mortar, and when they bee small, mix them with two pounds of sugar being finely beaten, adding two or three spoonefuls of rose-water, and that will keep your almonds from oiling: when your paste is beaten fine, drive it thin with a rolling pin, and so lay it on a bottom of wafers; then raise up a little edge on the side, and so bake it; then yce it with rose-water and sugar, then put it into the oven againe, and when you see your yce is risen up and drie, then take it out of the oven and garnish it with pretie conceipts, as birdes and beasts being cast out of standing-moldes. Sticke long confits upright into it, cast bisket and carrowaies in it, and so serve it: you may also print of this march-pane paste in your moldes for banqueting dishes. And of this paste our comfit makers at this day make their letters, knots, armes, escutcheons, beasts, birds, and other fancies.[22]

William Rabisha

William Rabisha or Rabysha was an interesting man, possibly a Yorkshire born Parliamentary captain, once awarded one hundred

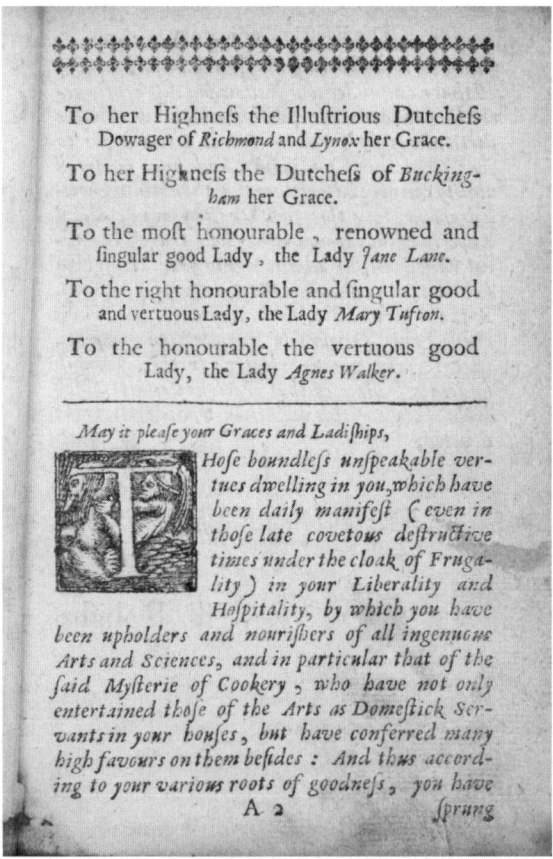

Figure 6. William Rabisha's *The Whole Body of Cookery Dissected*.

pounds for providing crucial political information from Ireland to England in 1649. He wrote on subjects as diverse as the condemnation of capital punishment, unorthodox Biblical scholarly works and of course, he wrote on cookery. The confusion between Rabisha and Rabysha becomes compounded with the knowledge that his book, *The Whole Body of Cookery Dissected* (1661), was a blatantly Royalist cookbook. The one-time Parliamentarian hero suddenly adopted a more Cavalier – in its literal meaning – approach to politics, as the end of the English Civil War culminated in the restoration of King Charles II.[23] If Rabisha and Rabysha are one and the same man, and the fact that both the Parliamentarian and the converted Royalist used the same publisher, Giles Calvert, suggests they may well be, William Rabisha must have lived an extremely diverse life, one that he changed and adapted to his own political advantage.

Like Robert May, Rabisha dedicated *The Whole Body of Cookery Dissected* to some of his former employers, including the Duchess of Richmond, Lady Jane Lane, Lady Mary Tuston and Lady Agnes Walker. Rabisha also suggests that he was brought up in a noble household, from whence he learned his trade, and that he was well-travelled, referring to his 'long travels in several kingdoms'.[24] Perhaps he was a military man once, after all. In his opening chapter, 'To the Reader', Rabisha certainly goes on to emphasise – to a much greater extent perhaps than is necessary – his courtly connections and his service to the king in exile during the war. However you perceive William Rabisha, there is no denying that his book, like only a handful at the time, seeks to elevate cookery into art form, one that requires training, skill and knowledge. His recipe for Italian pudding, given below, reflects both the continental trends of the period, and demonstrates an early eye for detail at this turning point in time for recipe writing.

A baked Pudding after the Italian fashion, corrected.

> Take a penny white loaf or two, and cut it in the manner of dice: put to it half a pound of Beef suet minced small, half a pound of Raisins of the sun stoned, a little sugar, six sliced Dates, a grain of Musk, the Marrow of two bones, season it with Cloves, Mace, Nutmeg, salt and Rose-water, then beat three Eggs with about half

> a pint of Cream, and put it to your bread and other ingredients, and stir it together softly that you break not the bread, nor Marrow: then slice some thin pieces of Apple into the bottom of your dish, that you bake it in, and put your Pudding theron: bake it in an oven not so hot as for Manchet: when it's enough, stick it with Cittern and strow it with Sugar.[25]

Thomas Dawson

Born in the mid-sixteenth century, Dawson wrote a range of popular books focussing on housekeeping and cooking, including: *The Good Huswifes Jewell* (1585), *The Good Hus-wifes Handmaid for the Kitchen* (1594), *The Booke of Carving and Sewing* (1597) and his *Booke of Cookerie* (1620). Typically of this period, Dawson covered everything from medicinal recipes and treatments, to drinks and cooking. What Dawson is perhaps most well-known for is his invention of the trifle. Although similar desserts existed in the sixteenth century and fruit and cream fools were the springboard for sugary, creamy desserts flavoured with fruits or ginger and flavoured waters, Dawson was by all accounts the first writer to christen the dish as a 'trifle'. In his book, *The Good Huswifes Jewell,* he includes the following recipe:

To make a Trifle.

> Take a pinte of thicke Creame, and season it with Suger and Ginger, and Rosewater, so stirre it as you would then haue it, and make it luke warme in a dish on a Chafingdishe and coales, and after put it into a siluer peece or a bowle, and so serue it to the boorde.

It is worth mentioning here that John Partridge was a similar writer to Dawson at the time and equally as popular. Among other manuals, he wrote *The Widdowes Treasure*, a mix of culinary and medicinal advice written specifically on behalf of a woman, probably a noble woman who provided Partridge with all of the information with which to compile his manuscript. Many women were either not able to write, or not empowered enough to write their own works during this period. It would be another century before the boom in women recipe writers emerged. Here is Partridge's recipe for dried pears:

Dried Peares

To make drie Peares. Take faire [spring] water and Rosewater according to the quantitie of your Peares, then take Honey as muche as you thinke good and put in your Peares, then let them seethe very softly that thei breake not, then take them out and put them in a Collander, and let them dreaine, then when you drawe your bread put them into the Oven in some earthen panne, and if they be not drie at the first, put them in againe until they be drie, then barrel them.[26]

Early Female Culinarians

During the early medieval period, female cooks would very rarely be employed in service. However, they would often have supported their husbands who were, particularly in the preparation process of cooking. Women were more likely to have been street cooks, selling their cooked items and speciality products, whilst dodging the fines for selling either overpriced or contaminated hotmeat and fish.[27] For obvious reasons, perhaps, there are few female cooks who have survived the annals of medieval historical reference, although two – interestingly both German women – have succeeded in leaving a small legacy.

Maria Sophie Schellhammer and Anna Wecker

The first is Maria Sophia Schellhammer who was one of six children born to Hermann and Anna Maria Conring in Germany around 1647. She represents one of the few early modernist female cooks of her generation. Like many who ended up writing or cooking professionally, following on from their housekeeping positions, Maria did just that, with tremendous support from her husband, also a writer and publisher (although his main profession was that of chemist and professor of medicine).[28] By 1697 she had written and also made successful *Die wohl unterwiesene Köchin* ('The well-informed cook'), known later as *Das*

Brandenburgische Koch-Buch ('The Brandenburg cookbook'), despite there being few references to actual Brandenburg cuisine.

Schellhammer's noteworthy confection and distilling recipes have often been credited to that of her husband, whose knowledge in these areas would undoubtedly have influenced her work. She was also an early advocate for porcelain, recommending that dessert courses were best served in porcelain wares.[29]

The other early German author of cookbooks was Anna Wecker or Weckerin, who was also married to a man of medicine. Born some 100 years prior to Schellhammer, she published the first cookbook authored

Figure 7. Anna Wecker's *Ein Köstlich new Kochbuch*.

by a woman in Germany. (The first unpublished one was by Sabina Welserin, whose manuscript cookbook of 1553 was only published in 1980.) The title of Wecker's bestselling book was *Ein Köstlich new Kochbuch* ('A delicious new cookbook'). As many cookbooks of this age did, it had an extraordinarily long subtitle, which when translated reads something like this:

> Of many kinds of meals consisting of vegetables, fruit, meat, poultry, game, fish and pastries. Not only for healthy people, but also and especially for infirm people who suffer from various sicknesses and weaknesses, and also for pregnant women, post-partum women, and other people inflicted by some illness. These recipes can be prepared in an artistic manner and are useful as well.[30]

Below is Anna's original recipe for roasted eel, the title roughly translated as 'almost gorgeous and good'.

Ein Aal zu braten/ fast herrlich vnd gut.

Wann der Aal abgezogen vnd bereitet wie er seyn soll/ so lege die stu:eck auch eine stund in ein guten Essig/ Pfeffer vnnd Saltz/ so werden sie fast keck vnnd scho:en blaw/ alsdann hab ein klein Vogelspießlein/ stecke die Stu:eck eins den langen Weg/ das ander vberzwerch daran vnnd allweg Salvey darzwischen/ oder Lorberbla:etter/ wann du sie haben kanst/ bestrewe jhn mit wenig Saltz vnd Pfeffer/ lege den spies gegen dem fewer/ brats wie Vo:egel/ stelle ein bratpfann vnder/ mache das Schmaltz heiß/ bereit eine bru:eh wie vor oben/ ohn allein kein brot vnnd Na:egelein/ thu es in die bratpfannen/ begeuß jmmerzu/ vnd wann es auff sein stat gebraten/ so nimb ein frische Butter/ betreuff jhn wol mit durch ein heissen schaumlo:effell/ vnder dessen habe bereit ein Schu:essel mit weissem Zucker vnd reinem geriebnem Brot/ wol mit Zimet vnnd Zucker bereit (Du magst wol fu:er das su:esse Schmaltz mit Pomerantzen wie die Koppen betreuffen) darnach bestrewe es mit dem brot/ daß fein bro:eslecht wird/ darnach lege es in ein warme blatten/ vnd die bru:eh in der pfannen daran/ das feyste sol aber abgenommen werden/ du magst Brot darinnen behen/ wanns wol braun ist/ du magst allerdings bereiten wie die Koppen/ es ist ein herrlich Essen/ vnd werden jhr vil nicht also gebraten.

For those readers who don't understand German, the recipe, from my rather crude translation suggests marinating the eel for an hour or so in a good vinegar, with salt and pepper, coating it in chicken or goose fat (*Schmaltz*), and then frying it in a pan, followed by roasting it in butter with white sugar and breadcrumbs. I have never found eel particularly appealing, but if this translation is anything to go by, my interest in Anna's recipe for this most slippery of fish, has definitely increased my interest in eel.

Wecker's book was reprinted many times and was largely inspired by the work she carried out cooking for her husband's patients, who she visited together with him, making copious notes for each ailment and its prescribed treatment. Following the death of her husband, she was encouraged by the medical fraternity to continue with her work and to ensure that all her research and culinary skills for treating the sick were communicated widely. She achieved this by compiling her notes and recipes into book form, even adding additional recipes which had little to do with their healing properties, ensuring that *Ein Köstlich new Kochbuch* found its place in the kitchens of all aspiring cooks, not just those seeking treatments. She advocated the need for the practical application of cooking, in order to become good at it:

> Nobody ought to be constrained through my book to prepare and to apply exactly the prescribed recipes according to the outlined quantity and amount. On the contrary, reasonable people will consider, in light of the advice of experienced doctors and on the basis of their own knowledge, the nature, physical composition, age, time, place, habits, even the previous life of the patients, and other circumstances, and will know how to adapt the recipes in a reasonable manner and according to the [patient's] needs.[31]

Here speaks a truly professional and modest practitioner of culinary specialism.

Hannah Woolley

Hannah Woolley (also spelt Wolley) was born around 1623. Hannah's work appears to have received a bit of a revival during the Victorian period and then again in the early twentieth century, with a number of references to *The Queen-like Closet* and the avant-garde nature of the woman herself and her work appearing in the media. Within this context she is frequently associated with other pioneering and successful women, and held in esteem as a symbol of the burgeoning women's movement at this time.

With a complex background and mixed beginnings, Hannah was orphaned at fourteen, though amazingly she established a small school by the age of fifteen and subsequently had a successful career as a governess. *The Ladies Directory* and *The Cook's Guide* were published in 1661 and 1664 respectively, not long after she and her husband started offering tuition and boarding to some sixty students in Free Grammar Schools located in first Essex and then London. It was *The Queen-like Closet* of 1674 that appears to have made the most significant impression of all her books. It is also a book that was republished in a number of new editions, and even translated into German. Forced to live with her son after outliving two husbands, Hannah made and sold remedies, practised as an amateur physician and trained other women in this art, whilst continuing to be published. All the time she was doggedly promoting the importance of a scholarly training for all women.[32]

She may well have been the first professional female food writer, earning money from her publications and she provided private tuition to women specifically affected by the Civil War and the Restoration, who had no other option than to go into service.[33]

Hannah wrote the following poem at the beginning of *The Queen-like Closet:*

> Ladies, I do here present you (yet)
> That which sure will well content
> A Queen-like Closet rich and brave
> (Such) not many Ladies have:
> Or Cabinet, in which doth set
> Jems richer than in Karkanet;
> (They) only Eies and Fancies please,
> These keep your Bodies in good ease;
> They please the Taste, also the Eye;
> Would I might be a stander by:

Yet rather I would wish to eat,
Since 'bout them I my Brains do beat:
And 'tis but reason you may say,
If that I come within your way;
I sit here sad while you are merry,
Eating Dainties, drinking Perry;

Figure 8. Frontispiece of Hannah Woolley's *The Queen-like Closet*.

But I'm content you should so feed,
So I may have to serve my need.

The frontispiece of *The Queen-like Closet* depicts five individual views of the kitchen and shows women tackling different tasks, like mixing, cooking, bottling and baking. She concludes with another poem, reminding her readers that if they didn't like what they have just read, then not to blame her. A sort of don't shoot the writer proclamation, emphasising how hard she has worked to provide women with such a helpful guide, that they should undoubtedly find useful. Her frank, no-nonsense style is clearly a reflection of her strong, forward-thinking character.

Jang Gye-hyang

Jang Gye-hyang (1598-1680) was a Korean noblewoman, who wrote the first cookbook to be written by a woman in East Asia, around 1670.[34] *Eumsik dimibang* ('Ways to discern tastes of food'), is also the oldest surviving Korean cookbook. According to Pae-Yong Yi (2008), the handwritten version of the book is also graced with a Chinese title – *Gyugon sieuibang* ('A lady's guidebook'). It is understood that this was added at a later date, in order to give the publication more authority. Lady Jang used native Korean recipes in the Korean language. It contains recipes for a variety of dishes, alcoholic and non-alcoholic drinks and fermented foods, some of which were handed down to her and some of which are original to the author. Part one of *Eumsik dimibang* contains recipes for cooking around 93 types of food including 11 main courses, 55 side dishes and 25 desserts from rice cakes to honeyed cookies.[35]

Jang Gye-hyang was in her early seventies when she started writing *Eumsik dimibang*. In the preface of her book she writes: 'All men and women eat and drink, but a few know the sense of taste.'

Today, the tour guides for the Korean village of Seokgye, where Jang lived and worked, provide a wealth of information on this poetess, author and humanitarian of the seventeenth century. One of the seven sons she raised became a minister to the king at the royal court and if you visit this remote village it is possible to stay in the very house that Jang and her husband built for their family. It is also possible to visit the village museum and restaurant dedicated to her book, which serves the exact same recipes and caters to a lucky few when they open their doors once a week.[36]

A significant percentage of *Eumsik dimibang* focuses on home brewing, which was integral to Korean hospitality in the seventeenth century. Entertaining was extremely important and it would have been the duty of the woman of the house to ensure there was enough brewed alcohol available on tap to satisfy this social nicety. *Gwahaju* is a summer wine, brewed in the spring, mixed with a hard liquor called *soju*, to aid preservation. Lady Jang provides a recipe for this flavoursome beverage which starts by pouring boiled water over four litres of malt powder, before letting it rest overnight. In the morning, the mixture is put through a sieve, before being added to twenty litres of rice, which has been washed, steamed and cooled. After three days, fourteen cups of the *soju* is poured onto the mixture and left to ferment for a further seven days, by which time the resulting 'hot and sweet' wine is ready for consumption.

Great European Influencers

Bartolomeo Scappi

As in other European countries, in Italy, the houses of the wealthy and nobility relied heavily on the kitchen staff, who were integral to the social and domestic success of the family. The master cook was a craftsman, highly prized and generously paid, considered a necessity from medieval to early twentieth-century times.

The Renaissance Italian cook from Lombardy, Bartolomeo Scappi is an example of one such cook who worked for cardinals and Popes. He wrote one of the first popularist recipe books around 1570, the *Opera dell'arte del cucinare*. The book contains a number of rich and unique hand-engraved illustrated examples of early tools and methods for cooking on open hearths. Scappi describes meals prepared whilst in service, including a dinner for the Roman Emperor Charles V with over a dozen different courses. It is understood from the writings of Scappi's biographer and translator of *Opera dell'arte del cucinare,* Terence Scully, that Scappi learned his craft as an apprentice, through extensive observation and widespread travel. This knowledge also enabled him to source the best ingredients, from the best locations – 'if the honey is from Spain it will always be better than ours'.[37] His handy hints, as a well-seasoned (pardon the pun), experienced and knowledgeable cook provide an interesting insight into the specifics of cooking and eating of the time, such as his advice on storing a pie for up to four days in the summer months to ten days in winter. Ah, the joys of storage prior to refrigeration. In fact, he wrote extensively about food that could be cooked or prepared in advance and reheated or simply stored safely for a later date. This sort of knowledge would be extremely useful to cooks working in large, busy households, who could prepare in advance and reduce the amount of work required in the kitchen. Scappi also had a preference for one pot cooking in a testo (a flat earthenware dish), in order to retain moisture and aid continuous basting. Scappi revealed his secrets to cooking success, those little additions that all cooks throughout the centuries have strived to learn, in an attempt to create a perfect or slightly different tasting staple dish. He was an advocate of sweet and sour, citrus juices and sugar, cinnamon in abundance and largely pork infused dishes using a variety of pig-related products, as the foundation for most savoury dishes.

It was Scappi's wish to leave a culinary legacy, a record of his lifetime's work and practical experience. *Opera dell'arte del cucinare* is a beautifully crafted book that provides a wonderful insight into the world of high-level European cooking practices of the sixteenth

Figure 9. Portrait of Bartolomeo Scappi, *Opera di Bartolomeo Scappi.*

century. It demonstrates the accuracy of cooking at this period, with the use of precise quantities and measurements, and it emphasises the importance of hygiene in the kitchen and the need for the right cooking utensils and tools. This book is an exceedingly important record of the achievements – and they do seem quite sophisticated – reached in medieval cooking.

The text in Italian is taken from Scappi's *Opera dell'arte del cucinare*, while the text in English is provided by Terence Scully:

(Per fare tortelletti con la polpa di cappone) [...] uno sfoglio di pasta alquanto sottile, fatto di fior di farina, acqua di rose, sale, butiro, zuccaro, & acqua tepida [...]

(To prepare tortellini with capon flesh [...] a rather thin sheet of dough made of flour, rosewater, salt, butter, sugar and warm water [...]

Per far minestra di tagliatelli
Impastinosi due libre di fior di farina con tre uoua, & acqua tepida, & mescolisi bene sopra una tavola per lo spatio d'un quarto d'hora, & dapoi stendasi sottilmente con il bastone, & lascisi alquanto risciugare il sfoglio, & rimondinosi con lo sperone le parti piu grosse, che son gli orlicci, & quando sarà asciutto però non troppo, perche crepe rebbe, spoluerizzisi di fior di farina con il fetaccio, accioche non si attacchi, piglisi poi il bastone della pasta, & comincisi da un capo, & riuolgasi tutto lo sfoglio sopra il bastone leggiermente, cauisi il bastone, e taglisi lo sfoglio cosi riuolto per lo trauerso con un coltello largo sottile, e tagliati che saranno, slarghinosi, & lassinosi alquanto rasciugare, & asciutti che saranno, fettaccisi fuora per lo criuello il farinaccio, & facciasene minestra con brodo grasso di carne, o con latte, & butiro, & cotti che saranno, seruanosi caldi con cascio, zuccaro, & cannella, & uolendone far lasagne taglisi la pasta sul bastone per lungo, & compartasi la detta pasta in due parti parimente per lungo, e taglisi in quadretti, & faccianosi cuocere in brodo di lepre, ouero di grua, o d'altra carna, o latte, & seruanosi calde con cascio, zuccaro, & cannella.[38]

Early Modernist and New World Culinarians 47

To prepare a thick soup of tagliatelle

Work two pounds of flour, three eggs and warm water into a dough, kneading it on a table for a quarter of an hour. Roll it out thin with a pin and let the sheet of dough dry a little. With a cutting wheel trim away the irregular parts, the fringes. When it has dried, though not too much because it would break up, sprinkle it with flour through the sifter so it will not stick. Then take the rolling pin and, beginning at one end, wrap the whole sheet loosely onto the pin, draw the pin out and cut the rolled-up dough crosswise with a broad, thin knife. When they are cut, broaden them. Let them dry out a little and, when they are dry, filter off the excess flour through a sieve. Make up a soup of them with a fat meat broth, or milk and butter. When they are cooked, serve them hot with cheese, sugar and cinnamon. If you want to make lasagne of them, cut the dough lengthwise on the pin, and likewise divide it lengthwise in two, and cut that into little squares. Cook them in the broth of a hare, a crane or some other meat, or in milk. Serve them hot with cheese, sugar and cinnamon.[39]

Figure 10. Francesco Procopio dei Coltelli.

To me, the extraordinary attention to detail and precise instructions, reflect a recipe book that was well ahead of its time.

Francesco Procopio dei Coltelli

Another well-known Italian, Francesco Procopio dei Coltelli, who was actually born in Sicily in 1651, founded the oldest surviving café in Paris, Café Procope, which he opened during his time there training to become a cook. It was Procopio's vision to create an establishment as glamorous as possible, to encourage customers to want to linger. And glamorous it was. Coffee and Procopio's novelty ice cream was served in the finest silver, the tables were made of solid marble, vast chandeliers adorned the ceilings and elaborate, decorative mirrors filled the walls. The waiting staff were dressed in the finest fur-trimmed hats and long flowing kaftans, a cultural Armenian reference (due to the owner before Procopio being Armenian) that would have been oh so de rigueur in

Figure 11. *Café Procope*, Paris, 1900.

seventeenth century Paris. Initially launched on the rue de Tournon, the café moved premises to what is now known as rue de l'Ancienne-Comédie, where it has traded continuously for almost 350 years. The café once served as the city's premier hangout for actors who performed at the nearby famous Comédie-Française, a relationship which led to Procopio offering a stand for light refreshments providing the theatre audience with general sundries to be enjoyed throughout performances. Café Procope was to spearhead the Parisian café society, with some three hundred and fifty odd similar establishments, modelled on the Italian's theme, opening less than fifty years after across the city.[40] Procopio is also credited with popularising modern ice cream, adding sugar and mixing salt into ice in order to retain its freezing properties. He represents perhaps not only the first known barista, but also the archetypal, Italian migrant artisan ice-cream maker, making gelato accessible to the masses.

Regularly patronised by great writers such as Voltaire and Balzac (the former rumoured to drink up to 40 cups of blended coffee and chocolate on a daily basis), it is understood that the traditional encyclopaedia that we are familiar with today was conceived at Café Procope. Ongoing conversations over endless cups of coffee between its creators Denis Diderot and Jean le Rond d'Alembert during the eighteenth century, resulted in an accessible, comprehensive reference work, the *Encyclopédie*. The model of a meeting place similar to his café, with free newspapers, writing paper and quills that Procopio provided his customers with, may well have influenced those who followed him.[41]

Messrs François Massialot and La Varenne

François Massialot wrote the very grand *Le Cuisinier royal et bourgeois* (*The Court and Country Cook*), first published in 1691, offering an insight into the kitchens of Versailles during the reign of Louis XIV. In this book Massialot describes one particular banquet in detail, hosted by the king's war minister in 1690. Those in attendance included various key members of the royal family. The first service revealed twelve types of soup, together with entrées from exquisite pâtés to roast meats. This was also the time of the meal when small hors d'oeuvres would be put out to munch on alongside the main dishes, like tiny seasoned birds or tasty sausages. The second service for this most courtly of dinners consisted of twenty-two platters of roast beef, mutton, pig, and a variety of poultry, together with an assortment of salads and numerous entremets, from game pies to blancmanges, beignets (doughnuts) and tarts. This gastronomic feast concluded with a choice of foie gras, truffles, crème brûlée or sweet omelettes, amongst other tasty treats. Interestingly Massialot omitted the fruit and confectionery course descriptions, as this was put together by the confectioners opposed to *Le Cuisinier royal*.[42]

Incidently Massialot is credited with the invention of crème brûlée – literally 'burnt cream' – which was actually a milk-based baked pudding, rather than the cream based bain-marie cooked dish we are familiar with today. His *Le Cuisinier royal* was translated into English in 1702 under the title, *The Court and Country Cook*. Here his original recipe confusingly omits sugar as the main ingredient of the dish, instead casually mentioning it at a much later stage in the recipe. This is something you will see all the time in old recipes when they start talking about ingredients halfway through the method, when the ingredient was never listed in the first place. I find it is on the same level of frustration that I often get with modern-day recipes, when you roll up your sleeves and start out with good intentions, only to read part way through the instructions that something needs to be marinated overnight, or chilled in the fridge for several hours, when the reality is that your dish needs to be made and ready to eat in the next thirty minutes or so.

Burnt Cream

> Take four or five Yolks of Eggs, according to the bigness of your Dish or Plate; and beat them well in a Stew-pan with as much Flower as you can take up between Fingers; pouring in Milk by degrees to the quantity of about a Quart: Then put into it a small Stick of Cinnamon with some green Lemmon peel cut small and likewise some candy'd. Orange peel may also be minc'd as that of Lemmon, and then 'tis call'd Burnt Cream with Orange. To render it more delicious, pounded Pistachoes or Almonds may be added,

with a little Orange-flower-water. Then set your Cream upon the Furnace and stir it continually, taking care that it do not stick to the bottom. When it is well boil'd set a Dish or Plate upon a Furnace, and having pour'd the Cream into it, let it boil again till you perceive it to stick to the side of the Dish: Then it being set aside, and well suga'd on the top, besides the Sugar that is put into it; take the Fire-shovel heated red hot, and at the same time burn the Cream with it, to give it a fine Gold colour. To garnish it make use of Feuillantins small Fleurons or Meringues, or other cut Pastry-works of crackling Crust. Ice your cream if you please, or else let it be serv'd up otherwise, but always among the Intermesses.[43]

Another of the pioneering French cooks of the mid-seventeenth

Figure 12. Frontispiece to an edition of
François Pierre de La Varenne's *Le Cuisinier françois*.

century was François Pierre de La Varenne. Born in 1615, his ground-breaking publication and the first of three bestsellers, *Le Cuisinier françois* (*The French Cook*) of 1651, was possibly the book that revolutionised the way in which French people cooked and ate, becoming the inspiration for a whole new sustainable generation of cooking methods and techniques. La Varenne was essentially the founder of French classical cooking at just thirty-five years of age, previously having spent a lucrative ten-year career, as master cook in service to the Marquis d'Uxelles.[44] Very little is known about this avant-garde leader of French culinary style, other than that he was trained as a basic kitchen skivvy in the kitchens of Catherine de Bourbon, sister of Henry IV, and did an apprenticeship in Florence, Italy before going to work for the Marquis d'Uxelles, whose namesake incidentally lives on in one of La Varenne's most famous of dishes, duxelles of mushrooms. La Varenne also invented the principle of the roux – mixing fat and flour to thicken sauces – and from that, the essential Bechamel.[45] La Varenne's subsequent books, *Le Pâtissier françois* (*The French Pastry Chef*) and *Le Parfaict confiturier* (*The French Confectioner*), continued to reinforce this new programme of culinary thought. Examples of some of La Varenne's classics from *The French Cook*, which are now standard cultural dishes, are boeuf à la mode, omelettes, ragouts and bisques. Here is his very simple recipe for boeuf à la mode:

> *Battez-le bien & lardez avec du gros lard, puis le mettez cuire dans un pot avec bon bouillon, un bouquet, & toutes sortes d'épices, & le tout étant bien consommé, serves avec la sauce.*

Translated, it reads:

> Pound it well, lard it with pork fat, then put it to cook in a pot with bouillon, a bouquet of herbs and all sorts of spices. When everything is boiled down, serve with the sauce.

La Varenne's short, concise, detail free recipe style, is indicative of one aimed at other professional cooks, who would already understand the basic principles of cooking.[46]

Stanisław Czerniecki

His 1682 *Compendium ferculorum* ('A collection of dishes') is thought to be one of the earliest surviving published Polish cookery books. The very first was actually translated from a Czech publication in 1544, titled *Kuchmistrzostwo* ('The art of cooking and cellaring'), published by Helena Unglerowa, about whom I can find very little information, apart from the fact that she was the wife of a well-known printer, living in Krakow and that they owned a bookshop together, which the widowed Helena ran single-handedly for many years.[47] This makes Czerniecki's the first Polish language original. Czerniecki appears to have had a number of notable roles, including governor of Krakow, royal secretary and head chef at the Polish court in the service of the Lubomirski family, to whom he was utterly devoted.[48] He worked here from about the age of fifteen. Czerniecki's dedication to Princess Helena Lubomirski in his *Compendium* reads:

> Since there was no one before me who wanted to show the world such a needful thing in our Polish language, I dared, under the protection of my Lady and Greatly Merciful Benefactress with my ineptitude, to write *Compendium ferculorum* or a collection of dishes, and show it to the Polish world.

Compendium ferculorum is not just a recipe book, it is a celebration of culinary taste, a detailed account of everything, from what utensils to use in the kitchen, to how to store foods and how to deliver a successful banquet, from the quality of the entertainment to the level of service, right down to advice relating to the big clean up after an event. Czerniecki was also very particular about the specific qualities a cook should aspire to:

> He should be neat and tidy, with a good head of hair, well-combed, short at the back and sides; he should have clean hands, his fingernails should be trimmed, he should wear a white apron; he should not be quarrelsome, he should be sober, submissive, brisk; he should have a good understanding of flavour, a sound knowledge of ingredients and utensils, together with a willingness to serve everyone.[49]

In 1689, following a distinguished military career, Czerniecki became a landowner, purchasing an entire village, Wola Nieszkowska, in southern Poland. It is now apparently quite a popular ski resort, but it once represented home to generations of Czernieckis.[50] Czerniecki's *Compendium* of some three hundred main recipes in three sections – meat, fish and dairy – includes a variety of bizarre dishes: capon in a bottle, literally a small fowl cooked in a glass container with whisked eggs; lampreys (like small eels) cooked with gingerbread and cherry juice; and beaver's tail boiled in salt and vinegar, garlic and butter. Thankfully the beaver is now a protected animal, but even if it was readily available, I'm certain that its tail would not be the choicest cut to indulge in. The following recipe for Polish rosół, is probably about as timeless as you can get, in terms of traditional Polish fayre. It remains one of the most popular national soups, served at both special events and at family dinners. Here is Czerniecki's version, roughly translated into English:

> This is the way to cook polish rosół: take beef meat or veal, hazel grouse or partridge, pigeon and whatever meat that in rosół can be cooked. Soak it, lay in pot, then strain and pour over meat, add parsley, butter, salt, and skim well. One have to know what to put in rosół to not stink of water or wind, that is parsley, dill, onion or garlic, nutmeg or rosmarin or pepper to taste. Lime will not spoil any rosół as well.[51]

Lancelot de Casteau

Lancelot, a Belgian ecclesiastical cook, served three prince-bishops during the 1500s and wrote one outstanding recipe book, *Ouverture de cuisine* ('Opening the kitchen') in 1604. This unique manual represents possibly the first original collection of international recipes that was not a copied reworking of a medieval book, a practice common at the time. There is only one known surviving original copy which can be found in the archives of the Royal Library of Belgium. Casteau makes reference to a new kind of pastry, reminiscent only of a few other cookery writers of his period, most notably Scappi. This early version of puff pastry is attributed to the Spanish by Casteau, although it is typically credited to the Middle East and popularized by the French or Italians. Lancelot's recipe, like others of that period includes flour, eggs, butter, water and spices rolled into flat sheets and folded over four or five times, layered with melted pork fat.[52]

The Renaissance influence of Italian cuisine, sweeping across Europe at that time is also prominent throughout Casteau's book, including *raphioulles* (ravioli), eighteen recipes for Italian *tortes/tourtes* and that most Italian of classics, *la mostarda di Cremona*. This is perhaps even more understandable considering Casteau's home town of Liège sat along the trade route between Italy and the Low Countries (Belgium, the Netherlands, and Luxembourg).[53] Here is Casteau's recipe to make Cremone mustard, which is almost identical to today's authentic Italian version:

> Take half a pound of orange peels candied in sugar, half a pound of quince preserved in sugar or marmalade, & chop them all well together very small: then take half a pint of mustard well thick, then take melted sugar with rose water, & put therein some turnsole, & let it boil together to give good red color, & let it boil like syrup, & mix therein that which you have chopped, & mix the mustard with, put enough syrup, & serve in little plates three or four spoons for setting at the table with roasts.[54]

Like many of his contemporaries, Casteau also recognised the late medieval shift in the role of women and cooking, and offered a little 'advice' for them:

> Like many Women who willingly meddle with Cooking, as one finds, working in a kitchen better than other Cooks, in many styles & fashions; But for the pleasure of the Ladies there will be found there a little opening for knowing how they should conduct their affairs, to know what one must have for a meat dish, & what a meat dish is.[55]

Perhaps most delightful of all is that Casteau includes the bill of fare at the end of his *Ouverture de Cuisine,* which he prepared for Robert de Berges' ceremonial royal entry. The visual scope of this banquet is perhaps best summed up with the detailed description of the four lavish accompanying displays, which appear to have consisted of a lot of butter.

> There was in the palace accommodation for fourteen plates of meat: the table of the Prince was of five plates.
>
> The second table was of six plates.
>
> The third table of three plates of meats.
>
> For the first service.
> Guinea fowl boiled with oysters, & cardoons, Spanish salad.
> Roast bustard. Tart of blanc mangier.
> Boiled leg of mutton.
> Sweet kid, & roasted oranges.
> Marrow of beef in pottage.
> Suckling pies of partridges.
> Fat roasted veal in *adobe*. Roasted heron.
> Hare in pottage.
> Cold venison pie.
> Roasted crane with olives. Boiled partridge with capers. Roasted crane bird.
> Roasted boar. Breast of veal stuffed and boiled.
> Roasted mutton & *remorasque*.
> Boiled redressed veal. Roasted plovers.
> Stag in pottage. Capon in Hungarian pottage. Roasted water *pegasine*.
> Little birds in pottage.
> Roasted duck in dodine sauce.
>
> Second service.
> Roasted pheasant, royal sauce.
> Fat roasted veal. Pies of kid.
> Roasted stag. Ravioli of beef marrow. Roasted *hulpe*.
> Crane bird in pottage.
> Roasted *begasse*. Capon pies.
> Roasted bittern. Boar in pottage.
> Roasted goat.

Creamed veal tart.
Roasted partridges in pine nut sauce.
Roasted hare.
Roasted swan in *Cremonese* sauce.
Roasted egret. Roasted wood fowl.
Blanc mangier ravioli leaves.
Roasted *lepelaire*. Redressed roasted veal.
Angry pie. Kid in pottage.
English pies.
Stuffed boiled pigeon. Duck in pottage.
Roasted *cerselle*. Redressed leg of
mutton. Roasted wild birds.

Third service.
Redressed wood fowl pies.
Cold roasted bustard. Pheasant pie.
Molded blanc mangier.
Dressed, molded jelly.
Cold roasted wild swan.
Pork jelly.
Redressed partridge pie.
Cold roasted guinea fowl.
Partridge pie, roasted crane.
Oysters in pottage, pigeon pies.
Bologna sausage. Boar pies.
Mushrooms in pottage. Roasted stag.
Boiled sturgeon. Goat pies.
Leg of *Mayence*.
Boiled Boar *hurres*.
Heron pie. Boiled Potato.
Stag pies. Lace jelly.
Anchovies. Bustard pies.
Trout in *adobe*. Lobster.
Guinea fowl pie. Larded jelly.
Hulpe pie. Roasted oysters.
Bittern pie. English *brenne*.
Seulette in *adobe*. Duck pie.
Egret pie. Turbot in *adobe*.
Sturgeon *cafiade*. Hare pie.
Smoked beef tongue. Roasted

Boar. Red deer in *adobe*. Mushroom fritters,
Crane pie. Boiled piece of Boar.
All the cold roasted venison was with gilded feet, & all the redressed pies gilded, & carrying banners.
All the lords were defrayed, each came to the palace seeking their raw meat, & all that they had need, spices & sugar.

Fourth service.
Large gilded marzipan. *Genua* pie.
Liquid sweets. Sugared waffles
Quince pies. Roman pipes.
White marmalade. Clear white jelly
Pistachine. Royal tart.
Long pipes. Orange pie.
Almond lard. May butter.
Wafers. Clear red jelly.
Sugared almonds. Apple pie.
Candied cinnamon. *Moustacholle*.
Dried sugar. *Bugnole* fritters.
Sugar pies. *Samblette*.
Palamitte. Molded marmalade.
Cream tart. Fish preserves.
Orange preserves with flowers.
Ice jelly. Offal puffs.
Large sugared biscuit, Eel fritter.
Sugared *crenelle*. Large *castelin*.
Candied capers. Candied pears.
Snow on rosemary. Raw apples.
Anise. Parmesan. Hungarian candied prunes, puff cakes. Chestnuts.
Morquin. Rosquille. Biscotelle.

There were four parks of two feet square, environed in a hedge of butter.

The first was Adam & Eve made of butter, a serpent on a tree, & a running fountain, with little animals all-around of butter.

The second park was the love of Pyramus & Thisbee, the lion by the fountain, & the trees all around environed in a hedge of butter.

The third park the hunt of Acteon, & the nymphs with Diana at the fountain, & then of the little dogs of butter.

The fourth park was two wild men, who battled one another with the masses by a fountain, & little lions of butter all around: each park had four banners.[56]

Francisco Martinez Montino

Perhaps the most influential Spanish cookbook of the 1600s was *Arte de Cozina, Pasteleria, Vizcocheria y Conserveria* ('The art of cooking, baking, patisseries and conserving') written in 1611 by Francisco Martinez Montino. He began his career as an apprentice working for the sister of Philip II of Spain. Incidentally Philip II is said to have demanded a daily ration of sugared pears and peaches, along with servings of white pudding, three times a week.[57] In fact, from everything I have read, the whole lineal pattern of bad eating amongst all the King Philips seemed to have contributed to their downfall.

Montino worked as grand cuisinier to both Philip III and IV. Philip IV quite famously died of uremia, a failure of the kidneys which is greatly influenced by diet. He was known to eat extremely high levels of meat and animal fats.[58] Undoubtedly Montino would have had to prepare these types of dishes in large quantities. The king suffered a very slow physical decline, which perhaps could have been alleviated with a radical change of diet.

Like many Catholics at that time, Montino was a pious man. In Manuel Fernández y González's *El cocinero de su majestad: Memorias del tiempo de Felipe III* ('His majesty's cook: memoirs of Philip III's time'), we are informed that he attended Mass every evening at 8 o'clock, at the Santo Domingo el Real.[59] This strange little account, which appears to be part fictional and partly based on some genuine facts acquired during Montino's service in the court of Philip III, also implies that Margaret of Austria, the king's wife, was secretly in love with their head cook. The narrative revolves around a plot in which Montino goes on a quest to seek the identity of a young man who introduces himself one day as his nephew. The text weaves in and out of all sorts of complicated episodes, culminating in Montino losing his wife, while his daughter elopes with an unsuitable lad. Why Fernández y González chose Francisco as his protagonist, together with such a complex storyline, in which the central figure is so beset by tragedy, is not clear. But it does certainly infer that Francisco Martinez Montino was perhaps a much more thought-provoking character than I imagined.

Below is Montino's 1611 recipe for 'Frog Pie':

> From frogs you can make a pie, soak them in a bit of fresh fat and toss on top a bit of hot water, and a little bit of greens, salt and let it boil. Then take them out with a skimmer, and season with all spices and salt and place in a vessel with a large co's butter, and when they are cooked, beat some egg yolks with lemon juice and add some broth in which you have purged the frogs, and fill your pie and thicken in the same way that you do to season English empanadas of frogs, soaking the frogs with your fat and onions and you can add all the spices and a little wine and a little verjuice and stew them.[60]

Montino suggested that the most important aspects of being a good cook involved maintaining cleanliness, having good taste buds and a good palette, and what roughly translates as 'readiness', by which he probably meant being prepared.

By 1760 *Arte de Cozina, Pasteleria, Vizcocheria y Conserveria* had made it to twenty-two editions.

Don Quixote, written during Montino's career at the Spanish royal court, is wonderfully illustrative of Spanish cuisine during this shifting period in culinary progression. The food served at the wedding of Camacho is representative of many traditional elements of medieval cooking, however, the detailed descriptions of the staff involved, intense preparation and level of attention, are all indicative of the augmentation of the new culinary movement.[61]

For me, it has to be the wall of cheese that I find the most impressive here, in Cervantes' piquant description of a wedding feast:

> The first object that presented itself to the eyes of Sancho, was an entire bullock spitted whole, upon an elm, roasting by a fire of wood

of the size of a middling mountain, and round it, six pots, but not such pots as are cast in common moulds, for, they were half jars, and each of them contained a whole shamble of meat; whole sheep found room in them, and were stowed as commodiously as if they had been so many pigeons. There was an innumerable quantity of cased hares, and ready plucked fowls that hung about the branches of the trees, ready to be swallowed up in these receivers; and an infinite number of wild fowl, with vast quantities of venison, were likewise hanging about the trees, for the air to cool them. Sancho himself told above threescore skins, which, as it was afterwards discovered, were full of rich wines, every skin containing above twenty-four quarts. Loaves of the whitest bread were piled up like heaps of wheat on a threshing floor; and such a quantity of cheese ranged in the form of bricks, as seemed a wall; two pans, as wide as cauldrons, and larger than a dyer's vat, full of oil, were ready for frying their fritters and pancakes; and when fried, they took them out with strong peels, and dipped them in another pot that stood by full of prepared honey. The cooks, men and women, amounted to about fifty, clean, good humoured, and all busy; in the belly of the roasting bullock, were sewed a dozen sucking pigs, to make it tender and savoury. Spices of all sorts, which seemed to have been bought by wholesale and not by retail, stood in a vast chest.[62]

It should be noted that the reference to 'Spices of all sorts' here would also include items like candied orange peel, sugar and almonds.

Maintaining the Spanish theme, it would be careless not to include Diego Granado as an example of early Modernist European culinary intelligence. His gigantic *Libro del arte de cozina* ('A book on the art of cooking') predated Montino's work by about twelve years. It also significantly plagiarised (almost word for word) the Spanish cook, Ruperto de Nola's very early manual of 1520, *Libre del coch* ('A cook's book') This was a sort of policy document for future workers of the king – both kitchen and general household – to adopt. Nola, who was head cook to Don Ferrante (Ferdinand I of Naples) from 1458 to 1494, is important within the context of the whole discourse on culinary history, in that he advocated the need for cooking to be elevated to the status of culinary art. The word 'moderno' occurs with some frequency within the titles of his recipes, already establishing awareness of the turning tide in cooking at this time. He also attributes a wealth of international dishes from other cultures, like Moorish and Jewish recipes, as inspiration for the evolution of national Spanish cuisine.[63] *Libre del Coch* provides wonderful written documentation of how food for royalty was prepared, cooked and served in sixteenth century Spain. A rare example indeed. In case you're wondering why a Spanish cook and Spanish writer of Spanish recipes was serving an Italian district, run by a Spanish King, the simple answer is that Naples fell in and out of ownership of the Spanish Empire during this era.

Here is Nola's intriguing recipe for 'Pottage which is called *Higate* because it is made from figs', translated from his *Libre del Coch*:

Potaje Que Se Dice Higate Porque Se Hace De Higos

Fig and Bacon Soup

Take white and black figs and put them in cold water, or tepid which would be better; and with this water wash the figs very well, and remove the stems; and when they are very clean and washed, set them to gently fry with good, very fatty bacon; and when they have gently fried for a while, take good hen's broth or mutton broth, and cast it in little by little, in such a manner that it can cook for an hour and a half; and while it cooks, cast all these spices upon it in the pot, which should be well-ground: sugar, ginger, cinnamon, and pepper, and other good spices; and if the pottage is of black figs, cast in a little saffron, so that it has a yellow color; and when it is half cooked, stir it with a *haravillo*, like someone stirring gourds, in such a manner that it will be thick; and do not remove your hand from them until they are well-thickened, tasting it for saltiness and sourness and sweetness; and when it is removed from the fire, let it rest a little while; and prepare dishes, and cast sugar and cinnamon upon them.[64]

American Settlers

In terms of early American colonists, food was dependent on the region and type of migrational influence. Jamestown in Virginia was an area heavily populated by the English, New York by the Dutch, while the Spanish settled in Florida's St Augustine and the French in South

Early Modernist and New World Culinarians   63

Carolina. Often Europeans adapted or integrated Native American recipes, alongside their own traditional meals.

Amelia Simmons' book *American Cookery* is considered the first published work of early American cuisine, and was published in 1796. The leader of the first Plymouth Pilgrim colony to arrive in Massachusetts in 1620, William Bradford wrote a journal documenting the first thirty to forty years of their experiences. Written partly in the first and partly in the third person, presumably to make the journal sound more authoritative, it is sometimes confusing, but provides a detailed and informative illustration of the pilgrims' struggle from arrival to early settlement. Bradford talks about the harsh shortage of food, which was subsidised by further ships arriving later to the colony, bringing much needed cattle amongst other things. They did, however, eat lobsters in abundance and in fact Bradford informs us the settlers diet mostly consisted of fish, without bread or vegetables, as a consequence of still learning to farm the land. Following the first harvest, everyone received 'a quarter of a pound of bread a day'.[65] *Mourt's Relation*, a similar journal from that time compiled mostly by Edward Winslow, describes a meal settlers ate with a small community of native Americans, who he recalls 'entertained us with joy, in the best manner they could, giving us a kind of bread called by them *maizium*'. They ate this together with 'the spawn of shads', followed by boiled acorns,[66] the former being an open water fish – its spawn, undoubtedly the roe eggs.

Squanto

Squanto (circa 1585-1622), was a Native American from the Patuxet tribe. He taught the early Plymouth Pilgrim settlers how to hunt, where to fish and cultivate the land for food, using the resources available. He recommended manuring the ground with herrings, which were in great abundance. He was well travelled, initially captured as a slave and taken to Spain. He even lived in England for some time and spoke the English language. Squanto is often associated with the first Thanksgiving tradition, although there remains a great deal of contention around the origins of this annual American holiday.

Figure 13. Squanto teaching Plymouth colonists.

Many believe it to coincide with Native Indians and Pilgrims coming together to feast after their first corn harvest, successfully achieved by settlers and Squanto working the land together. The other less idealistic discourse around Thanksgiving, involves a great massacre of the Pequot tribe, led by English and Dutch mercenaries following their annual corn festival. The next day was decreed one of 'Thanksgiving', owing to the vast number of Native Indians that were successfully slaughtered. The turkey is native to the Americas, as are the traditional corn and squash accompaniments. A contract was drawn up between Squanto and the Pilgrims, including agreements not to physically hurt or offend each other and to leave all weapons behind before entering respective camps and so on.[67] Sickness and disease through lack of food and poor diet was a constant threat to these early settlers and without the help of Squanto undoubtedly many more would have perished sooner.

Among early established colonists there was a preference for British cuisine, reproduced from British recipe books, one of the most popular being Hannah Glasse's *The Art of Cookery Made Plain and Easy*. More about Hannah and Amelia Simmons can be found in chapter two. It should also be noted that depending on the colony and geographical region, cooking was done in accordance with the availability of local crops and type of agriculture, alongside the influences of the migrant communities themselves. For example, the French settlers deported to Louisiana during the eighteenth century influenced the way food was cooked in this state, and evidence of their style of cooking still exists today. Certainly, the French chef Louis Eustache Ude's *The French Cook* of 1813, would have graced the shelves of the fashionable Louisiana households.

William Sherman

Bake houses were the first commercial food retail businesses to be established in the colonies. One of the earliest colonial bakers was William Sherman. He lived in the Coke-Garrett house, Williamsburg. He sold this around 1708 (also around the time of his death) to a Mr. Joseph Chermeson, who was interestingly then granted a license to open an 'Ordinary' – in other words a cook shop – on this site. This suggests that the property was already being utilised as some sort of business involving the retail of food, and may have been where Sherman operated as a baker.[68] Although the inventory of his estate, including curtains, a looking glass, several dishes and tankards, a punch bowl and small kettle amongst other items, does not reveal much evidence of him ever having owed any significant baking equipment. The first bakers of Colonial America would have relied heavily on corn and rye, with no proper leaveners. Nuts and molasses were used primarily to flavour. The following recipe for cornbread was published in 1867, but was acquired some forty years before this from a southern state hotelier:

> Scald the corn meal in boiling hot water, just as much as will barely wet it, make up the dough with sweet, rich milks, and work it well and put it to bake in a hot oven or stove; it is important that the stove be hot, and the baking done quickly, or the bread will have a dry and insipid taste. The dough should be formed into what the

old Virginians call dodgers: 2 and ½ inches long, 1 and a ½ wide, 1 and ¼ inches thick; or, it is excellent baked on a griddle in cakes 3 inches in diameter. The milk has the effect of browning the crust handsomely. Eaten hot with Alderney milk...'[69]

The Armitages

It was difficult to determine whether the story of the Armitages should be recounted in the chapter addressing forgotten notable cooks, or here as an example of very early food and drink trading. As so much documented American culinary history revolves around the eighteenth century, it seemed important to clarify that there was plenty of activity occurring earlier than this. Of course, there was. People have always needed to eat and drink, both in the domestic and work environment. Understandably, many taverns serving food, or establishing themselves on the British model of Ordinaries, set themselves up in key locations convenient to serve the local community and cater to weary travellers. It is understood that one of the first cook shops to serve meals – The Anchor – was opened in the colonies in the early to mid-1600s, and eventually licensed to 'Goody' Armitage, in the city of Lynn, north of downtown Boston, Massachusetts. The following poem is from Lynn's early industrial era, and is still in common parlance today.

Lynn, Lynn, city of sin
You never come out the way you went in.
Ask for water they give you a gin
the girls say no but always give in

By the seventeenth century, female licensees were often frowned upon, as was the case with Goody, who was revoked permission to 'drawe wine'. Goody – or Jane as she is referred to in the records – put forward a petition to the General Court in 1643, to hand custody of the cook shop over from her husband to her. The reason for this is not entirely clear, other than that it appears Joseph Armitage got into financial difficulties of some sort. The petition was signed by some of leading men in the community at the time, together with two ministers. Jane's husband Joseph was originally a tailor, who, prior to the petition was still the licence holder for The Anchor.[70] It appears that The Anchor either continued to sell alcohol illegally, or chose to wait a number of years before petitioning the court for a number of old financial expenses owed to Joseph in 1669, for entertainment services provided to local dignitaries. These included eleven shillings and four pence owed by Governor John Endecott for beer and wine, six shillings and eight pence from Simon Bradstreete for beer and wine, one shilling and four pence owed by Thomas Bradbury et al for the cost of dinner… And so the list went on. Joseph died in 1680. The cost of his burial is recorded as fourteen shillings, while the wine and cider that was consumed at his funeral totalled two pounds, around £200 in today's money. This certainly denotes where his priorities lay, even in death.[71]

Chapter Two

Women Cooks of the Enlightenment and Empire

1700 to 1900 was a time when the publication of recipe books was at its most prolific. The new middle classes were enjoying the availability and accessibility of varied and exotic foods, whilst indulging in a love-hate relationship with French cuisine. The wealthy got wealthier and the poor became more dependent. As the centuries progressed, industrialization and innovation began to dominate British society and with it food production and cookery evolved. A number of influential women emerged in the field of cooking and cookery literature from the slightly tragic Hannah Glasse, to Eliza Acton and her arguably less creative, yet more sensationalised contemporary, Isabella Beeton.

Depending on class of course, traditionally the role of women written about during the eighteenth century suggests that they were constrained by family and largely remained subjugated and marginalized. But in trade, retail and business generally, many thrived and left their mark on society. By the Victorian period, British cookery writers began to incorporate more firsthand experiences of foreign cuisine, as a consequence of new opportunities for travel and access to different countries and cultures. There remained an ongoing glut of French cookery books, inherited from the migrant cooks of the French revolution and sustained by the overriding belief that the French were the most advanced gastronomic pioneers in the world. However, Britain's global empirical endeavours were beginning to influence cooking and cookery writing generally, with recipes for curry and sea turtles dressed in the West Indian manner dominating the new culinary scene.[1]

This was the age of learning, training and trading, and women turned to cookery lessons in their droves, either to seek employment, keep up with the trends, or to learn more about household matters. Liners sped across the oceans in record time and increased migration and a desire to learn from experience, encouraging the Georgians through to the Edwardians to explore and advance.

One of the great cooking crusaders of the time was Margaret Pearson.

Margaret Pearson

Pearson trained at the illustrious National Training School for Cookery, founded in 1874. From here she moved to Scotland, as superintendent of the Dundee School of Cookery. By 1886 she was working in the colonies of Australia, preaching the word of good culinary principles to the masses.[2] An observer of one of her lectures in Melbourne in 1888, noted that it was attended by 'maids and matrons of every degree in the social scale from the general servant, who wishes to qualify for the more important office of cook, to the lady of fashion, who, for the moment, has "taken up cookery" as her latest and most engrossing fad'.[3]

Clearly fired up by her trade, that same year Pearson wrote *Cookery Recipes for the People*, an instant bestseller with over 16,000 copies sold. A brief review appeared in the *Williamstown Chronicle* (Australia), on 29 June 1889, which read: 'This is a thoroughly practical and trustworthy book, and embraces all kinds of cooking.' *Cookery Recipes for the People* was also released under the title *Australian Cookery*. Essentially, this was a compendium of recipes that Margaret taught as part of a series of lectures and demonstrations she delivered on behalf of the Metropolitan Gas Co. during the 1888 Centennial Exhibition in Melbourne, marking one hundred years of European settlement. *Australian Cookery* is a very rare book indeed, which I would dearly love to get my hands on. A review in the Hobart newspaper, *The Mercury*, on 7 February 1890, described the book as:

> a practical one, the directions being plain and brief, and the recipes generally such as people of moderate means really require. Miss Pearson's book will be welcome in many households.

Figure 14. Cookery class at the Working Men's College, Melbourne.

Even rarer still is her *Australian Household Book: on Fruits, Canning, Preserving, Drinks and Light Summer Dishes*, written in 1890, and the only copy I can find resides in the archives of the State Library, Victoria.

Margaret was appointed to run cookery lessons at the Melbourne Working Men's College, but aimed at women and girls rather than actual working men. Here, together with her colleague Harriet Wicken who was equally well-known in her own right, Margaret taught and delivered demonstrations alongside participation in the numerous International Exhibitions, which were so popular during the nineteenth

Women Cooks of the Enlightenment

century. They could promote cookery using the science of invention, gadgetry and new technology.[4] A notice for one of her courses, whilst at the Working Men's College, read:

> Miss Pearson, South Kensington, Diploma, Instructress of Cookery at the Working Men's College and Principal Schools, Convents, etc. Melbourne, purposes giving a course of ten demonstration lessons on Cookery at Bendigo, commencing in October. The course will consist of high-class Soups, Stocks, Gravies, Boning Fowl or Turkey, Galantines, Larding, Stewing, Frying, Grilling, Roasting, etc. Sweet and Savory Jellies, Creams, Puddings, Souffles, Omelettes, Pastry, Cakes, etc, etc. A lesson will also be given in Sickroom Cookery, and on Canning and Preserving Fruits…All work done in the presence of the students.[5]

In 1932 the press in both Pearson's native Scotland and homeland of Australia were advertising a book called *Fifty Meals Without an Oven*, written by a Margaret Pearson – on sale for two shillings. *The Shepparton Advertiser* described it thus:

> A new book of recipes, called 'Fifty Meals Without an Oven', has just been published. The recipes, which have been compiled by Margaret Pearson, are designed especially for the bachelor girl or for the housewife in charge of a small flat who does most of her cooking over a little gas griller which has no oven. All the recipes require the use of a grill and one gas ring only. There are menus for fifty days, and each one is different. While the book will appeal specially to the cooks for whom Miss Pearson has compiled it, the little book will also make a wider appeal because of its recipes.

I managed with great glee to acquire a first edition of this book. But this soon turned to disappointment when I examined what presumably is supposed to be a picture of Pearson included. The photograph is of a young woman, dressed in what appears to be typical 1930s attire and her introduction is signed as if writing from London. The year *Fifty Meals* was written, our Margaret, although still active, would have been in her eighties and not living in London. If anyone reading this can refute this, I would very much like to know. That being said, the young

Margaret Pearson's little book is very good indeed and I would very much like to know more about this obscure cookery writer of the 1930s.

Our Margaret settled in Brisbane, Australia where she lived past the age of ninety. She led an extraordinary life, initially working as a

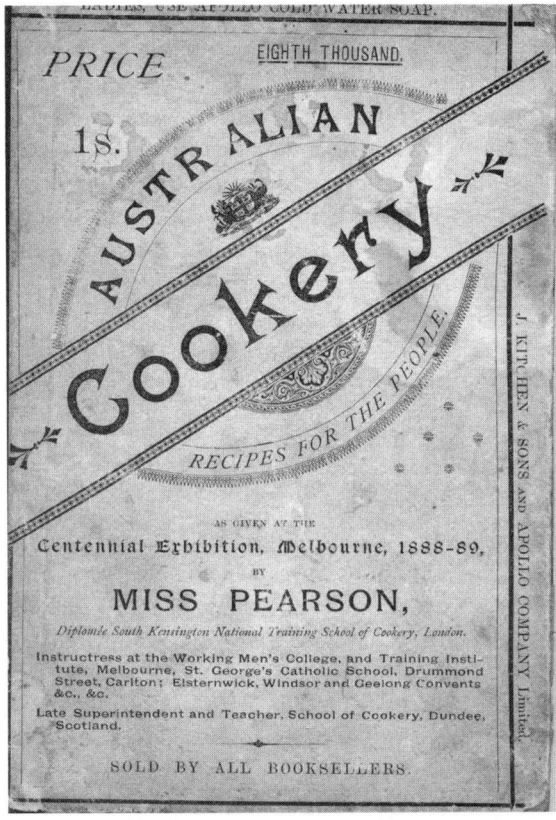

Figure 15. Cover of Margaret Pearson's *Australian Cookery*.

governess in Scotland, following a boarding school education, which lead to a broad career in cookery and cookery writing. An accomplished woman in many ways, throughout her life, she taught a variety of subjects including music, painting, drawing and French. She was also a talented musician, specialising in the organ and guitar. A seasoned traveller, Margaret had conquered the whole of Australia, Scotland, Ireland and a little of England. She was still in paid employment up to the age of eighty. As an old lady, she was physically described as having 'snowy white hair, neatly brushed back from her face, and blue eyes gazing intently from behind horn-rimmed glasses' and being 'dainty'.[6]

Encarnación Pinedo

Born in 1848, Pinedo is probably the latest cook historically to appear in this chapter. She wrote the first cookbook to be published in the United States by a Hispanic, *El Cocinero Español* ('The Spanish cook'). It remains the only surviving account of what early Spanish settlers ate in California,[7] therefore, making Encarnación Pinedo a very special contributor to culinary history. Written in 1898, *El Cocinero Español* is a whopping eight hundred and eighty recipes strong, at least, including both Spanish and Mexican dishes as well as European recipes. She disregarded much of what was eaten by other American settlers, in terms of 'Yankee' dishes. Historically, her family had suffered considerable losses at the hands of New Englanders and local vigilantes, of both lives and land. Undoubtedly, maintaining her Mexican cultural identity was of great significance for Encarnación as United States imperialism continued to quash their communities. In giving her compendium of recipes the title of 'Spanish', Encarnación was attempting to better legitimize her role in society by association with a more respected European heritage.[8] Pinedo kept a journal of daily life in Alta California during the 1850s, which she wrote up in 1901 for Santa Clara College. Much of it is based on religious observations, but it provides a wealth of information about how communities interacted and lived in an everyday way. She mentions the great banquet that accompanied a local wedding and toasts to the bride and groom that were sung in rhyme. Pinedo talks at length about the Native Indians, who held great parties, painted all in red, adorned with many beads and bangles. Food was rationed out on a weekly basis which you either queued for, or, if you were an unmarried woman, supplies would be taken directly to your residence. Ships from Boston moored twice a year, with various cargoes, from food to stockings, porcelain and glassware, which was available for purchase. Farming was obviously integral to survival and Encarnación writes detailed accounts of the process of ploughing and harvesting, notably commenting on the complications involved with managing a seven-year drought.[9]

Encarnación Pinedo never married and having lost her father when she was very young and her mother in her twenties, she lived out her life with her sister's family, who were comfortably well-off. This was due in part to Pinedo's brother-in-law being a European, who was able to secure steady bourgeois employment.

Dan Strehl has translated various sections of *El Cocinero Español* publishing it in 2005 under the title *Encarnación's Kitchen: Mexican Recipes from Nineteenth Century California.*

I couldn't resist including Pinedo's recipe here for Enchiladas – the ultimate Mexican comfort food, in my humble opinion:

Enchiladas de Maiz à la Mexicana

Make the nixtamal [a process of preparing corn which is soaked and cooked in an alkaline substance, like limewater] with five pounds of white corn and two tablespoons of lime. Boil the corn until it acquires a white color, stirring frequently so it takes on a good color. Remove it from the fire, and rinse in several changes of water, rubbing the corn with your hands to remove the skins. Grind the nixtamal, adding a half pound of flour for five pounds of ground corn, a little salt, a piece of lard, and warm water.

    Knead the dough until it has a good consistency. Make small balls; rest on a napkin for five minutes.

    Lightly grease a comal [a type of griddle] or stovetop with lard and put on a tortilla; as soon as it is set, give it a turn, taking it off the moment it starts to bubble. Put the tortillas on a plate and then fry each one in a frying pan in very hot lard.

    Drain the tortillas as they are removed from the oil. The bathe them in a sauce of red chile fried in a little lard with sesame seed and oregano. Chop four onions very fine. Pour boiling water over them, rinse immediately with cold water, and drain completely.

    Slice some olives in strips, Mexican sausage, [and] grated Dutch cheese or slices of fresh cheese.

    As soon as you fry each tortilla, drain it and pass through the chile sauce. Set it on a plate and put on the onion, olives, sausage, and grated or sliced cheese.

Roll up the tortilla, and place each enchilada in the serving dish.

When the plate is filled, cover the enchiladas with a lid and place in the oven, and serve very hot.

There are some who prefer to fry the chile in olive oil.[10]

Elizabeth Raffald

Elizabeth Raffald née Whitaker (1733-81) remains one of the eighteenth century's most memorable and versatile English cookery writers. Born in Doncaster and on receiving a fair education, she was employed by Lady Elizabeth Warburton for three years as Housekeeper of Arley Hall, Cheshire, until her marriage to the gardener. She had nine children, owned her own shop working as a Confectioner and training other women in her art. After the publication of her successful cookbook, she ran several Inns across Manchester and Salford (although some failed). As if that wasn't enough, Raffald tried her hand at journalism and invested in Salford's first newspaper, as well as compiling the first trade directory for Manchester.

Having initially traded in Fennell Street, as the owner of a Register Office, providing families with domestic servants, Raffald opened her confectionery shop near the once famous Bulls Head pub in the Market Place, Manchester. For a number of years during the eighteenth century, it was the only inn in the city where you could purchase wine. Her shop, as the *Manchester Mercury* of 1766 proclaimed, sold jellies, creams and other sugary treats that were 'as good and as cheap as in London'.[11] According to Roy Shipperbottom in *Cooks & Other People: Proceedings of the Oxford Symposium on Food and Cookery*, by 1768 the range of products had extended to:

> Canterbury, Shrewsbury and Derbyshire Brawn, Newcastle Salmon, Yorkshire hams, Tongues and Chaps, Potted Woodcocks, Char and Potted Meats, Portable Soups for Travellers…fresh Mushroom Catchup, Walnut Catchup, Lemon Pickle and Browning for made dishes, Picked Mushrooms, Barberrys, Mangos, and other sorts of pickles; dry and wet sweetmeats, Plumb cakes for weddings and Christenings, and all sorts of Cakes, Mackroons and Biskets, Jellies, Creams, Flummery, Gold and Silver Webs for covering sweetmeats,

and all other decorations for cold Entertainments.

Raffald's *The Experienced English Housekeeper*, 1769, boasted some 900 original recipes, 'whole proper province they are',[12] although future editions did contain other less original recipes. The publication was dedicated to her former employer, Lady Elizabeth Warburton of Arley Hall in Cheshire.

Elizabeth's husband, John Raffald, became the publican at the King's Head Inn in Chapel Street, Salford, and in their later years, they were the proprietors of the Manchester Coffee Exchange,[13] where John was Master, and Elizabeth was in the kitchen.[14]

Elizabeth died of what would probably now have been labelled a

Figure 16.
Frontispiece of Elizabeth Raffald's *The Experienced English Housekeeper*.

stroke in 1781. Her legacy, however, extended across the Atlantic, as she is remembered in several American newspaper articles. One published in the early twentieth century recalled the fact that *The English Housekeeper* ran to two editions in the same year due to its popularity. It also noted that she sold the rights to a third edition for the sum of 7,000 dollars. The book ran for a further thirty-six editions, suggesting that her decision to relinquish the rights was a rather poor one. The article also praised her efforts with producing the first directory for the city of Manchester in 1772, a project that ran every year until her death.[15]

In 1773 Elizabeth proposed her local directory would achieve the following:

> ...in order to make such a useful Work as correct as possible, to send proper and intelligent Persons round the Town, to take down the Name, Business, and Place of Abode of every Gentleman, Tradesman, and Shop-Keeper, as well as of others whose Business or Employment has any tendency to public Notice: the Proprietor therefore humbly requests, that everyone will please to give the necessary Information to the persons appointed, that she may be enabled to give an accurate Edition of a Work so advantageous to such a large, populous, and Trading Town as this is...[16]

Raffald's *English Housekeeper* contains heavily detailed instructions. Her 'sweet patties' are credited as the first Eccles cake recipe, an adaption of an existing ancient recipe.[17] Eventually the boiled calves feet were thankfully eliminated:

Sweet Patties

> TAKE the meat of a boiled calf s-foot, two large apples, and one ounce of candied orange; chop them very small; grate half a nutmeg; mix them with the yolk of an egg, a spoonful of French brandy and a quarter of a pound of currants clean washed and dried; make a good puff paste, roll it in different shapes as the fried ones, and fill them the same way; you may either bake or fry them. They are a pretty side dish for supper.[18]

Elizabeth frequently promoted her commercial activities, which were well documented in the newspapers of the time. What I like about Raffald in particular is that she spent the vast majority of her working life in Manchester – a welcome change from the endless London-centric cooks whose lives have been the most thoroughly recorded.

Another non London-centric English female celebrity cook was Maria Rundell, who lived most of her life in Bath before retiring to Lausanne in Switzerland.

Maria Rundell

Rundell's 1806 book *A New System of Domestic Cookery*, is said to be the second book only in Britain and America in which a butchery diagram was published. Maria's recipes, like Raffald's, proved to be very popular, with at least sixty-seven editions printed between 1806 and 1846. Essentially the book was a manual for poorly skilled domestics, aimed at the wealthier classes and based on Rundell's own tips and recommendations to be passed down to her daughters. One of the reasons why a butchery diagram was included can be attributed to the fact that fewer women were aware of the definitions and anatomical locations of all the various cuts of meat. This is testimony to nineteenth century urbanization, with families no longer travelling to public markets, preferring to rely on their local butchers to supply and deliver regular meat consignments. In this respect, Rundell's book can be viewed as an example of the changing times.[19] Maria just missed out on the dawn of the Victorian era, but she reached the age of eighty-three, having lived a relatively long life indeed for the period, srraddling both the eighteenth and nineteenth centuries. The book was a huge commercial success, for which sadly she received only a fraction of her earnings, due to an acrimonious relationship with her publisher, which ended in court.[20] While living in Swansea in 1806, Mrs Rundell collected various recipes for cookery and suggestions for household management for the benefit of her married daughters. She sent the manuscript to the publisher, John Murray, of whose family she was an old friend. He suggested the title *Domestic Cookery* and had the work carefully revised by competent editors and added engravings. Amongst these editors was Dr Charles Taylor, of the Society of Arts. The book was eventually published as *A New System of Domestic Cookery* in 1806, and had an immense success. Between five and ten thousand copies were printed annually. It became one of Murray's most valuable commissions. In 1812, when he bought the lease on his house, part of the security was dependant on the copyright of the book.

In addition to *A New System of Domestic Cookery*, *The New Family Receipt Book*, *American Domestic Cookery* and *The Experienced American Housekeeper*, she wrote a little-known manual on pregnancy and childcare in 1810, which can be found in the archives of the Wellcome Library and a work of fiction, *Letters Addressed to Two Absent Daughters*, published in 1814.

The following obituary was posted in the Gentleman's Magazine and Historical Chronicle of 1829:

> At Lausanne, aged 83, Maria-Eliza, widow of Thos.Rundell, esq. of Bath, and only child of Abel Johnstone Ketelby esq. of Ludlow.

And The Gentleman's Magazine of 1823 informs us that Thomas Rundell's brother Philip, was a partner in the eminent firm of Rundell & Bridge, silversmiths and jewellers, which was long established on Ludgate Hill, London, suppling snuff-boxes to the value of 8,205l. 15s. To foreign ministers at the coronation of George IV.[21]

Rundell had a number of children and her frequent correspondence with the socialite and courtier, Mary Hamilton reveals her constant efforts to ensure they were all kept well educated according to their abilities and integrated appropriately into Georgian society. She advises Hamilton when travelling with young children to carry a bottle of victuals 'made quite hot, and wrapped in flannels, & a cap, so that they may be fed if waking'. She also recommended that 'a crust of bread would likewise…be proper to carry with you to amuse the young lady in the chaise between changes'.[22] This abundance of maternal care and knowledge is very evident throughout *A New System of Domestic*

Cookery, which includes basic instructions on childcare and healthy eating advice for growing children.[23]

Ivan Day wrote in the *Strand Magazine* that King George I was sometimes nicknamed 'The Pudding King', as the royal family ate plum pudding as part of the Christmas Day meal in 1911. George III was also called 'brown George', perhaps for wearing a brown wig (he certainly had a very impressive one with long locks in various paintings, including one by Sir Godfrey Kneller), or for unfashionably requesting brown bread to be consumed in the royal household and bread was sometimes incorporated into puddings, so perhaps the two became intertwined. Whatever the real story is behind King George and puddings, Maria Rundell's 'George Pudding', in her manual *Domestic Cookery*, is a fine pudding fit for any King (or Queen).

A George Pudding

> Boil very tender a handful of whole rice in a small quantity of milk, with a large piece of lemon peel. Let it drain; then mix with it a dozen of good sized apples, boiled to pulp as dry as possible: add a glass of white wine, the yolks of five eggs, two ounces of orange and citron cut thin; make it pretty sweet. Line a mould or basin with a very good paste: beat the five whites of the eggs to a very strong froth, and mix with the other ingredients; fill the mould, and bake it of a fine bright colour. Serve it with the bottom upward with the following sauce: two glasses of wine, a spoonful of sugar, the yolks of two eggs, and a bit of butter as large as a walnut; simmer without boiling, and pour to and from the saucepan, till of a proper thickness; and put in the dish.[24]

Amelia Simmons

Many people associate Amelia Simmons' 1796 publication *American Cookery* as the first American cookbook, highlighting transatlantic changes in cooking equipment and terminology. The cookery book is important, appearing twenty years after American Independence, but it was William Parks who must be credited with the first American culinary text, with his specialist publication of Eliza Smith's *The Compleat Housewife,* some 54 years before Amelia Simmons even contemplated this notion, which was designed to exclude recipes 'the ingredients or materials for which are not to be had in this country'.[25]

A printer and newspaper man, little is known about Parks, other than his roots were originally from Shropshire, England. He pioneered the first printing house in Maryland, before initiating a weekly newspaper in Williamsburg, called the *Virginia Gazette*. Not a man particularly passionate about cookery, his published works were eclectic to say the least from colonial statutes, to *Typographia, an ode on printing* (1730) and the equally enthralling sounding *The Office and Authority of a Justice of the Peace* (1736).[26]

Aside from Parks' colonial edition of *The Compleat Housewife*, up until the nineteenth century, the majority of early American settlers had to be satisfied with inherited British or other European recipe books. Amelia Simmons's *American Cookery* of 1796 is thought to be the first notable cookery book of American authorship. Eliza Smith's *The Compleat Housewife*, printed in Williamsburg in 1742, is thought to be the first cookbook published in the colonies, while Susannah Carter's 1772 *The Frugal Housewife* became popular in Boston. Nonetheless, all these early publications remained largely rehashed versions of English works. American variations on British recipes were essential to the needs of New World settlers, whose methods of cooking, cooking terminology and utensils all needed adapting to the changes taking place in colonial America. *American Cookery* presents us with molasses, rather than treacle and emptins instead of yeast. Even the type of ingredients varied greatly from those of their European counterparts. As with many cookery writers of that time, much of Amelia's work was plagiarized. Nonetheless its content set the stage for further similar works within the genre of uniquely American gastronomic literature.[27]

Very little is known about Amelia, except that she was a simply educated orphan, accomplished in the art of cookery, who wrote for the benefit of both the wealthy and poorer classes and was probably from the Hudson River Valley region of America. In the preface to *American Cookery*, Simmons reflects on the unfortunate position of many orphans, forced into domestic service, a hint perhaps to her own situation. The surname Simmons has its origins in the south west of England. A high incidence of parental deaths was recorded in the southern colonies from childbirth or disease during this period, which may account for Simmons being an orphan. It is estimated that around 75 percent of southern children lost at least one parent during childhood. Frequently, orphaned children were 'bound-out' or were in receipt of an apprenticeship to train in a skilled profession.[28] Alternatively, Amelia may have travelled to America as an already orphaned indentured slave, perhaps a kitchen worker. One must also take into account the fact it was not uncommon for many cookery writers during the eighteenth and nineteenth centuries to remain anonymous or provide a pseudonym, making it possible that the Amelia Simmons of *American Cookery* may have never even existed. The book however was issued with Federal Copyright, the same year as publication, classified as a State Department record in the name of Amelia Simmons, orphan and American.[29]

Some of Amelia's uniquely American recipes include those using indigenous foods like cornmeal to make 'Johnnycakes', a flat-bread that some attribute to Rhode Island, New England and 'Indian Slapjacks', a type of pancake, known commonly as 'flapjack' today. Although, there is evidence to suggest that the origins of the word flapjack can be traced back at least to 1500s England, as quoted in Shakespeare:

> Come, thou shalt go home, and we'll have flesh for holidays, fish for fasting-days, and moreo'er puddings and flap-jacks, and thou shalt be welcome.[30]

Similarly, cornmeal was not particular to Native America and is documented in many countries as a cheap substitute for flour or oatmeal. Johnnycakes may even be a derivative of the English 'jannock', a type of oatmeal bread meaning straightforward or genuine and deriving from early Dutch settlers in Lancashire during the 1500s.[31]

There are also recipes for pumpkins and squash which were then only native to North America. The closest vegetable available in Britain to the pumpkin in the 1700s would have been the turnip or mangelwurzle. Incidentally, both were used as lanterns in traditional Hallow'een English folklore, way before the pumpkin craze of the twentieth century.

Other migrant phrases that had obviously worked their way into the early American language and are to be found in *American Cookery* include the Dutch words 'koekje' (or, as Simmons puts it, 'cookey'), termed 'little cakes' or 'cakes' in British culinary literature at the time, and 'slaw', meaning salad.[32]

Here is Simmons' recipe for 'Another Christmas Cookey':

> To three pound of flour, sprinkle a tea cup of fine powdered coriander seed, rub in one pound of butter, and one and half pound sugar, dissolve one tea spoonful of pearlash in a tea cup of milk, kneed all together well, roll three quarters of an inch thick, and cut or stamp into shape and size you please, bake slowly fifteen or twenty minutes; tho' hard and dry at first, if put in an earthern pot, and dry cellar, or damp room, they will be finer, softer and better when six months old.[33]

To most of us the thought of eating six-month old biscuits, sounds rather unappetising. Having tried and tested old biscuit recipes myself, although I cannot vouch for the taste, I can confirm that they often stay physically appealing for many months, undoubtedly preserved by the vast quantities of sugar used in the baking process.

Mary Randolph

Another hugely inspirational cook, this time of the nineteenth century, was Mary Randolph, whose 1824 publication *The Virginia House-Wife* became one of the most influential cookery books of the century. Randolph's ancestral connections include the fact that her father was a second cousin of Thomas Jefferson, and her recipes were diverse, moving from Virginian classics to traditional European dishes, interspersed with a nod to Elizabethan and Jacobean influences, copied down from early English inherited recipes.

Born in 1762, Mary's emphasis was always on ensuring that women spent as limited amount of time as possible in the kitchen, to free themselves up for other activities. Unlike other cookery writers of the time Mary Randolph did not live rurally or on a plantation, but in the city of Richmond and cooked for travellers and guests in her boarding house, as well as for family and influential friends.[34] She used traditional Virginian practices and local Virginian produce, giving her the reputation as one of the best cooks in Virginia at the time. Randolph's boarding house was situated on Cary Street, which would later become the well-known Columbian Hotel and subsequent commodity exchange, the Columbian Block. It is described in Samuel Mordecai's *Virginia, Especially Richmond, in By-gone Days* (1860) as 'a quiet spot, with very few houses in its immediate vicinity'. The boarding house itself attracted a loyal following, with Mary at the heart of it as the charming, funny and entertaining landlady. It is here that rumours abound about Mary inventing a type of refrigerator (a name given to it by her apparently), which kept all of her thirsty customers' drinks cool. And legend has it that one of her guests made off with the prototype, patented it and the rest is history.[35]

The Virginia House-wife was penned much later, when the Randolph's moved to Washington. Undoubtedly many of the recipes contained in the book would have been those prepared and served up to her boarding house customers. Mary, affectionately known as 'Queen Molly' died in 1828 and her life and work were largely forgotten until her gravestone was discovered in the late 1920s, sparking a revived interest.

As to be expected, many Southern State recipe books of the eighteenth and nineteenth centuries include Creole inspired dishes, like Catfish stew, which has remained a popular national dish to this day. Mary's recipe for Catfish Soup, in *The Virginia House-Wife*, is a wonderful example of this iconic dish:

Catfish Soup

An excellent dish for those who have not imbibed a needless prejudice against those delicious fish.

Take two large or four small white catfish that have been caught in deep water, cut off the heads, and skin and clean the bodies; cut each in three parts, put them in a pot, with a pound of lean bacon, a large onion cut up, a handful of parsley chopped small, some pepper and salt, pour in a sufficient quantity of water, and stew them till the fish are quite tender but not broken; beat the yelks of four fresh eggs, add to them a large spoonful of butter, two of flour, and half a pint of rich milk; make all these warm and thicken the soup, take out the bacon, and put some of the fish in your tureen, pour in the soup, and serve it up.[36]

Abby Fisher

In 1660 the total number of recorded slaves in Virginia and Maryland stood at around 1,700. By 1680, this had increased to some 4,000.[37] Abby Fisher was of mixed race and born into slavery in the 1830s, most likely a kitchen-hand, a role from which she learned all her skills. She retained much of her knowledge of traditional plantation cooking methods. Following a difficult move to San Francisco, Abby, her husband and their ever increasing brood of children finally settled into a new life and she became a successful caterer to wealthy urban locals, during the latter part of the late 1800s. Together with her husband, Abby also built up a hugely lucrative pickle and preserve manufacturing business. Her dedication, reputation and talents gained her a diploma and various medals for her work. She dictated her recipes to the forward-thinking radical Women's Co-Operative Printing Office, who in turn compiled and published what is now considered to be the first original soul food cookery book, *What Mrs Fisher Knows About Old Southern Cooking*.[38] Abby was a socially savvy, respected and thoroughly ambitious woman, whose skills and determination have entrenched her life and work within the American cultural culinary archives.

Whilst her story is probably a familiar one to most Americans interested in the heritage of cooking, it was to me one of the few eye-openers for this book. I had never heard of Abby Fisher before and strongly believe that there must be a much bigger book to present this fascinating narrative and surely a screen play.

I felt somewhat sad to read that later census records for both Abby and her husband see them both listed as 'white', opposed to their former 'mulatto' identity. I can only imagine their complicated personal/socio/political reasons for choosing to think of themselves as white, which in itself makes for such a wider historical discourse, one not just concerning food. *What Mrs Fisher Knows* originally consisted of 160 recipes, within thirteen categories. Having been through several editions over the years this recipe for Fisher's Jumberlie (undoubtedly an adulteration of Jambalaya), just completely resonates simple southern American Creole cooking for me:

Jumberlie – A Creole Dish

> Take one chicken and cut it up, separating every joint, and adding to it one pint of cleanly-washed rice. Take about half a dozen large tomatoes, scalding them well and taking the skins off with a knife. Cut them in small pieces and put them with the chicken in a pot or large porcelain saucepan. Then cut in small pieces of sweet ham and add to the rest, seasoning high with pepper and salt. It will cook in twenty-five minutes. Do not put any water on it.[39]

Fannie Farmer

Miss Farmer, remained just that – a fiery redheaded Spinster, dedicated to her art and nothing but zealous in all her enterprises. She suffered physically throughout her life from having polio at an early age, and subsequent strokes left her with some paralysis. Despite her parents' wishes for all their children to embark on academic careers, due to her illness, Fannie enrolled at the prestigious Boston Cooking School in 1887 when she was 30. She ended up staying for some fifteen years, as both student and teacher, before establishing her own training school, Miss Farmer's School of Cookery in 1902. Her *Boston Cooking-School Cook Book* became a staple of most American households and is still in print under the titled *The Fannie Farmer Cookbook*. It is perhaps best recognised for its precision, in terms of reinforcing the importance of measurements and quantities, previously so prone to conjecture in most cooking manuals of the century before. Her knowledge, and her scientific and experimental attitude towards food and cooking, is also captured in the many lucrative articles she wrote for the magazine *Woman's Home Companion,* from 1905.

Farmer differed from her pioneering peers at the time, women who were already trading and basking in the American culinary boom

Women Cooks of the Enlightenment

years of the late nineteenth century, including Mary Lincoln, Marion Harland, Christine Herrick, Janet Mckenzie Hill, Elizabeth O. Hiller and countless others. Instead of promoting domestic science as a means of improving one's time better in the home and kitchen and therefore empowering oneself from the drudgeries of the past, Fannie Farmer exuded a passion for food and the creativity it could inspire. She cared little for moderation or exacting portion and calorie control. Her recipes encouraged enjoyment and an unconditional appreciation of food in all its marvellous combinations.[40] This apparent enthusiasm however, did not extend to wastefulness. This was a subject which remained a huge bugbear to Miss Farmer, as demonstrated in her 1911 article – which incidentally already introduced her as a 'world-famous exponent of scientific cooking'. The article, dramatically titled '$20,000,000 Thrown Away', appeared in the *Bridgeport Evening Farmer*, 16 December 1911. As the title suggests, Miss Farmer details the modern carelessness concerning food wastage, noting that the majority of her cookery school students have no regard for properly peeling vegetables and fruit, resulting in great piles of needless peelings. This

Figure 17. Fannie Farmer, Memorial in Medford, Massachusetts, USA.

was a habit, she claimed, extended to hotels and hospitals, the latter she had once witnessed squandering enough leftovers in two or three days – the equivalent to feeding an institution for a whole day. Cutting the crusts off toast and sandwiches particularly horrified her, and she would remind her readers that such scraps could be used 'to make the finest bread puddings'. Her biggest gripe it seems is with the kitchens of the average middle-class family, who she encouraged to make milk last longer by letting it go sour in order to make a range of batters and cottage cheeses. She also suggested keeping the whites of the eggs instead of throwing them away, for frosting cakes, if only the yolk was required.

What I found particularly interesting about these rather castigating ramblings, is that they are still so pertinent to today's society. We currently battle endlessly with global debates about spendthrift habits and wastefulness. Farmer believed the average household bill could be reduced by a tenth, if everybody just spent a little more time being resourceful in the kitchen, a lesson many of us could learn from today, in our throwaway disposable culture. No doubt Miss Farmer would be doing 360 degree turns under the ground (despite the fact that she was in fact cremated) if she could witness just how disgustingly wasteful western society has become.

Urbanization and mass migration during the late nineteenth century altered the way in which cooking skills were passed on and indeed how food was consumed. Culinary connections were misplaced. Mothers no longer passed on their knowledge and skills to their daughters, and traditional dishes became fused or evolved into more continentally influenced fare. These changes combined with rapidly advancing technology in the kitchen would undoubtedly have elevated the popularity and need for good practical cookery books and solid training. Whilst the chemist Ellen Richards must be credited with linking cookery to science, it is Farmer perhaps who fundamentally made this notion popular. The haute cuisine of the last century, although still revered, was in many ways deconstructed and simplified, a process adopted by Farmer in her lectures, writing and teaching. It has been said that she could not rest at the dinner table if she came across a sauce whose flavours she failed to identify, without properly dissecting

Women Cooks of the Enlightenment

the ingredients. *The Boston Cooking-School Cook Book* in its various forms, sold in excess of several million. Farmer's obituary, an ironic commentary piece written in the *Evening Public Ledger*, 25 February 1915, is testament to her unique fame:

> Great women have lived before, and will live after this. Some of them have written great poems, great plays and novels. Some of them have founded empires, or have born and reared the men who did the coarse work of founding an empire. Others have summoned their peerless powers to reform. Still others, unhappily, to waste and wreckage. But certainly not among these latter belongs Fannie Farmer. She was the Henry Wadsworth Longfellow of the gas range…Fannie Farmer ministered to the humble emotions of the average. Not for her the glittering effrontery of the 'à la's', the tinkling timbales of this or of that, the lordly champignon, the aristocratic oignon, nor the sybaritic sauce supreme. No, as it is not the Lucullus of ancient Rome, nor yet his modern counterpart at Newport, who makes the world, so Fannie Farmer saw that the real furtherance of human destiny rests upon the broad and capable shoulders of the Joseph Smiths and the Benjamin Browns, who do the world's work and who need their evening steak to keep them brave and blithe and strong. And for them she wrote accordingly.

So, here is Fannie Farmer's recipe for broiled beefsteak:

The best cuts of beef for broiling are porterhouse, sirloin, cross-cut of rump steaks, and second and third cuts from top of round. Porterhouse and sirloin cuts are the most expensive, on account of the great loss in bone and fat, although price per pound is about the same as for cross-cut of rump. Round steak is very juicy, but, having coarser fibre, is not as tender. Steaks should be cut at least an inch thick, and from that to one and one- half inches. The flank end of sirloin steak should be removed before cooking. It may be put in soup kettle, or lean part may be chopped and utilized for meat cakes; fat tried out and clarified for shortening.

To Broil Steak. Wipe with a cloth wrung out of cold water, and trim off superfluous fat. With some of the fat grease a wire broiler, place meat in broiler (having fat edge next to handle), and broil over a clear fire, turning every ten seconds for the first minute, that surface may be well seared, thus preventing escape of juices. After the first minute, turn occasionally until well cooked on both sides. Steak cut one inch thick will take five minutes, if liked rare; six minutes, if well done. Remove to hot platter, spread with butter, and sprinkle with salt and pepper.[41]

Agnes Bertha Marshall

Crossing back over the Atlantic again now, the Victorian and Edwardian eras were witness to many dedicated and talented ladies who, like Fannie Farmer, were most definitely in the right place at the right time in this period of culinary evolution. Another great woman was my all-time heroine, Agnes Bertha Marshall. Considering her wide spanning entrepreneurial career, the life of Agnes Marshall is not nearly celebrated and cherished enough. This in part can be attributed to a great fire which destroyed most of the Marshall archives. While many women were writing and teaching about the subject of cookery during this time, some were also inventing, teaching and lecturing. Reminiscent of Raffald a century before, Agnes born 1855, the only daughter of John Smith from Walthamstow, married Alfred William Marshall in 1878, who on his death in 1917 was cited as a 'food specialist', living at the address of the cookery school, leaving a number of financial bequests to his employees.

Together with her husband, the couple opened Marshall's School of Cookery in Mortimer Street, London, in 1883, which boasted to be 'the largest and most successful school of its kind in the world'.[42]

Marshall's trained budding cooks in the art of both French and English cuisine – and Fannie Farmer would have been delighted to hear that the school prided itself on squandering 'no waste'.[43]

Initially, the institution ran small intimate classes led by Marshall herself. As word circulated about her great abilities and its reputation as the best school to train as a cook, the venture quickly needed to look for larger premises. What was particularly special about Marshall's is that it transcended class, with students ranging from duchesses to dairy maids. Attached to the school was an employment agency, enabling newly qualified cookery teachers, who each graduated with a diploma after several years' study, to seek work if they so wished from fee paying registered households looking for domestic staff. There was also a 'cook shop' on site selling an array of the latest kitchen utensils and gadgetry and exhibiting the latest gas and electric stoves. In addition to inventing items for the kitchen, Agnes had her own brand of basic cooking ingredients including a special gelatine leaf which proved to be very popular. This, together with an assortment of other groceries, all manufactured by Agnes herself. were sold in a shop within the cookery school confines. This shop led into a printing and editing suite where all of Marshall's recipe books were published. The exhibition hall would be laid out for large functions to showcase the work of the

Figure 18. Agnes Bertha Marshall.

students and Mrs Marshall's own culinary creations. Having also toured America, Agnes's achievements were well known across the Atlantic. The *Washington Times* of 1 May 1898 described the scene during one exhibition for invited patrons:

> The hall is filled with long tables set luxuriously, as for dinners, luncheons, suppers or breakfasts. The most recent patterns in menus, floral and fruit decorations, the arrangements of roses and the lighting of tables are displayed, and the whole exhibition is accompanied by a series of lectures on the culinary art.

What I wouldn't do to step back in time and spend just a day absorbing Agnes's fantastical culinary empire? She had it all. Not only was Mrs Marshall one of the shrewdest, most talented and entrepreneurial women of her time, but she was beautiful with it. The one portrait that survives of her shows a stunning, young, fine featured woman, standing tall and elegantly attired. The *Western Morning News* of December 1887 describes Agnes during one of her lectures as 'a fascinating fairy who waved, not wand, but magic knife, spoon.'

Agnes wrote four books: *Ices Plain and Fancy: The Book of Ices* (1885), *Mrs A. B. Marshall's Book of Cookery* (1888), *Mrs A. B. Marshall's Larger Cookery Book of Extra Recipes* (1891) and *Fancy Ices* (1894).

With her books, most notably focusing on ices, it's little wonder that Agnes made the practice of chilled desserts her specialism. It has often been quoted that Marshall invented the edible ice cream cone. While she probably pre-empted the American claim to invention during the early twentieth century, it would appear that the French were already delighting in ice cream cones at least as early as 1807. A print by the Parisian artist Philibert-Louis Debucourt, of a seated lady indulging in an ice cream filled cornet clearly illustrates this fact. But Agnes did popularise the ice-cream cone by including them in her recipes, an item which had previously been unpublished in that way before. Her patent ice-cream maker – nothing more than a hand-cranked drum with a paddle, had the ability to make ice cream in three minutes. Clearly her inventions were much more prolific, as the press and advertisements of the time imply, including Marshall's patent ice caves, ice moulds and 'IVEL' safety cooking utensils, which were demonstrated at the Corn

Women Cooks of the Enlightenment

Exchange in Bedford in 1888. The British press during the latter part of the nineteenth century is full of advertisements and notices regarding Agnes's school, her merchandise, books and various lectures and demonstrations. Her publicity machine was vast and her reputation impeccable.

Here is Agnes's spicy ice recipe for Ginger Bombe, taken from her *Book of Ices*:

Figure 19. Marshall's Patent Freezer.

Prepare a custard made with half a pint of milk, boiled with one lemon-peel and 3 ounces of castor sugar; when the milk boils, mix it on to 4 raw yolks of eggs and as much ginger as will cover a threepenny piece, thicken over the fire and tammy, (sieve) then add the juice of 1 lemon and 6 drops of vanilla essence, and when cool freeze; when partly frozen, add half a pint of whipped cream sweetened with a saltspoonful of castor sugar; line the bombe mould with this, and have 3 ounces of preserved ginger cut in dice and put in the centre; fill up with more custard, and freeze for 1 ½ hours in the cave. Turn out and serve on a napkin or dish-paper'.[44]

Agnes Marshall died in 1905 following complications after falling off a horse, at the age of forty-nine, her talents cut so short. Who knows what culinary endeavours she would have continued to achieve? Her husband must have maintained aspects of the business after her death as advertisements still existed for the school. There are also examples of vintage kitchen products, such as Marshall's bottled food colourings manufactured by A. B. Marshall Ltd still circulating the vintage market-place, as late as the 1950s. According to John Deith,[45] Marshall's became a limited company in 1921, a very prosperous and successful one which finally folded around 1954. The cookery school closed its doors in 1939, along with its periodical, *The Table.* Deith also implies that Agnes and her husband Alfred were experiencing marital problems not long before she died and that he was having an affair with her personal secretary, who Agnes fired following a terrible row.

Although very little is known about how she trained in the art of cookery, an interview with her husband in the *Pall Mall Gazette* of 1886, reveals that she studied in Paris and Vienna from a very young age.

She carried out a number of lecturing tours around the country, one which took her as far as Dundee in 1892 and to Exeter in 1887, titled 'A Pretty Luncheon' where we are informed by the press at the time that she provided demonstrations to crowded audiences.[46] From 1886 the Marshall's embarked on the production of their weekly periodical, *The Table.* This included articles on food, cookery and Gastronomy, with a new recipe appearing in each edition over the first six months of publication. It cost 3d and was well received nationally.[47]

Agnes was embroiled in a court case during the 1880s, over threatening letters sent to her by a William Waudley from Leamington who accused her of not responding to his wife regarding a position of employment. He spoke libellously about Marshall's School of Cookery. The letters were deemed to be of 'a very objectionable character'. What became of Mr Waudley is unknown, but he was a former inmate at East Riding Asylum.[48] Agnes's high profile persona in the media is perhaps testament to this incident and is reminiscent of today's social media trolling.

Like so many others, Agnes has always been overshadowed by the legacy of her contemporary Isabella Beeton, whose publisher is said to have bought the rights to the Marshall books in order to quell the successes of Agnes, in favour of promoting Beeton to the masses. Coincidently the Marshall archives were also in the possession of Ward Lock, the same publishers, when the fire took hold in the 1950s. It is unlikely that the fire was deliberate, and the destruction of the Marshall archives remains another of history's unexplainable mysteries. Sadly, we are all familiar with Beeton, who is held up as the exemplar for all things food and cookery related during the Victorian period, when the reality was that there were many others far more deserving of being remembered.

Isabella Beeton

Isabella Mayson was born in 1836, educated in Germany and then married a wealthy publisher, Samuel Beeton in 1856. The first edition of the legendary *Mrs Beeton's Book of Household Management* was published in 1861, by her husband, who sold the rights to Ward Lock after her death, when he was short of funds. Ward Lock continued to promote her work well after her death, which led the public to think that she was still alive and happily cooking up new experimental delights in the kitchen. There was a great deal of rumour, speculation and innuendo around the woman herself and her family. It wasn't really until the 1930s that her life and work began to take some sort of physical shape, with the unveiling a photograph of her at the National Portrait Gallery. The image generated public debate and speculation, fired up by the writings of her son Sir Mayson Beeton, who seemed to be on a mission at this time to provide a lasting legacy for both his parents. It emerged that *Mrs Beeton's Book of Household Management* was a compilation of Beeton's monthly jottings submitted as part of her husband's publication *The Englishwoman's Domestic Magazine*.[50]

The only reason I have included Beeton in this book is because of her legendary status, a status which I absolutely feel is unworthy of her. Beeton wrote one helpful guide for housekeepers. It was founded on the recipes of others and clearly demonstrates that her knowledge of cooking was poor. Amongst a long list of howlers, she recommends three quarters of an hour parboiling time for sliced carrots. Her recipes are rich beyond the normal excesses of the age and she was rather out of touch with what constituted the average family needs.

Figure 20.
Frontispiece of *Mrs Beeton's Book of Household Management*.

Stewed Carrots

Ingredients. – 7 or 8 large carrots, 1 teacupful of broth, pepper and salt to taste, ½ teacupful of cream, thickening of butter and flour.
Mode. – Scrape the carrots nicely; half-boil, and slice them into a stewpan; add the broth, pepper and salt, and cream; simmer till tender, and be careful the carrots are not broken. A few minutes before serving, mix a little flour with about 1 oz. of butter; thicken the gravy with this; let it just boil up, and serve.
Time. – About ¾ hour to parboil the carrots, about 20 minutes to cook them after they are sliced.
Average cost, 6d to 8d per bunch of 18
Sufficient for 5 or 6 persons.
Seasonable. – Young carrots from April to June old ones at any time.[51]

Undeniably the book was well promoted and became a huge bestseller. It is also nicely written and well presented. However, there were many other great cookery and household manuals at the time written by far superior, talented, trained and knowledgeable women. Many of these books did not receive the notoriety or publicity of Beeton's work and have since been consigned to the archives. If Mrs Beeton had lived a longer life, then perhaps she would have demonstrated further talents.

Eliza Leslie

Eliza Leslie was affectionately termed Miss Leslie and born in Philadelphia in 1787, before moving to England for a short period and then back to the States where her mother ran a number of boarding houses. Her father was a watchmaker, and a close friend of Benjamin Franklin and Thomas Jefferson. She toyed with writing as an adolescent, but destroyed all of her early work at the age of fourteen on becoming disillusioned with pastoral poetry and prose.

Her next attempt at writing was in the form of copying out all of the recipes she learned attending the famed cookery school of Mrs Goodfellow. She circulated these to friends, which proved very popular and led to her first cookery book *Seventy-Five Receipts for Pastry, Cakes, and Sweetmeats* first published in 1828.[51]

She was an advocate for proper etiquette, which is reflected in her later work and also provides us with an interesting insight into the do's and don'ts of mealtime etiquette. *Miss Leslie's Behaviour Book* stated:

> It is ungenteel to go to the breakfast table in any costume approaching to full dress. There must be no flowers or ribbons in the hair.

> No lady looks worse than when gnawing a bone, even of game or poultry. Few *ladies* do it. In fact, nothing should be sucked or gnawed in public.[52]

And of course, understandably:

> It is an affectation of ultra-fashion to eat pie with a fork, and has a very awkward and inconvenient look. Cut it up first with your knife and fork both; then proceed to eat it with the fork in your right hand. Much of this determined fork exercise may be considered foolish. But it is fashionable.[53]

And my absolute favourite, which I know my young son would really appreciate:

> The chattering of children all dinner time is a great annoyance to grown people. The shrill voice of a child can be distinguished annoyingly amid those of a whole company. They should be made to understand that if they talk at table they are to be immediately taken away to finish their dinner in the nursery.[54]

She was a frequent contributor to *The Columbian Lady's and Gentleman's Magazine* and even launched her own periodical in 1843 *Miss Leslie's Magazine*, subtitled *The Home Book of Fashion, Literature and Domestic Economy*, which despite its glowing reviews in the media lasted about a year before publication ceased.

Women Cooks of the Enlightenment

Figure 21. Eliza Leslie.

Elizabeth Goodfellow

Elizabeth Goodfellow's recipes lived vicariously through her students, like Leslie and adoring fans. There is at least one manual dedicated specifically to her by name, which appears to be her voice directly speaking to the reader: *Mrs Goodfellow's Cookery as it Should Be*, the first publication of which I can find advertisements for date from 1853, a couple of years after her death. It serves rather as an homage to her theories and recollected recipes, with the preface providing us with a reminder of her work:

> Besides this advantage of being a practical cook, she obtained some of the best receipts from experienced housekeepers of the south, who understood well the art of compounding good things. Many

of the receipts are from Europe, presented to her by travelling friends, and experimented on by the authoress, and adapted to American palates.[55]

Eliza Leslie maintained that *Mrs Goodfellow's Cookery as it Should Be* was not an accurate reflection of the eminent trainer's work or recipes. Despite this, it proved to be a popular publication and ran to four editions.[56]

It was Elizabeth's pastry-shop, from which she also ran her cookery school that made her a noteworthy culinary icon. Her high-end business attracted wealthy clients requiring private catering and she specialized in elaborate and fancy cakes, puddings, pastries and desserts. It also provided a training ground from the early 1800s for Philadelphia's most elite young ladies. Born in 1768, Elizabeth married three times and lived into her eighties. Descended from a family of early British settlers, her instruction manuals and recipes were almost entirely inspired by the British cooking sorority including Maria Eliza Rundell, Hannah Glasse and Elizabeth Raffald. Her business was originally, and for many years, located in Philadelphia's Dock Street with access to all the markets and luxury imported goods, attracting a busy and active exchange of trades.[57] Goodfellow's was not the first cookery school in America, but it was undoubtedly the one that appears to have left any kind of lasting legacy, possibly due to the number of years it traded and the type of clientele it attracted.

Goodfellow's lemon pudding recipe became the prototype American staple for lemon meringue pie:

Lemon Pudding

One lemon with a smooth thin rind.
Three eggs.
A quarter pound of powdered white sugar.
A quarter pound of fresh butter – washed.
A table-spoonful of white wine and brandy, mixed.
A tea-spoonful of rose-water.
Five ounces of sifted flour and a quarter of a pound of fresh butter for the paste.

Grate the yellow part of the rind of a small fresh lemon. Then cut the lemon in half, and squeeze the juice into the plate that contains the grated rind, carefully taking out all the seeds. Mix the juice and rind together.

Put a quarter of a pound of powdered white sugar into a deep earthen pan, and cut up in it a quarter of a pound of the best fresh butter. If the weather is very cold, set the pan near the fire, for a few minutes, to soften the butter but do not allow it to melt or it will be heavy. Stir the butter and sugar together, with a stick or wooden spoon, till it is perfectly light and of the consistence of cream. Put the eggs into a shallow broad pan, and beat them with an egg-beater or rods, till they are quite smooth, and as thick as a boiled custard. Then stir the eggs, gradually, into the pan of butter and sugar. Add the liquor and rose-water by degrees, and then stir in, gradually, the juice and grated rind of the lemon. Stir the whole very hard after all the ingredients are in.

Have ready a puff-paste made of five ounces of sifted flour and a quarter of a pound of fresh butter. The paste must be made with as little water as possible. Roll it out in a circular sheet, thin in the centre, and thicker towards the edges, and just large enough to cover the bottom, sides and edges of a soup-plate. Butter the soup-plate very well and lay the paste in it making it neat and even round the broad edge of the plate. With a sharp knife, trim off the superfluous dough and notch the edges. Put in the mixture with a spoon, and bake the pudding about half an hour in a moderate oven. It should be baked of a very light brown. If the oven is too hot, the paste will not have time to rise well. If too cold, it will be clammy. When the pudding is cool, grate loaf sugar over it. Before using lemons for any purpose, always roll them awhile with your hand on a table. This will cause them to yield a larger quantity of juice.[58]

Hannah Glasse

Goodfellow was inspired by British-born Hannah Glasse, who was in turn inspired by many others when writing her recipes for the public. Hannah just missed out on being included in the chapter on early Modernists in this book, being born in 1708. But there is no doubt that she left her mark on female culinary history, albeit she was a little like Beeton in that she was not formally trained and really only found fame through one book. She ended her days in poverty, despite leaving a legacy as one of the earliest British female writers to spot a gap in the middle-class market for good, plain, no-nonsense cookery. Transcending class as she did, Glasse had enough knowledge of fashionable cooking practices and trends which she combined with simple instructions and uncomplicated ingredients. She was vehemently criticised in the media by respected cooks of the time such as Ann Cook and even by Samuel Johnson, for her lack of credentials and uncultivated style. But then, Johnson also said that no woman could write a cookery book, often threatening to write one himself. Unlike many of her contemporaries at that time, she did not run a cookery school. Rather, her talents for making money leaned more towards needlework.[59] Glasse wrote a couple of books, but none so popular as *The Art of Cookery Made Plain and Easy*. It is perhaps her abandonment of high culture within this work which makes her so unique for the period. It has been implied that Glasse included the first known recipe for curry to appear in an English cookbook, which is devoid of any traditional Indian spices, yet contained all the flavour.[60] Glasse, as with Goodfellow's endorsement, crossed into the American market with ease and popularity. Her book was one of the top eighteenth-century cookbooks to be found in Virginian homes at that time, with *The Art of Cookery* in circulation across America from 1765 onwards.

Unlike Beeton's disregard for cooking vegetables appropriately, Glasse maintained that 'All things that are green should have a little crispness, for if they are over-boiled, they neither have any sweetness or beauty.'[61]

Glasse's no-nonsense style is very engaging, as demonstrated below with her recipe for roasted ham or gammon. The simplicity with which she delivers her recipes, must have been appealing to the mass market of burgeoning middle classes during this era.

To roast a Ham or Gammon

TAKE off the swerd, or what we call the skin, or rind, and lay it in lukewarm water for two or three hours; then lay it in a pan, pour

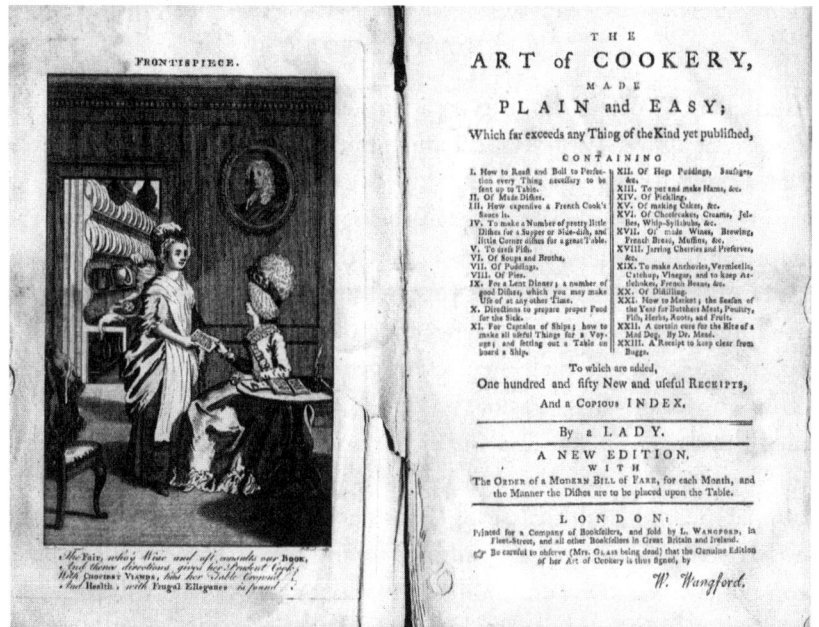

Figure 22. Frontispiece and title page of Hannah Glasse's
The Art of Cookery Made Plain and Easy.

upon it a quart of canary [canary wine], and let it steep in it for ten or twelve hours. When you have spitted it, put some sheets of white paper over the fat side, pour the canary in which it was soaked in the dripping-pan, and baste with it all the time it is roasting; when it is roasted enough, pull off the paper, and dredge it well with crumbled bread and parsley shred fine; make the fire brisk, and brown it well. If you eat it hot garnish it with raspings of bread: if cold, serve it on a clean napkin, and garnish it with parsley for a second course. Or thus: Take off the skin of the ham or gammon, when you have half boiled it, and dredge it with oatmeal sifted very fine, baste it with butter, then roast it gently two hours; stir up your fire and brown it quick; when so done dish it up, and pour brown gravy in the dish. Garnish with bread raspings if hot, if cold garnish with parsley.[62]

Maria Parloa

Maria Parloa's obituaries of 1909 are testament to her legacy, with their consistent appreciation, respect and genuine affection for this first true American celebrity cook.

How much individual credit belongs to Maria Parloa for the improvement which took place in American home cooking in the late nineteenth century is difficult to say. But, the fact that she was one of the foremost advocates of a saner diet and contributed materially to a culinary reform of which the present generation is enjoying the benefit is in no doubt. Miss Parloa was one of the first to apply scientific methods to cooking and to instill the principles of domestic economy in American homes. Through her books and lectures she vigourously campaigned for healthier eating, making her a household name. By the early twentieth century, unhealthy cooking habits had not diappeared completely, but they undoubtedly were not so prevalent. The frying pan was used less and the broiler became more popular. Breakfasts grew simpler, with hot breads and meats no longer a burden on the digestive system. More thought was put into the preparation of food for the table. Dinner and its careful composition became the main focus of the day.[63]

Possibly the most prolific of female cookery book writers with a bountiful and varied career, Maria Parloa wrote at least ten guides, manuals and recipe compilations. Like many of the male cooks of the century before, Parloa took it upon herself to broaden her knowledge and experience of her subject, travelling throughout Europe seeking inspiration and acquiring new culinary techniques. Living and working at a slightly later date than many of the women in this chapter, Parloa benefitted from many of the trappings of a more contemporary celebrity life. This included product and brand endorsements, magazine articles and culinary experiments, on both sides of the Atlantic. Born in Massachusetts in 1843, then possibly orphaned from an early age, we learn from her first bestseller – *The Appledore Cook Book*, initially published in 1872 – that Maria 'had years of experience as a cook in private families and hotels', reassuring her readers that she knew 'the wants of the masses, [feeling] competent to supply them'.[64] Apparently,

Women Cooks of the Enlightenment

Maria was employed as a pastry cook at a number of resort hotels in New Hampshire; including the eponymous hotel of her first book, throughout the 1860s and the first half of the 1870s.[65] From her own small cookery school which she ran in Boston from 1877, to teaching at the infamous Boston Cooking School, before moving to New York in 1883, to open yet another training establishment, Maria's talents and energy did not stop there. She part-owned the popular periodical the *Ladies' Home Journal*, in addition to contributing to domestic science and home economics magazines across Europe and America.[66]

Parloa's lectures must have been engaging. At one, delivered at the College of Pharmacy in New York in 1883, she was reportedly accompanied on stage by a whole dressed side of beef weighing 400 pounds, together with a butcher, ready to cut and demonstrate on her cue.[67]

It is hard to skim a newspaper from either the United Kingdom, the United States or even Australia during the nineteenth and early twentieth centuries without finding some reference to Parloa, including quotes lifted from domestic manuals, to household hints, announcements of up-and-coming lectures or advertisements for endorsed products like Royal Baking Powder and Liebig's Beef Extract. She was everywhere.

Aside from the appealing title, which rather promises pantomime larks and *Carry On* capers, *Camp Cookery: How to Live in Camp*, is a book full of ideas for cooking and eating outdoors. It's like a marriage between Jamie Oliver and Bear Grylls – simple, fresh ingredients, cooked in primitive ways. However, you can't help but chuckle about the fact that halfway through Maria starts referring to range and oven cooking, as if she's either abandoned the whole open fire option, or is just assuming that the average camper would have these sorts of facilities at the ready, turning the book into a sort of camping in the back garden type of guide. Her recipe for traditional clam-bake redeems the book for me:

> First, make an oven of flat stones placed together in the form of a square, on a flat surface about two and a half feet square; around the edge of these, place other stones to form a bin. Fill this oven with small kindlings, such as can be gathered on the beach. On these,

pile a few armfuls of larger sticks, crosswise, so that the top can be well covered with stones about the size of one's two hands. Start the fire, and allow it to burn down until the stones, which were on top of the wood, settle into the oven. Clean out all the cinders with a poker or stick; for, if allowed to remain, the smoke from them will spoil the bake. This must be done very quickly, that the oven may not cool. Cover the oven with fresh seaweed about an inch and one-half thick. On the seaweed, spread the clams so the vegetables, &c., may be placed on top of them: then, in order, put on onions, sweet or Irish potatoes, or both, green corn, then the (blue or cod) fish, and a live lobster, if one can be had; if not a boiled one, which will be very nice warmed up in this way....Cover the whole bake with a piece of cheap cotton cloth, to keep out dirt; then cover all with seaweed until no steam escapes. Bake thirty-five minutes...and all hands fall to, and help themselves.[68]

Sarah Tyson Rorer

Sarah Tyson Rorer, also affectionately known as Sallie, is one of the great pioneering women of culinary repute in this chapter. She was still active right into the twentieth century. By then, the media had become a powerful tool, and by the early 1900s Ms. Rorer features frequently and shamelessly. She appears not only to be the queen of food conservation, but she endorsed anything from lard to canning jars. She also maintained lucrative partnerships with manufacturers such as *Moore's Ranges*, for which she wrote a useful Thermometer Guide, a copy of which was sold with every range. Some writers have described her as the 'first American dietician' and the newspapers frequently christened her 'The Country's Foremost Cook'. She is even noted in a British newspaper of 1928, in an article listing the latest acquisitions for Falkirk Public Library, who proudly announced their new copy of *Mrs Rorer's Vegetable Cookery and Meat Substitutes*.[69]

Sarah became an instructor and then took over the operational side of a cookery school that was established in Philadelphia in 1879. She renamed it the Philadelphia Cooking School. [70]

Rorer was also integral to the running of the Pennsylvania branch of rural America's adult education movement, 'Chautauqua'. She published over twenty books and was editor of the renowned *Table*

Women Cooks of the Enlightenment

Talk periodical for a number of years. Her drive for healthy eating was synonymous with an age obsessed with diet, combined with a need to ration prudently during wartime. She also made some fairly pointed and forward-thinking statements that many could still benefit from today, such as 'There is nothing in cake to give you brain and muscle unless you get the latter from beating the cake'.[71]

I am particularly fond of Sarah Rorer's chapter titled 'Dinner-Giving for Sensible People', in her *Philadelphia Cook Book*. Rather than listing the sort of things to avoid that may induce madness in your guests, as the title implies this section advises on the nature of dinner parties and how to make them more productive, enjoyable and economical. Rorer provides a number of menus, with which to achieve this:

Dinner (Spring)

Julienne Soup

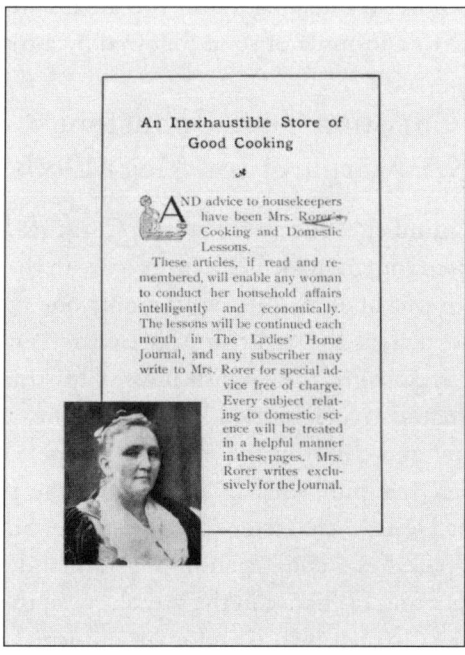

Figure 23. Sarah Tyson Rorer.

Oysters à la crème
Roast Lamb, mint sauce, peas, new potatoes
Lettuce, French dressing
Crackers and cheese
Black coffee

Dinner (Winter)

Oysters on the Half shell
Consommé Cream macaroni
Boiled leg of mutton, caper sauce currant jelly
Mashed potatoes, peas, cauliflower
Lettuce with French Dressing
Water crackers, Neufchâtel [a type of French cheese]
Lemon sponge
Black coffee

With regard to dinner parties, she suggests inviting no more than six to eight guests, to never try making a dish you are unfamiliar with and to basically adhere to a formula of soup followed by a roast.[72]

Christina Jane Johnstone AKA Margaret (or Meg) Dods

Despite writing a number of successful novels, Christina Johnstone was a woman whose pseudonym made her a curiosity with the press; she has earned her place in this book despite writing only one cookery book.

Sometimes nicknamed the Scottish Mrs Beeton (rather insulting, for all manner of reasons) in the English press, Christina was a liberal activist an early feminist. She married John Johnstone, a schoolmaster and later the owner and editor of the *Inverness Courier*. Her *Cook and Housewife's Manual* was published in 1862 under the pseudonym of Mistress Margaret Dods (a character conjured up by Sir Walter Scott in a novel which parodies a congregation of gourmand).[73] Johnstone shows great humour and brilliance in the way she used the characters in Scott's book not just for her own pseudonym but for the fictionalised introduction to her book. Her work was so good that it was thought Scott himself must have written it. What is most interesting about this book, is that many well-respected journalists hailed it as a masterpiece, an ingenious coupling of modern French cuisine and old British cooking. Here are just a few quotes from the press at the time: 'It contains all that the most exquisite epicure could desire to know' (*New Scots Magazine*), 'A valuable compendium of culinary knowledge' (*The Courant*), 'Well deserves to be in the hands of every housewife in the kingdom' (*The Scotsman*).[74]

The absolute best aspect of this book is Johnstone's chapter on Scottish national dishes, my particular favourite being Skink, which she describes as being 'an old Scotch stew-soup'. This is now most commonly known as Cullen Skink, a soup made of haddock, but in the seventeenth century, it was often made with shin of beef, as in Robert May's 1660 recipe from *An Accomplishtd Cook*. This is Johsntone's version from the nineteenth century:

> Take two legs of beef, put them on with two gallons of water, let them boil for six hours, taking care to skim the soup well all the time, as the gravy should be very clear and bright; then strain the liquor from the meat, take the sinewy part from the meat, and lay it aside till your soup is ready to serve up. Cut the sinews about an inch long. Have some vegetables cut, such as carrots, turnips, leeks, onions, celery, lettuce, cabbage shred small, and green pease, when to be had. Blanch the whole in water for ten minutes. Put the whole into the soup and boil till quite tender. Serve up the sinews in the tureen with the soup. Season the soup with salt and pepper before dishing it.
>
> *Obs.* – Herbs may be used in these soups and white pease (boilers) are by many thought an improvement.[75]

Other noteworthy women who made an impact on the early Scottish culinary scene include Susanna MacIver, a cookery teacher based in Edinburgh during the eighteenth century who published her popular manual on *Cookery and Pastry* in the 1770s, some twenty years after Elizabeth Cleland established a training school in her own house, in the same city. Cleland's *A New and Easy Method of Cookery* was designed to accompany her lessons, and it boasted sections on gravies, soups and broths, fish and sauces, potting and hams, pies and pastries and wines and distilling.[76] MacIver's 1789 version of *Cookery and Pastry* informs us that certain positions in her life have enabled her to become 'conversant in cookery'. We could assume that this means she worked in kitchen service, before transferring her skills to the teaching of cookery, directed at 'the genteel and middling ranks of life'. Here is MacIver's recipe for calf-brain cakes, a popular eighteenth century dish:

To make Brain Cakes

> When the head is cloven, take out the brains; take out any strings that may be amongst them, and cast them well with a knife; then put in a little raw egg, a scrape of nutmeg, and a little salt, and mix them with flour to make them stick together; cast them smooth; then drop them like biscuits into a pan of boiling butter, and fry them on both sides a fine brown.
>
> Lambs brains are done in the same manner.[77]

There are numerous female culinarians of this period, although history has left many of them devoid of documentation. Very little is known about Susannah Carter, for example, other than that her book, *The Frugal Housewife,* was published around 1765. As well as being published in London – the title page reveals that Carter was from Clerkenwell – the book was reproduced for the American market, making it to six editions before 1803, and it is considered to be one of the main inspirations behind Amelia Simmons' own iconic work. In 1841 there is a record of a death of a Susannah Carter, who had owned the *Black Bull Inn* in Stratford by Bow, a position she had held for some forty-two years, or since 1797-99 making her date of birth around 1742-44. This Susannah Carter was greatly respected in the community and a popular member of the *Licensed Victuallers' Society*. Whether our two Susannahs are the same remains speculative.[78]

Mary Holland published her *Complete Economical Cook and Frugal Housewife* circa 1824. An earlier work of Holland was circulating around 1800, titled *The Complete British Cook*.[79] All her books tell us is that she was a 'professed cook'. However, and more importantly, there is a small reference to her being Principal Woman Cook to the *Corporation of London* in a newspaper advertisement of 1800.[80] I cannot find sufficient references to her in the London Metropolitan Archives.

Chapter Three

Eminent Gastronomes

It was during the eighteenth century that cookery began to become an independent area of study in its own right, separate from the old medieval alliance with medicine. Cooking is officially understood to have become classified as an art in 1764, when instead of being subcategorized as 'medical' or 'science and arts', it was alternatively listed as an 'art' in the second volume of the publication *Traite des livres rares*. In addition, Perrot's catalogue of 1776 transferred the subject of cooking from the 'medicine' category, into that of the aristocratic arts.[1]

Many writers have noted the radical transformation in cooking and recipe writing in France, which essentially started during the late 1600s. Nonetheless, the transformation did not just relate to France, but to large areas of Europe and countries which had some European influences. It was a new culture of cuisine that was light, flavoursome and cleverly arranged, served in the more sophisticated Russian style, opposed to the old French style of piling dozens of dishes on the table at once.

Haute cuisine has been reputed to have evolved from the Italians, largely based on a story involving Catherine de Medici's inspiring cooks accompanying her to France in the mid-sixteenth century (the same logic applied to why ice cream suddenly became so popular). This is probably a dubious, if not rather romantic rationale. It is more probable that cooks around the seventeenth century were becoming true, dedicated professionals in their own field. They started to create elaborate and time-consuming dishes for the new wave of commercialism – rich, opulent meals, to compliment the grand and lavish new restaurants that were emerging.

The rise of leisure time and an increased interest in the culinary arts signified a cultural shift, with food and cooking being integral to it. French cooks were in demand everywhere during this period, from Russia, to England, Germany and Spain, as they emigrated far and wide, partly to meet the demand in employment and to escape political persecutions in their own countries. Cooks were also establishing themselves as independent businesses, Beauvilliers being one of the first, while writing recipe books to accompany and promote their ventures.[2]

Within this same transformative culture, gastronomy began to evolve as a study in its own right, motivated by the notion that food could be an art form in itself, both in theory and practice. There emerged a science of eating, combined with the inventive and creative nature of food. The definitive gourmand at the time, Brillat-Savarin, was not only the first real food aficionado, but someone who saw that herbivores and carnivores were healthier than those who ate grain and bread, in his treatise *The Physiology of Taste,* in 1825. He was followed by a band of men who would probably be known as 'foodies' today, men like Grimod de La Reynière and later Maurice Sailland. By the nineteenth century, food and cooking had become a branch of good taste, intrinsic to modern society.

Prince Curnonsky

'Prince' Curnonsky, whose real name was Maurice Sailland, is probably the most contemporary of the gastronomes that I have included here and possibly the most acclaimed gastronomic writer of the twentieth century. I am not even going to bother to explain why he was nicknamed 'Curnonsky', as there appear to be about ten different speculative suggestions published on this subject, each one slightly duller than the last.

Unlike many of the other big names referenced in this book, Sailland was not a cook, but his influence was so considerable that I felt compelled to include him. His obituary of 1956, following a tragic fall from his third-floor apartment, hails him as a witty, modest, highly likeable and knowledgeable man. He remained true to his convictions that French cuisine was the finest in the world, until a visit to China, after which he declared Chinese food a very close second. He believed in simple dishes of only two courses and that only one type of wine should be drunk with a meal. He ate just one meal a day, happily waiting the fourteen hours a good cassoulet could take to cook, just to experience the intense flavours. He published almost seventy books in his lifetime and founded the *Académie des gastronomes* in 1930, for the benefit of his peers and fellow gastronomes.[3]

Sailland feared that France had become too standardised with its menus, catering for tourists with unrefined tastes, rather than producing good quality exclusive French dishes. I have to admit we have found this as a family ourselves; travelling regularly to South-West France, that for every one fabulous restaurant, there are ten others that only serve fr*i*tes, with a number of accompaniments, most often moules, steak hach*é* or, heaven forbid, pizza.

Sailland's *La France gastronomique*, co-written with Marcel Rouff, became a classic ironic piece of culinary literature after his death. It represents a compendium of his gastronomic tours of France by car, in 1908, with Sailland allegedly writing under the pseudonym Bibendum, after the Michelin Man character, Bibendum, from the car company's tyre advertisements, which went back to 1898. He was an early advocate of the Michelin Guide, merging automobile travel and gastronomy together.[4] He urged his readers to eat regionally, to experience dishes in the correct area. Sailland divided cuisine into four predominant categories: *haute cuisine,* high-end restaurant food, *cuisine bourgeoise*, which was home food prepared and cooked by skilled housewives, *cuisine régionale*, traditional provincial cooking and local specialities, and finally *cuisine improvisée* which essentially included spontaneous, freshly caught or picked produce, cooked in a simple way.[5]

Whether it was the stuff of urban legends or not, it is thought that some eighty or more restaurants across Paris would reserve a table for Sailland every evening, on the off-chance that he might visit and critique the place. Very little can be gleaned about his private life, other than he was a bachelor and possibly an orphaned child, who became so overweight in later life, that he would often require help from others. That single meal a day must have been one heck of a meal.

Alexandre Balthazar Laurent Grimod de La Reynière

Sailland followed in the footsteps of possibly the most famous and first French food critic, Alexandre Balthazar Laurent Grimod de La Reynière, a trained lawyer from a long line of tax collectors, wealthy ones at that, who left him a substantial inheritance. He was an eccentric, born with malformed hands, and his missing fingers were covered by gloves which hid his prostheses. Sadly, he was banished from the family home, by his mother and father who were ashamed of their son's affliction. Grimod returned to his inherited mansion on the death of his father and it was here that he truly unleashed his eccentricity and passion for food and drink by staging lavish and often surreal dinner parties, one of which

Figure 24. Alexandre Balthazar Laurent Grimod de La Reynière.

involved pseudo-funerals for the guests. It was said that black cloths hung in the dining room, a coffin resplendent in the middle of the table and the room surrounded by lit candles, one for each day of the year.[6] These events generated both scandal and awe across society and contributed even more to the shame of his family.

Grimod's next venture was to establish the *Almanach des Gourmands* in 1803, a guide to the best eateries in Paris, with contributions from a panel of reviewers, who tasted and tested the work of chefs throughout the city. The periodical was heralded a masterpiece, with reviews covering everything from preparation to technique, and even the origin of the ingredients. Like the content of consumer sites such as *Trip Advisor* today, diners and the cooks themselves openly criticised the *Almanach*'s bias, prejudices and lack of discretion. As a consequence, Grimod was taken to court and forced to cease publication in 1812.[7] He was an observer and chronicler of the amazing historical shift in the gastronomic revolution, but his curious personality and inability to acknowledge his own limits perhaps drove Grimod into exile, and he died at his rural retreat, allegedly during Christmas dinner, on 25 December, 1837.[8]

Finding an accessible fully translated edition of Grimod's work is difficult. A number of translated extracts from the *Almanach des Gourmands* are published in Denise Gigante's, *Gusto*. In particular, his opinions on the subject of hosts are some of of the most entertaining:

> The table is a hub around which all reputations are formed; it is a theatre where there never is a flop; and without a doubt, plays would never fail if, on opening night, their authors could give a dinner in the orchestra...money alone does not suffice to have a fine table. While one who spends much may serve miserable fare, another with mediocre fortune may give excellent dinners. All depends on the care, knowledge and studies one has undertaken in all aspects of the art of dining. Like all other callings, that of host requires an apprenticeship, and it is far easier to acquire an immense fortune quickly than to know how to do it justice...Spending your life rinsing glasses does not make you a wine connoisseur, nor does giving out plates to everyone mean that you know how to organise a good meal...the first indispensable quality of a man anxious to serve food and drink properly, is an extreme delicacy of

the palate, which allows the appreciation, in tasting, of a full range of flavours...It takes long years, unimpeachable relations, boundless activity, and constant watchfulness to cultivate and maintain a good cellar, without which one cannot earn the renown of a true host. Nine out of ten households in Paris serve bad wine, because this task is left to wine stewards, rascals whose stock comes from wine merchants who are even bigger rascals.[9]

Jean Anthelme Brillat-Savarin

'Gourmandism' is an act of judgement, by which we give preference to things which are agreeable to our taste over those which have not that quality.[10]

In addition to being a French eighteenth century magistrate and politician, Brillat-Savarin was one of the first in a long line of gastronomes who recommended swallowing forty to fifty oysters as an appetiser before a meal. While all like-minded food aficionados around him were busy writing cookery books or serving royalty, Savarin wrote about the very essence of food as an experience. He did this from the perspective of the impact on the senses – how food functions as a science, in terms of its chemistry and the process of one's appetite, the elements of food and the specifics of each method of cooking. He applied a straightforward, flippant style of language, writing a bit as you might expect him to speak. In many respects, Brillat-Savarin revolutionised the way in which people processed their thoughts about food by advocating the need to eat for pleasure, as opposed to necessity. It is both his informal, witty style – lines such as 'a day without cheese is like a beautiful woman with only one eye: in both cases, something is missing'[11] – together with his culinary wisdom and audacious manner, that has committed Brillat-Savarin to our memories. Speaking as one who would find life quite unbearable without cheese, how could you not find him engaging?

It would appear that eccentricity ran in the family. He had two sisters who lived in a country house belonging to him. Brillat-Savarin visited them regularly every September and October and this was the only time the ladies would leave their beds, remaining horizontal for

Figure 25. Jean Anthelme Brillat-Savarin.

ten months of the year. When he visited they lived a normal life, and when he left they retired back to bed. One of his sisters died at the remarkable age for that time of 99, allegedly in the midst of eating her dinner. Whether it was true or not it still makes for a great story – she was quoted as saying: 'Hurry up with the dessert', just moments before death took her.[12]

Brillat-Savarin's most famous work was his *Physiologie du goût* ('The Physiology of Taste') of 1825. Above all else this book highlights the fact that, despite the bravado and analytical dissection of the process of cooking, eating and drinking, he appreciated the very simplest of dishes as long as they were executed with style and proficiency. This is demonstrated in his recommended recipe for fondue, which he describes as being a 'soup dish' that 'consists only in frying eggs in cheese in proportions revealed by experience…It is a pleasant dish, quickly made and easily prepared for unexpected guests'.

Recipe for Fondue copied from the papers of M. Trollet Bailli of Mondon in Berne

> Calculate the number of eggs in proportion to the guests. Take one-third of the weight of Gruyère and one-sixth of the weight of butter. Beat the eggs and mingle them with the butter and cheese in a casserole. Put the kettle on a hot fire and stir it until the mixture is perfect. Put in more or less salt in proportion as the cheese is old or new. Serve it hot with good wine of which one should drink much. The feast will see sights.[13]

Hercules and James Hemmings

Hercules, Uncle Harkless or Uncle Hercules as he was also known, was chief cook to the first president of the United States, George Washington. His nicknames were acquired through slavery and in recognition of his unusual muscular strength. Despite his obsession for cleanliness and discipline in the kitchen, he was a well-respected and jovial man who was apparently quite fixated with his appearance, spending his wages on the finest white linens, silks and highly polished buckled shoes. His trademark attire included a velvet-collared coat, a fancy fob watch and a gold-headed cane to complete the ensemble. Hercules, by all accounts, was a veritable dandy.[14]

He was married to a dower slave (meaning a slave not owned, but inherited through marriage) named Lame Alice, a seamstress. They had three children together: Richmond (b.1777), Evey (b.1782) and Delia (b.1785). Alice died in 1787 leaving Hercules to raise his children. Hercules famously made his escape to freedom from slavery in 1797, during Washington's transition from Philadelphia to retirement in Mount Vernon, Virginia. Hercules was highly valued in the Washington household and was in receipt of many perks, from the gains of the sales of kitchen leftovers, to regular theatre tickets in the luxury of the presidential box.[15]

He escaped in tandem with Oney Judge, Martha Washington's

personal servant, although they both went their separate ways. At the time Martha wrote to her sister rather indignantly:

> Am obliged to be my own housekeeper which takes up the greatest part of my time – our cook Hercules went away so that I am as much at a loss for a cook as for a housekeeper – altogether I am sadly plagued.[16]

Washington himself commented:

> The running off of my cook has been a most inconvenient thing to this family, and what renders it more disagreeable, is that I had resolved never to become the master of another slave by purchase, but this resolution I fear I must break.

Washington continued his search for Hercules for some years, undoubtedly out of affection and regret, as well as the fact that his trusty, eccentric cook had also abandoned his six-year-old daughter.

George Washington was not an advocate of slavery and upon his death arranged for all of his enslaved staff to be granted their freedom.[17]

The president ate breakfast around seven to seven thirty, depending on the season, consisting of butter and honey corn cakes.[18]

Dinner was served typically around three or four in the afternoon in the Washington household, with tablecloths and glassware changed between courses. The first and second courses would consist of multiple dishes, all delivered to the table at the same time, in the early fashion for the French style of dining, from soup to shellfish and then meats and game. The third course consisted mostly of a selection of fruits and nuts. One diner from New York recalled the following account of his experience round the table during Washington's administration, which may well have been prepared by Hercules himself:

> At dinner have wine, porter and/or beer. After it we drank about three glasses…At dinner we had two pint globular decanters on table, after dinner large wine glasses. Port was brought in claret bottles…Menu…Leg boiled pork, top; goose, roast beef, round cold boiled beef, mutton chops, hominy, cabbage, potatoes, pickles, fried tripe, onions etc. Table cloth wiped, mince pies, tarts,

cheese; cloth of port, Madeira, two kinds nuts, apples, raisins, Three servants.[19]

These dinners were nearly always exclusively male. Diners were announced one by one as they entered the room, with Washington there to greet them at his usual spot in front of the fireplace. It is said that the president had a nostalgic fondness for old Dutch cooking and particularly enjoyed fish.[20]

Washington kept farmlands in excess of 8,000 acres, making the White House almost self-sufficient in meat and produce.

Hercules was not the only black slave to cook for a president of the United States, there was also the mixed-race slave, James Hemmings. Despite the fact that Thomas Jefferson was not inaugurated until 1801, the same year as James Hemmings' death, the mixed-race slave spent much of his life in service to Thomas Jefferson and his family.

Figure 26. Thomas Jefferson.

It was Jefferson's post as minister of France that laid the foundations of Hemmings' training in the art of cooking, paying for his education and tutoring in the French language. Following a number of prestigious apprenticeships, James Hemmings was eventually enrolled in Jefferson's kitchens as *chef de cuisine*. The president was somewhat of a gastronome himself and collected hundreds of recipes, a number of which were written in his own hand. The originals can be found in the archives of the Library of Congress. These include 'Biscuit de Savoye', 'Blanc Manger', 'Wine jellies', 'Haricots', 'Ice cream', 'Macarons', 'Meringues', 'Pour faire les pêches à l'eau de vie' (Brandied peaches), 'Petit's method of making coffee', and 'Nouilly à macaroni'. Below is Jefferson's transcripted recipe for macaroons:

> Pour boiling water on 1 pound of almonds and remove the skins. Wash them in cold water. Wipe them well with a towel. Put them through a food chopper, using finest grinder. Turn into a wooden bowl and add gradually ¾ of a pound of powdered sugar, beating thoroughly all the while with a wooden spoon. Add, one by one, the whites of 3 eggs, beating constantly to a smooth paste. Drop from the tip of a spoon on white paper, in small balls about the size of a nut. Bake fifteen to twenty minutes in a slow oven.[21]

Similar to Washington's self-sufficiency, Thomas Jefferson landscaped a vast garden that ran a thousand feet in length to 80 feet wide, cut into the mountains adjacent to his home. It was this land that provided his household with some 300 varieties of vegetables, as well as fruit from his orchard (or the 'The Fruitry' as the president called it), berries and vineyards, alongside a separate fenced enclosure for livestock.[22]

Samuel Fraunces

Fraunces was a steward and superintendent of the kitchen for George Washington and a tavern owner in New York. He was affectionately nicknamed 'Black Sam', but the origins of this name remain a mystery. Fraunces was undoubtedly a white man, if we are to believe in the legitimacy of the one surviving colour

Figure 27. Samuel Fraunces.

portrait of him. Born in the West Indies, he may have been of mixed race, or perhaps he had less prominent European features. His surname could have been French in origin, or a derivative of Frances/Francis, but his racial identity remains a bit of a mystery. He was however buried in an unmarked grave, which would have been unusual for a man of his standing during that period, unless he was considered to be of African descent, another woeful indication of the times. A few years ago Samuel's resting place was finally officially marked with an engraved memorial.[23]

The end of the Revolutionary War celebrations, attended by George Washington and his men, were held at Samuel Fraunces's Inn, known simply as Fraunces Tavern, in New York in 1783. It was a great buffet lunch including hot and cold meats, platters of bread and butter and

Figure 28. Fraunces Tavern, New York, 1900.

something called 'garden sauce'.[24]

I found an early nineteenth-century recipe to make sauce from garden greens, which may have been something similar, as it was used as an accompaniment to meats. This is perhaps what Fraunces served:

Poulets à la Jardinière
(From the Garden Greens which make the Sauce)

Make a sauce with a few slices of veal and ham, bits of carrots parsneps sliced onions and a few basil leaves; soak it until it catches a little, then put to it a glass of white wine, as much broth, two cloves, and one of garlick; boil slowly to reduce to a sauce, then sift and skim it; add some chopped scalded chervil, a bit of butter and flour, give it a boil, and serve under roasted chickens.[25]

There were also big tables with decanters of wine and glasses and a myriad of staff on hand to mark this historic, yet poignant and war weary moment. Fraunces Tavern remains today in all its original glory, with a small museum attached, narrating the story of its long legacy as an iconic building.

Shortly after Fraunces' appointment in 1789, the president's personal secretary, Tobias Lear, wrote to Washington's nephew and gave this account of him:

> ...a very excellent fellow he is [as superintendent of the kitchen] – he tosses up such a number of fine dishes that we are distracted in our choice when we set down to table, and [are] obliged to hold a long consultation upon the subject before we can determine what to attack. Oysters & Lobsters make a very conspicuous figure upon the table and never go off untouched.[26]

The president, however, frequently berated his cook for his lavish spending on ingredients and fresh goods. As president, Washington was entitled to an annual salary of 25,000 dollars a year and no expenses. He never drew on this salary, but continued to host fairly lavish state dinners and receptions. During breakfast one morning, he asked Samuel Fraunces how he had managed to acquire shad (a fish similar to herring) so early in the season. His steward admitted he had paid two dollars for it, at which point the president erupted, stating: 'Two dollars! I can never encourage such extravagance at my table!'[27]

Samuel and Hercules would have worked for the president at the same time, with Hercules trained underneath his superior. It has been written that Hercules greatly admired his mentor, to the extent that he would even dress in the same flamboyant manner. Fraunces was also privy to a number of meetings where secret political issues were discussed, linking him with informant activities and he raised funds for American prisoners of war. He was a great deal more than a kitchen steward and innkeeper, with his obituary of 1795 stating: 'Society has sustained the loss of an honest man, and the poor, a valuable friend.'[28]

Antoine Beauvilliers

Antoine Beauvilliers made the early transition from an employee of a royal household to a businessman. He opened his restaurant La

Grande Taverne de Londres (named in homage to the London Tavern, see chapter four) in the Palais-Royal in 1782, later moving to premises at number 20 rue de Richelieu, Paris. Its success was slow burning, but as his reputation increased, Beauvillier's business was said by 1814 to rival that of the great Véry (named after the brothers who ran it), which was considered the leading restaurant of its era, patronised by the likes of famous novelists such as Balzac. He is said to have been completely without prejudice and remembered the names of faces of all his clientele, if they had visited two or three times, even some twenty years later. He circulated the dining room every night, apparently carrying a sword and engaging in witty banter with his customers, offering them advice on menu choices and recommending accompanying wines.[29]

There were nearly 200 dishes on the menu at La Grande Taverne de Londres including partridge with cabbage, veal chops and duck with turnips. The restaurant survived both war and stiff competition before finally closing its doors in 1825.[30] One observer wrote in 1814 that the restaurant was L-shaped, with about twenty tables laid. Different waiters had responsibility for around two or three tables at a time. At either end of the room there was a sort of bar area covered with fruits, presided over by elegantly dressed 'conversable and agreeable' women. These women would tally up the bills, with each item ordered relayed back to them by the waiters. Most astonishing of all was that every day between 500 to 700 punters would dine in this one room, each spending on average around ten francs a head. People came from all over the world, making the dining room a cacophony of diversity, from language to dress. This same observer provided an extract from the bill of fare (menu) during his visit in 1814, which included:

> Oysters as an entrée (at least a dozen or two), Beef – boiled, roasted and dressed in 10 different ways, Fowls, pigeons, turkeys, Partridges, Ducks etc., dressed in 44 ways. The veal was also dressed in 25 different ways, the mutton 19, Fish dishes in 31 ways. Desserts included preserves, fruits and cheeses.[31]

In 1814 Beauvilliers wrote what has become one of the most fabled volumes of French gastronomy, *L'Art du Cuisinier* (translated into

English in 1822 as *The Art of French Cookery*). Here is his recipe for Partridges with Cabbage. I would like to think this was very similar to the same dish that was regularly served at La Grande Taverne de Londres:

Chartreuse of Partridges with Cabbage
Perdrix aux Choux et en Chartreuse

Take three old partridges, prepare and truss them en poule; lard with large lard, season with salt, pepper, and fine spices, pounded and sifted aromatics, parsley and small onions minced; cover a stewpan with some parings of veal, two carrots, two onions, and half a clove of garlic; put in the partridges, cover with slices of lard, moisten with some good stock, let it boil, and cover it with a round of buttered paper and the cover of the stewpan; put it on a *paillasse* with fire over and under, give it about an hour and a quarter; in the mean time prepare the cabbage in the same manner as beef (*au choux*), in which cook a Bolognese sausage and a bit of petit lard; cut thirty red carrots, as many turnips, make them the size of a shilling, their length must be that of the mould used; blanch these roots; drain and cook them in *consommé* with a little sugar to take off the acid; having allowed the Bolognese and the *petit lard* to cool, butter a mould, put a round of paper in the bottom and a band round the sides reaching the top; cut the sausage in thin slices and the lard in dices of the same thickness put in the centre of the mould a slice of sausage then round it the dices of the *petit lard* and continue to cover it in this manner; then dress the sides of the mould with the formed carrots and turnips alternately very close together; press out the cabbage cover the bottom of the mould and the sides strengthening the wall; leave sufficient room in the middle for the partridges; put the breasts down, and fill up the mould with cabbage; press it well in so that it may be firm, and leave nothing over the edge of the mould put on a cover and put it in the *bain marie*; pass the seasoning through a gauze search; add three large spoonsful of reduced *espagnole* in the following manner: let it reduce skim bring it to half glaze; turn out the *chartreuse*; take the paper carefully off and spunge it all over with the corner of a cloth with the glaze, and sauce with it.[32]

Auguste Escoffier

Truly, one of the most renowned names in culinary history, Auguste Escoffier is the godfather of high-end French cuisine. His legacies include the Savoy Hotel in London, which he established with César Ritz, the ultimate cooking manual, *Le Guide culinaire* (translated into English in 1907 as *A Guide to Modern Cookery*), and the invention of a range of well-known dishes, one of the most famous of which being the Peach Melba.

Much has been written already about Escoffier and unlike many famous cooks, the culinary world was lucky enough to inherit his personal memoirs, *Souvenirs culinaires*, which were first published in 1985 by his grandson fifty years after his death. These intimate recollections – translated into English in 1996 by his great-granddaughter-in-law, Laurence Escoffier, under the title *Memories of My Life* – reveal the workings of his innovative and pragmatic mind (along with some fascinating society gossip). Born close to Nice in 1846, he was apprenticed first at Le Restaurant Français, which was run by his uncle, before a stint in Paris, which was followed by a noteworthy career as a military chef. Escoffier's earliest experiences of being inspired to cook are captured in his memoirs and offer a lovely glimpse into a simple, yet defining moment in his life:

> My first experiment with cooking dates from 1856. I was ten years old and had no idea at the time that I would one day become a chef. In those days, coffee was not a common beverage; one treated oneself to this stimulating concoction only in certain circumstances. One morning, before she left for Nice, I watched my grandmother prepare coffee for herself in the traditional way. I waited for her to leave and then faithfully repeated her procedure so that I too could taste this coffee that I had heard so much about.
>
> Sometime later, I heard a group of women discussing ways of making coffee. The conversation took place at an evening gathering at our home, in front of a warm fire, and each lady had her own version. When they had all finished giving their ideas on the subject, I announced. 'It really doesn't take much to know how to make coffee!' and told them about my small sin of curiosity. At first they scolded me a little, but in the end they all laughed, and

my grandmother kissed me and whispered in my ear, 'You'll make a good cook!'³³

Aside from *Le Guide culinaire* (1903), Escoffier's other publications included: *Le Carnet d'épicure* (*'A gourmet's notebook'*), a monthly magazine published between 1911 and 1914; *Le Livre de menus* (1912), a book of recipes intended as a companion volume to the *Guide*; *L'Aide-Mémoire culinaire* (1919), a pocket aid for the professional chef; two books aimed at those on restrained means, *Le Riz* ('Rice') in 1927, and *La Morue* ('Cod') in 1929; and *Ma Cuisine* (1934), a classic book of recipes.

Escoffier was a visionary, a man who looked beyond the art of cooking, towards the wider elements of all that eating and dining involved. He

Figure 29. Auguste Escoffier.

was instrumental in establishing the modern-day functionality of commercial kitchens. His *brigade de cuisine* revolutionized the different working elements required in the kitchen. His system provided each cook with their own station, where the plate moved from one to the other, gradually being assembled and all overseen by the *chef de partie*. This form of ranking was undoubtedly influenced by Escoffier's time spent in the army. He introduced structure and discipline to a profession where there had largely been chaos and disorder.

The high-class hotel restaurant industry dominated the nineteenth century. It was the partnership team of Auguste Escoffier and César Ritz who took this trend to new spheres of excellence. Having been thrown together into the hotel business on the French Riviera and then Germany, Ritz chose Escoffier as his executive chef for the Savoy Hotel. The success of this pairing cemented their partnership. Escoffier designed and developed the kitchens and recruited the best staff to work in Ritz's European-wide hotel syndicate.

It was during this period that Escoffier created dishes and menus for some of the world's most famous people: there was *fraises à la Sarah Bernhardt* for the celebrated actress, and *pêche Melba* for the opera singer Dame Nellie Melba (for whom he also crafted a special Melba toast).

Having spent around ten years making the Savoy a global success, Ritz was accused of fraudulent activity and dismissed, but staff loyalty was so strong that many key workers, including Escoffier, chose to follow him to his next endeavour, the Carlton Hotel.[34] His speciality sauces were often highlighted in the press during his lifetime; in particular his Sauce Robert, which you could enjoy either by dining at the Carlton Hotel, or by purchasing Escoffier's own ready-made version in the shops. Sauce Robert was not Escoffier's creation. It has its origins in medieval cooking and appears in many ancient texts, as well as permeating French popular culture during the eighteenth and nineteenth centuries.[35]

Nonetheless he revived it and made it the condiment of popular choice during the early twentieth century. The following recipe is from a later edition of *Le Guide culinaire*:

Finely mince a large onion and put it into a stewpan with butter. Fry the onion gently and without letting it acquire any colour. Dilute with one-third pint of white wine, reduce the latter by one-third, add one pint of half-glaze, and leave to simmer for twenty minutes. When dishing up, finish the sauce with one tablespoonful of meat glaze, one tablespoonful of mustard, and one pinch of powdered sugar. If, when finished, the sauce has to wait, it should be kept warm in a bain-marie, as it must not boil again. This sauce – of a spicy flavour – is best suited to grilled and boiled pork. It may also be used for a mince of the same meat.[36]

Escoffier was a gentle, calm practitioner who frowned upon any type of bad behaviour in the kitchen. Staff were expected to be polite and professional, with any disagreements settled outside of the working areas. Staff spoke in whispers and orders from the dining room were announced cordially, rather than barked out.[37]

After his death in 1935, people became less interested in culinary practices, preoccupied as they were with war and a rapidly changing society, but his contemporary ideas and theories on adaptation in cooking, in terms of following the trends of the public, have withstood the test of time and been adopted by the broader catering industry and innovative practitioners today.

Escoffier's original recipe, together with the story that accompanied the origin of the Peach Melba, can be found in his memoirs:

Original Recipe for *La Pêche Melba*

(For 6)

Choose 6 tender and perfectly ripe peaches. The Montreuil peach, for example, is perfect for this dessert. Blanch the peaches for 2 seconds in boiling water, remove them immediately with a slotted spoon, and place them in iced water for a few seconds. Peel them and place them on a plate, sprinkle them with a little sugar, and refrigerate them. Prepare a litre of very creamy vanilla ice cream and a purée of 250 grams of very fresh ripe raspberries crushed through a fine sieve and mixed with 150 grams of powdered sugar. Refrigerate.

To serve: fill a silver timbale with the vanilla ice cream. Delicately place the peaches on top of the ice cream and cover with the raspberry purée. Optionally, during the almond season, one can add a few slivers of fresh almonds on top, but never use dried almonds. Presentation: Embed the silver timbale in an ice sculpture and add a lace of spun sugar over the peaches (optional).

Note: Blanching the peaches in boiling water and immediately cooling them in iced water has the effect of keeping them fresh for several hours and preventing them from blackening, which is of great importance for large restaurants; if, however, it is necessary to keep the peaches until the next day, they must be placed in an earthenware dish and covered with boiling syrup.

Escoffier informs us that he first put this dish on the menu to celebrate the opening of the Carlton Hotel, although he had served it to Nellie Melba herself after she had delighted the famous French chef with her performance in Wagner's *Lohengrin* at Covent Garden in the 1890s. He had cooked for her when she stayed at The Savoy, dining in the restaurant with friends after her performance. Escoffier recreated the magical swan that appears during the first act of *Lohengrin*, as an ice sculpture that formed the centrepiece for the dessert. Nellie Melba was delighted, and is said to have remembered and talked fondly of the night *pêche Melba* was presented to her for the rest of her life.[38]

Jules Gouffé

The Gouffé name extended to Jules's two brothers Alphonse, one-time head pastry cook to Queen Victoria and Hippolyte, head chef to Count André Schouvallof of Russia. Their passion and talents were undoubtedly inherited from the time they spent working for their father, Louis Gouffé, a pastry cook himself, who owned a pâtisserie in Paris where they learnt the trade. It was here that Jules would meet his future mentor, Antonin Carême. Carême was so impressed with a window display that Jules had created for his father's shop, which he saw when he happened to be walking past, that he approached Louis

Figure 30. Jules Gouffé.

about recruiting his son. For the next part of his life, Jules Gouffé would work as apprentice to Carême, engaged at the Austrian embassy, from just seventeen years of age.[39] He then progressed to the Palais des Tuileries, where he stayed under Carême's tutelage before purchasing his own shop around 1840.

Nicknamed *l'apôtre de la cuisine décorative* ('the apostle of the decorative kitchen'), Gouffé became head chef of the Paris Jockey Club; one of Europe's most celebrated eating societies. He was persuaded to come out of early retirement by his colleagues having worked in his own successful pâtisserie, at number 3 rue du Faubourg Saint-Honoré, Paris from circa 1840 to 1855, manager to some 28 employees.[40] (Incidently, this address is now currently home to the fashion house Dolce & Gabbana.)

During his time at the Jockey Club, Gouffé had an apprentice by the name of Alexandre Thevenot who went on to become a renowned chef to royalty in his own right during the latter part of the 1800s.[41] While I have been unable to source a menu cooked by Gouffé during his time at the illustrious Club, while he was still employed there a memorable dinner was organized, revolving around rather controversial ingredients, certainly foods that would have been illegal to consume in England at that time. The meal was prepared by the French epicure, Baron Brisse. During the Siege of Paris in 1870, all food imports were bockaded by the Germans, and the poplation on occasion turned to dog, and rat, and this menu shows how desperate the chef was. It consisted of the following:

> Hors d'oeuvre. Radishes, herring marine, o*nions à la Provençale*, slightly salted butter gherkins and olives.
> First course. Soup of slightly salted horse, with vegetables; ass-flesh cutlets, with carrots; mule's liver, *saute aux champignons*; horse's lights, with white sauce; *carp à la matelotte*; fried gudgeons; celery heads with seasoning.
> Second course. Quarter of a dog braised; leg of dog roasted; rats cooked upon the ashes; rat pie, with mushrooms; *eel à la broche*, salad of celery and small salad.
> Dessert. Dutch cheese, apples, pears, marmalade au Kirsch, *gateau d'Italie au fromage de Chester*.

Apparently the dinner was heralded as being 'a complete success'.[42]

The Paris Jockey Club was at the forefront of radical and fashionable cuisine, but the palate for horse I believe was still a more niche area of gastronomy, as indeed it was in England. I have however read about queues for dog meat and specialist dog meat butchers being prevalent in Paris during the late nineteenth and early twentieth centuries. Thankfully Gouffé does not include any recipes for either in his books, but undeniably he would have had to cook it for his clientele at one stage of his career, considering the exotic appetites of some of the Paris Jockey Club members.

Having searched for Gouffé's presence during the 1867 International Exposition, the second of its kind to be held in Paris, it seems there are few references to him, or the dining experiences that were staged that year. It appears there was a very good reason for this. The organisers had originally planned an international gastronomy competition, a sort of cook-off against the supposed best chefs in the world, to be located on the Champ de Mars.

To accompany this challenge, Gouffé was tasked with designing, building and coordinating a huge state of the art, fully functioning kitchen, complete with separate stations for soup, sauces and roasts etc. Here every specialist in each sphere, from different nations, would cook their signature dish, to create the ultimate super, celebrity kitchen model. Salons and dining-rooms for visitors/judges, would then lead off from these spaces. Sadly, the plans did not come to fruition, as Napoleon's commissioners decided to sell every available square yard of the Champ de Mars to traders. The outcome, we are told, was a rather lacklustre mixture of 'a few indifferently provided cafés, and some cheap breakfasts and dinners'. This was such a wasted opportunity for both Gouffé and France to have showcased what could have been a marvellous culinary fusion of international expertise.[43]

In his later years, Gouffé set about leaving his legacy in the written word, producing four books, two of which have become the most notable: *Le Livre de cuisine* ('The royal cookery book') of 1867, and *Le Livre de pâtisserie* ('The royal book of pastry and confectionary') of 1873. The former approaches cooking from the perspective of the modest household to that of high-end grand cuisine – separating both domestic and ceremonial recipes into different sections. Published in several languages it became one of the great culinary manuals of the nineteenth century. Here is Gouffé's 'Household' recipe for Broiled Red Mullet. It demonstrates the progress of cookery writing dramatically in the mid-nineteenth century, from the level of description involving the preparation of the fish, to the precision involved with the ingredients and cooking times.

Broiled Red Mullet *À La Maître D'Hôtel*

Take 4 red mullet; remove the gills only (red mullet are dressed with the inside left in); cut off the fins; scrape, and dip the fish in water, quickly, not to soak them; wipe, and score them in the same way as Whiting; put them on a dish, with: 3 tablespoonfuls of salad oil, 2 pinches of salt, 2 small pinches of pepper, 1 onion cut in thin slices, and a few sprigs of parsley, say 1 oz; and steep them for half an hour; drain, and free them from onion and parsley; put them on the gridiron, over a sharp fire, for five minutes each side; serve, on a hot dish, with ½ lb of *Maître d'Hôtel* Butter under them. Red mullet are also served dressed with French white wine.[44]

Carême (Marie-Antoine or Antonin)

'The chef of kings and king of chefs'. Born in Paris in 1783, Marie Antoine Carême, who preferred to be called Antonin, was abandoned by his struggling family, of some speculated twenty-five members, at the age of ten, with no education and no money. Fate took him to the door of a pastry cook, seeking an apprenticeship. By seventeen he was working for the pâtissier Monsieur Bailly in the rue Vivienne, whose clientele included Napoleon and the first minister of France, Charles Talleyrand. For the latter, Carême worked a number of years as *chef de cuisine*. Like many French during the early 1800s, Carême fled to England and landed a prestigious position working for the Prince Regent in Brighton; however, this only lasted a matter of months due to homesickness. On returning to France he was recruited first by Alexander I, followed by a position with the British ambassador in Vienna, a return to France again, back to Vienna, and then a final position working for the banker, Baron de Rothschild, until his death in 1833.[45]

Carême diligently studied the past, attended lectures and researched the evolution of cooking. He was particularly frustrated at the lack of information relating to how the Romans ate. One book in particular, *Le Pâtissier pittoresque,* became very important to him, as it contained illustrations of architectural garden designs. These were the inspiration behind many of his elaborate creations. He studied and copied prints from the Bibliothèque Nationale while working as an apprentice for Sylvain Bailly, which led him to dream up Greek temple structures in marzipan, sugar and other romantic, decorative dishes. Yet his work was far from frivolous as he strove to blend flavours rather than contrast them, removing trimmings and side dishes, unnecessary condiments

Figure 31. M.A. Carême.

and sweetbread accompaniments. As Lady Morgan commented during one of Carême's dinners for Rothschild:

> To do justice to the science and research of a dinner so served would require a knowledge of the art equal to that which produced it; its character, however was that it was in season – that it was up to its time – that it was the spirit of the age...no trace of the wisdom of our ancestors in a single dish – no high-spiced sauces, no dark-brown gravies, no flavour of cayenne and allspice, no tincture of catsup and walnut pickle, no visible agency of those vulgar elements of cooking of the good old times, fire and water. Distillations of the most delicate viands, extracted in silver dews, with chemical precision.[46]

He was first assistant to Monsieur Laguipierre and Monsieur Robert, the head of the kitchen, for two years following the French Revolution, men he deeply respected and admired. With Laguipierre he learned to improvise under difficult conditions, working at the time for Murat, Marshal of France and husband to Napoleon's sister, Caroline, at the Elysée Palace. Undoubtedly it would have been difficult for kitchen staff at this time of political insecurity, when both money and resources were scarce. As Carême noted, Napoleon's kitchen staff had to become very resourceful with making their *sauces maigre* (skinny sauces):

> It is in a Lenten kitchen that the cleverness of a cook can shed a brilliant light. It was in the Elysée Imperial and by the example of the famous Laguipierre and Robert, that I was initiated into this fine branch of the art, and it is *inexpressible*. The years '93 and '94, in their terrible and devastating course, respected these strong heads (*ces fortes têtes*). When our valiant First Consul appeared at the head of affairs, our miseries and those of gastronorny finished. When the empire came one heard of soups and *entrées maigres*. The splendid *maigre* first appeared at the table of Princess Caroline Murat. This was the sanctuary of good cheer and Murat one of the first to do penitence. But what a penitence!⁴⁷

Carême was extremely fond of Laguipierre, who died virtually unknown, leaving nothing behind of his testimonies to great cooking. You can read a little more about this rather engaging man in the final chapter of the book.

His work for Napoleon was just a small part of Carême's professional career at this time. He worked in what were termed as 'extras', under short contracts, in a freelance capacity. So he would flit between the kitchens of Talleyrand, his shop on the rue de la Paix in Paris, and his desk to write his first book – *Histoire de la table romaine*.

The next chapter of Carême's life was spent travelling from one employer to the next, like a restless backpacker. Eight months working for the future King George IV, a stint with the Tsar Alexander I, based in Aix-la-Chapelle, next stop was Vienna in service to the English ambassador to Austria, a short futile trip to St Petersburg to work for the Tsar again, followed by a hugely convoluted chase across Europe to rekindle his working relationship with the English ambassador to

Austria and an endless wait of over a year anticipating working for Prince Esterházy of Hungary, who never turned up. Carême's final years of service were spent with Baron James de Rothschild, until semi-retiring in 1829. His last years were spent indulging in time with his wife and daughter, writing his books, experimenting with his beloved pastry work and securing his legacy for future generations.[48] Carême was adept at the art of self-promotion, determined as he was to raise himself out of the poverty he came from. His life and work were all about fiercely retaining independence, making big projects achievable and documenting his life's work in books. He was a machine, an innovator, a troubled, sad and lonely little boy in a man's body, orphaned and abandoned; looking for his next job, his next home, the next big accomplishment to take him forward. Perhaps always seeking acceptance.

He died in 1833 at just forty-nine. His death was one of the first to be publicly recognized as a disease of the lungs associated with early cooks, a consequence of years spent inhaling poisonous charcoal fumes.[49]

Carême's main publications, *Le Pâtissier royal parisien* (1815), *Le Maître d'hôtel français* (1822) and *Le Cuisinier parisien* (1828) were all highly acclaimed. He also left behind the tradition of wearing the chef's hat, for both safety purposes and to denote rank. Bakers and sauce cooks wore caps, supervising chefs wore small pleated toques, while the head chef traditionally balanced a tall, starched white toque, the number of pleats denoting the number of ways he knew how to cook an egg.[50] Carême's elaborate style of cooking meant he was as adept at creating highly complicated Greek temple constructions from sugar and making cakes for royal weddings. He is also credited with the invention of the vol-au-vent, although almost a century before François Marin had written a recipe for *Un de petits gateaux vole au vent*, which clearly disproves this. However, Carême was undeniably creating more versions of this small hollow case of pastry – both sweet and savoury – than his peers at the time. In *Le Pâtissier royal parisien*, which was translated into English as *The Royal Parisian Pastrycook and Confectioner* in 1834, he writes instructions over the course of three pages on how to create the best puff pastry to make vol-au-vents, offering tips and lengthy guidelines on how to prepare and cook the vol-au-vent cases.

Here is a tasty recipe for the filling of 'Vol-au-Vent à la Nesle', which features in section six:

Vol-au-Vent à la Nesle

Make some balls of poultry force-meat in small-coffee spoons, dip them in jelly broth, and after draining them on a napkin, place them regularly in the vol-au-vent, which fill up with a good ragout of cocks' combs and stones, lambs' sweetbreads, truffles mushrooms, lobsters' tails and four fine whole brains, and cover the whole with a German sauce.

And here is his recipe for German sauce, in case you were wandering:

German Sauce

This sauce is made by reducing the velouté in the following manner: Pour half of the velouté, and the same quantity of good jelly broth of poultry, with some parings of mushrooms and truffles (but very little salt) into a stewpan; place it on a fierce fire, and stir it with a wooden spoon until it boils; put it on the corner of the stove, cover it, and let it simmer for about an hour; then take off the fat, and put it back on the fire, stirring it continually with the wooden spoon. When the sauce is sufficiently thickened, and has acquired the appearance of a jelly, take the stewpan off the fire then mix the yolks of two eggs and a spoonful of cream and after passing them through a tammy [sieve], add a piece of butter as big as an egg, divided into small bits, and pour it altogether into the veloute, stirring it continually with the wooden spoon. When the whole has been well mixed put it on a moderate fire, continuing to stir it; and the moment it begins to boil up, take it immediately off the fire, and add the same quantity of butter that you used for thickening, with a little nutmeg.

N.B. This sauce should be made very thick.[51]

Louis Eustache Ude

Once labelled 'whimsical, good-natured [and] exorbitantly vain', Louis Eustache Ude was born into the court kitchens of Versailles in

Figure 32. Louis Eustache Ude.

1769. He had a string of vocations before settling on cook, from jeweller, hairdresser and engraver to haberdasher, printer, gambler and actor, all of which he considered easier to master than the art of cooking. Ude hungrily tore his way through early life, settling on a position as chef to Napoleon's mother before arriving in Liverpool at the bequest of the Earl of Sefton, somewhat more affectionately known as Lord Dashalong and quoted by Ude as 'one of the best master's man ever served'. It was here that Ude would remain for some years as *chef de cuisine* before moving to the royal kitchens of Frederick Augustus, the son of George III, and then acquiring the role of maître d'hôtel at the legendary gambling and gentlemen's retreat, Crockford's Club in London. He was paid a very generous 1,200 pounds a year to work at

Crockford's (around £65,000 in today's money). It was while employed at Crockford's that Ude became embroiled, amongst other altercations, in a legal case against him for contributing towards the consumption of grouse out of season, contravening the 1831 Game Act.[52]

Ude had a curious fascination for red mullet and was very particular about how it was cooked. It is also said he ate a slice of apricot tart every day and lavishly indulged his close friends and family annually on his birthday with a sumptuous evening feast. This was frequently wrecked by the menagerie of pets that he and his wife indulged in. Despite this extravagance, he publicly denounced the waste of food and urged people to only order what they knew they would like to eat, as well as recommending that large households should seek to serve up dishes that they were certain would satisfy everyone's palettes. In true stereotypical head chef style, Ude was a flamboyant, quick-tempered man who did not suffer fools gladly and there are many accounts of his rages recorded when in service. A diverse, temperamental and sometimes cruel man, Ude had a thick French accent, with a thick dark head of hair to match, and was both the darling and the scourge of the media throughout his lifetime.[53] His book *The French Cook,* of 1813, was published in countless editions over a number of years and represents the archetypal system of French cooking.

As Ude was so fond of apricot tart, I have included here, from *The French Cook*, his recipe for 'Apricot Cakes Trellised', which resemble small tarts, rather than cakes. Perhaps this was the sweet treat he was so addicted to:

Apricot Cakes Trellised

> Spread some puff-paste over the dresser trimmings; will do for these cakes; spread it equally on a large buttered baking sheet, by using the rolling pin as above. Spread some apricot marmalade over the paste equally, then cut some more paste long and narrow, roll it about the size of strong cord, and arrange it crossways like a trellis over the marmalade; put dorure over the bars lightly, and lastly bake in a moderately hot oven. When done cut it into small oblong squares and dress them on the dish one above the other.
>
> As there is an immense variety of paste cutters, select your own

Eminent Gastronomes

Figure 33. Charles Elmé Francatelli

forms; the paste is always the same. Decorate sometimes with almonds cut into different shapes, and sometimes with almonds coloured with green of spinach. It would be too tedious and minute to attempt even describing the various forms. The ingenuity of the practitioner will supply the ornaments, which must always be made of sweetmeat.[54]

Charles Elmé Francatelli

It is said that Francatelli's salads had a definitive flavour, achieved rather alarmingly by crushing a clove of garlic between his teeth and then breathing heavily onto the leaves on the plate.[55] This may have something to do with the fact that until the early twentieth century, garlic was actually considered inedible and offensive. By transmitting the fumes, opposed to physically adding garlic cloves, Francatelli got away with his attempts at flavouring this particular dish. He was also known for adding truffles to almost all his dishes, whether they were required or not.

Born in London in 1805 of Italian extraction and trained by the legendary Marie-Antoine Carême in France, Francatelli worked, amongst other positions, as *chef de cuisine* to the Earl of Chesterfield, Earl of Dudley, Lord Kinnaird, and Sir Rowland Errington, with a brief spell in the royal kitchens of Queen Victoria. Like all prominent cooks of the time, Francatelli was employed by a number of significant dining clubs including Crockford's, St James's, the Reform Club and the Freemason's Tavern, as well as writing several well-received books on cookery. It is understood that Francatelli's erratic, tempestuous behaviour is what got him dismissed from the royal kitchens. On 2 December 1841 it was reported that:

> On Tuesday last [30 November] a long investigation took place at the Board of Green Cloth, before the Lord Steward of her Majesty's Household, when nearly twenty persons of the Royal establishment were examined touching an affray between Mr Norton, the Deputy Comptroller of her Majesty's Household, and Mr. Francatelli, chief cook of the Royal kitchen.
>
> It is well known that broils, jealousies, and ill feeling, to a great extent, have been existing in the Royal establishment ever since the appointment (at the instance of his Royal Highness the Duke of Sussex) of the Hon. Charles Augustus Murray to the office of Comptroller of her Majesty's household. That gentleman, immediately on entering office, caused many old and valuable servants of the Royal Household to be pensioned, or sent to the rightabout, in order to make way for a large number of French servants, who now fill some of the principal offices in the Royal establishment.
>
> Mr Norton, by his judicious management, has done much towards allaying the ill-feeling among the servants, which this injudicious change naturally created, and, by his straightforward, manly conduct, has gained the respect of those over whom he has had control. Francatelli, on the contrary, has kept his department in continual broils, which have been the cause of many dismissals

and numerous complaints to the Lord Steward. On Monday last Mr Francatelli took an opportunity of insulting Mr Norton in the presence of all the Pages and about forty others, when high words ensued, which ended in a policeman being sent to take Francatelli into custody, but he managed to make his escape before the officer arrived. The result of the investigation was the suspension of Francatelli until the matter shall be laid before her Majesty and Prince Albert, when there is no doubt that measures will be adopted to prevent a recurrence of such disgraceful proceedings.

Apparently, the final decision to dismiss Francatelli was slow and he was granted three months' notice. He was replaced on 1 April 1842 by P.N. Morel, who was promoted from Francatelli's first master cook.[56]

Despite this very public disgrace, Francatelli's recipe for Christmas pudding was still being used – according to *The Cookery Book of Lady Clark of Tillypronie* (1909) – for the household of King Edward VII, so clearly there was little grudge attached to his eventual departure. In addition, Queen Victoria's obsession for Indian cuisine and her subsequent close relationship with her Indian chef, Abdul Karim, may originally have been sparked by Francatelli's variety of Indian curry recipes included in his book *The Modern Cook*, recipes that were potentially served to the Queen some forty years before Karim's arrival in 1887.

Francatelli's written works were a combination of themes, with practical guides promoting the benefits of healthy, economical cooking alongside sumptuously illustrated books showcasing his skills, such as *The Royal English and Foreign Confectionery Book,* published in 1862.

Always at the forefront of modern culinary progression, Francatelli was involved in one of the first public horse-eating experiments in history, on Friday, 27 December 1867, when he was tasked with cooking a pre-prepared eighteen-year-old horse to make soup, sausages and escalopes in herbs, amongst other dishes, served up to twenty-two willing test subjects at a leading West End hotel in London. Initially no butcher could be found to slaughter and cut the meat and when one finally complied, both he and the hotel hosting the event remained anonymous for fear that public prejudice would significantly impact on their businesses.

This controversial trial was a success with all who ate the horse, who declared it extremely palatable and succulent, with the flavour of game.[57] Despite public criticism, it seems that the event sparked a series of further horseflesh eating banquets across the country. From Ramsgate to Sheffield, small elite groups of men met to dine on this contentious meat until the Sale of Horseflesh Act was passed in 1889, making it illegal for anyone to sell horseflesh for human consumption. This undoubtedly would only have served to encourage the practice to retreat underground and demonstrates that the horsemeat controversy is an age-old issue and not just one for the modern-day tabloids.

Francatelli's obituaries from 1876 described him comparatively as both amiable, yet reminiscent of Henry VIII (not in a good way).

As this fiery Italian cook was so obsessed with truffles, it seems only fitting to include one of the many, many recipes of his that use this most coveted fungus. Taken from *The Modern Cook*, first published in 1845, this is Francatelli's recipe for Scallops of Partridges, with Truffles:

Scallops of Partridges, with Truffles

Fillet the partridges, remove the sinews from the fillets, and place them in a sautapan with some clarified butter; season with a little salt, and simmer them in the oven or over a slow fire for five minutes; the, turn them over, and when done on both sides, drain them upon a napkin, and cut them into scollops; place these on a stewpan with four ounces of truffles (previously simmered with a small piece of butter and glaze), and to these add some *Espagnole* sauce worked with a *fumet* made from the carcasses. Warm the scollops without boiling, dish them up in the form of a dome, garnish round with some *croquettes* made with the legs; or, the minion fillets may be reserved, and then decorated or fried in batter, used to place round the scallops.[58]

Alexis Benoit Soyer

The most written about of all the celebrated chefs of the eighteenth and nineteenth centuries and perhaps the most eccentric. Soyer was born in 1810 in Meaux-en-Brie – that of the eponymous cheese – and sadly

Figure 34. Alexis Benoit Soyer.

died at just 48 years of age, allegedly from contracting a fatal disease while working out in the field during the Crimean War. He had an eye for beauty and an eye for the ladies, but Soyer's short life was also tainted with tragedy. The death of his wife and stillborn child during a storm took its toll on him, and he would later descend into financial difficulty and personal illness, never truly recovering.

Said to have cut and made his own outlandish clothes from patterns he created himself, Soyer's physical appearance was, according to all accounts, unconventional to say the least. He was referred to as dressing like a 'zoug-zoug', perhaps after the Arabic tribe or popular performing circus troupes of the Victorian age. This costume was frequently paired with high boots, cut on the bias so that he resembled the leaning tower of Pisa, about to collapse. But most importantly, Soyer was a hearty, cheerful and very likeable man, remembered fondly by all who came in contact with him. So vast and varied was Soyer's career that it is worthy of a book in itself. Cook, writer, reformer, government advisor, philanthropist, designer and inventor…and so much more. Sadly, as much as he was admired and courted by society, he was also shamefully chastised for his lack of restraint, eccentric appearance and working-class background, which is perhaps why he has not been as sufficiently acknowledged in the annals of British history as he should have been.

Charles Dickens once said of Soyer that until he had tasted the renowned cook's food he had never properly dined, and never would again unless it was cooked by Soyer. Soyer was a man of considerable contradictions, serving refined food to wealthy Victorians, but also establishing missions in Ireland to feed the starving poor. He undertook humanitarian crusades during the Crimean War, inventing new methods of cooking for the military, and advising on budget cooking methods in his book *A Shilling Cookery for the People*. He was by no means a modest man though. His energy when it came to self-promotion was admirable. He sent endless letters to the press, his social commentaries mixed with promotions of his own work and advertisements for his latest activities. He was an object of derision for every satirist in London and parodied in the fiction of many a famous writer of the day.[59]

He was a colourful, flamboyant and hugely interesting character, perhaps physically best summed up by one of his few biographers, Helen Morris:

> Soyer's desire to be noticed, to be admired, above all to be extraordinary, grew ever more dominant. He tried not only to cook differently from everyone else, but to dress and talk and walk differently too…he was a plague to his tailor, his hatter and his cravat-maker, for he would not wear a single garment with either horizontal or perpendicular lines. His hats were specially built so that when clapped on at any angle they slanted in a coquettish way – in his own phrase, *à la zoug-zoug*. His coats had to be cut on the cross…His visiting card…was not a rectangle but a parallelogram; so was his cigar-case, and even the handle of his cane slanted obliquely.[60]

Considerably more than a dandy, the *Morning Chronicle* of 1858, reported in some detail on the methods adopted by Soyer. During one of his military cooking demonstrations he was able to prepare and serve stewed mutton, soups, beef puddings and dumplings, roast beef, fried potatoes, liver and bacon and rice pudding, amongst other dishes, to 300 men. He achieved this by using three or four cylindrical stoves. These were developed by the chef himself. With a lifespan of several years and light enough to be swung across the back of a horse for transportation, Soyer's *batterie de cuisine* became invaluable to the army and navy, replacing the heavy, expensive, inflexible and unreliable copper canisters of the past.

Soyer's *A Shilling Cookery for the People* was written to help inform poorer communities about the benefits of cooking economically. It is full of witty observations and handy hints and tips, as well as recounting examples of the many home visits Soyer undertook over the years, advising everyday labouring folk on their methods of cooking and helping them achieve the best results for the least outlay. He recommended that the poorer classes use wholemeal flour to make their bread. This would both increase the volume of the actual final product, as well as costing significantly less. Brown bread was historically always considered inferior in England, particularly during the Georgian age. By the early nineteenth century, wholemeal bread was beginning to become more widely accepted as a good and healthier alternative to the aristocratic refined white bread, so coveted by the masses. By the time Soyer wrote his *Shilling* cookery book in 1854, brown bread would certainly have become more accepted by the poor, though this wasn't the case in Ireland, as Soyer regretfully noted:

> In Ireland, amongst the poor, it is almost a disgrace to eat brown bread. During the year of the famine, being at Malahide, I saw a female, without shoes or stockings, go into a baker's shop, purchase two loaves, one white, and the other brown; the white she carried in her hand, the brown she hid under her everlasting cloak – her pride would not allow it to be seen. These ignorant people should be told that there is hardly a family in England but what have on their table for breakfast and tea a loaf of each kind of bread, white or brown.

Here is Alexis Soyer's recipe for Cottage Bread:

Cottage Bread No 1

Put into a large pan fourteen pounds of flour, add to one quart of warm water a quarter of a pint of brewer's yeast, or two ounces of German yeast, make a hole in the flour, and pour in the water and the yeast; stir it well up with a wooden spoon till it forms a thickish paste, throw a little flour over, and leave it in a warm room; in about one hour or seventy five minutes it will have risen and burst through the covering of flour, then add more warm water and four teaspoonfuls of salt, until it forms, when kneaded, a rather stiff dough; it cannot be too much worked; then let it remain covered with a cloth for about another hour, or an hour and a half; the time, as well as the quantity of water it takes, depends greatly on the quality of the flour. Cold water may be used in summer.

Then divide the dough into five pieces; if the flour is old and good they will weigh four pounds each, and take about one hour and forty minutes to bake; the oven should be well-heated and sufficiently large to bake the quantity of dough you make at one time; if the oven is small, make only half the quantity; the door should be well closed. If the bottom of the oven is too hot, a tile placed on it will prevent too much bottom crust; or a baking sheet, kept half an inch above the bottom of the oven, will have the same effect.[61]

Soyer was an extraordinarily gifted man, who effortlessly seems to have stamped his mark on culinary history, in the most dynamic, original and influencial way. The *Britannia and Eve* newspaper of 1951 reflected on the 100th anniversary of the Great Exhibition of 1851, during which Soyer contrived his astonishing 'Gastronomic Symposium of All Nations'. This was essentially a hugely flamboyant restaurant and 'pleasure resort', to replace the dull refreshment rooms provided by the exhibition organizers. For this purpose Soyer leased Gore House, a stately pile on Kensington Gore Road in London, directly across from Crystal Palace. Here he transformed the interior from quaint rooms and galleries into elaborate banqueting halls and temples, with detailed panoramas filling the walls of celebrities, both dead and alive. Soyer created magnificent floral grottos and pavilions in the grounds and, once completed, he welcomed the glitterati of London for private views, before inviting the world's media to attend a lavishly staged banquet. Gore House remained one of the most talked about venues in London, months before the Great Exhibition even began. Its dinner halls and restaurants served the capital city resplendent meals both day and night, with one 'Monster Pavillion of All Nations' seating 1,500 diners across 400 feet of ornately decorated table. It was anticipated that the great 'Symposium' would be sustained as a permanent fixture, but a visit from a magistrate to renew the licence put an end to Soyer's extravagant eatery, arriving as he did in the middle of a rather debauched night of over 700 revellers gorging and enjoying themselves to excess. The venue was closed down just a few days later.

From his astonishingly successful beginnings at the Reform Club, to his years of tireless inventing, campaigning for the poor and prolific writing, Alexis Soyer delivered it all with tremendous eccentricity, style and aptitude, the likes of which has never been matched.

Charles Ranhofer

Figure 35. Charles Ranhofer.

Charles Ranhofer is quoted as saying:

> What is more important than our food? Nothing. Then can there be any higher art than its proper preparation? Persons who eat three times a day often consider the art of cooking as a matter of little importance: but isn't a mistake in cooking that affects the health more vital than one in architecture that may offend the eye?[62]

An obituary for Ranhofer published in the *Evening Times*, 1899, describes him as a man who:

> supervised six or seven dinners in as many parts of New York city, sent refreshments for hundreds to the yacht races, and attended to the multitudinous details of the kitchen of Delmonico's all in one day. There was nothing in culinary art which he could not accomplish. If an order came to prepare a dinner within an hour he was never known to fail.

Figure 36. Delmonico's, New York, 1906.

Interestingly, whilst obituaries for him in the States site his birthplace as France, the British stipulated that he was German by birth.[63]

Delmonico's was already a highly fashionable, successful restaurant when Ranhofer became head chef in 1861. His famous book, *The Epicurean,* was the first definitive authority on haute cuisine in America. To the horror of his fellow cooks – and the restaurant itself – Ranhofer's book revealed all the secrets of Delmonico's recipes and exposed the mystery of gastronomic art for the benefit of everyone. With almost one hundred egg dishes alone – sixteen of which were variations on a scrambled theme – and some eight hundred illustrations, *The Epicurean* is certainly one of the most distinctive and thorough manuals of its era. It was even recorded in the 1895 edition of the prestigious *Appletons' Annual Cyclopaedia and Register of Important Events of the Year.*

Heralding from an established culinary family, Ranhofer trained in Paris from the age of twelve. He specialized in the art of pastry and, after having run several kitchens in France, moved to New York in 1856 to work for the Russian consul. He subsequently transferred to positions in both Washington and New Orleans, followed by a brief stint in Paris, before returning to New York again in 1861 to run Delmonico's, overseeing a kitchen staff of forty-six.[64] He was extremely disparaging of American cooking, declaring: 'It is a wonder that you have not entirely ruined the national digestion with your careless cooking and hasty eating'.[65] His most famous dish was Lobster à la Newburg. It is said he renamed the Baked Alaska as Alaska Florida, contrasting the heat of one state with the cold of another

The old Georgian style of *service à la française* in which all of the courses were placed on the table as part of an elaborate display, began to change during the early to mid-nineteenth century. It was replaced by the Russian process of dishes being brought to the table in a sequence – the style that we are still most familiar with today. The French were the first to adapt to this *service à la russe* method, followed swiftly by the English and the Americans. The American method differed slightly, although Ranhofer indicates that it was 'copied more or less from the French and Russian [whilst being] remodelled to the tastes and customs of this country'. He was known for his slick ability to manage the constant changeover of courses with precision timing, as outlined in *The Epicurean*:

> American service, like the Russian, must be served quickly and hot. As easily understood by the following card, a dinner of ten minute intervals can be served with fourteen courses in two hours and twenty minutes and if at eight minute intervals, in one hour and fifty-two minutes, the same as an eight-course dinner of ten minute intervals will take one hour and twenty minutes, so at eight minute intervals it will take one hour and four minutes.

Fourteen course dishes inevitably consisted of oysters, soups, fish, various vegetable dishes, a punch of some kind, often iced to cleanse the palette, followed by the roasted meats, cold meats and salads, and ending in a hot dessert and a cold dessert.[66]

Ranhofer made Delmonico's internationally famous. It became the place to visit for travellers, attracting a number of the most famous names in history: Charles Dickens, Oscar Wilde, Mark Twain, Theodore Roosevelt, even King Edward and Napoleon III.

Operated by the Delmonico family in New York, Delmonico's first opened its doors in 1827. It relocated several times before becoming established at number 2 South William Street. In the celebrity fuelled culture of today it is difficult to comprehend the importance of Delmonico's reputation at the time, as one of the first celebrity endorsed restaurants. It is understood that Oscar Wilde, then aged just twenty-seven, went directly to Delmonico's from the pier on his arrival in America in 1882.[67] One of the dishes he sampled was terrapin and he would later remark: 'Indeed, the two most remarkable bits of scenery in the States are undoubtedly Delmonico's and the Yosemite Valley.'[68]

Charles Dickens was honoured with a farewell dinner by the American press at Delmonico's, which concluded his visit in 1868, during which he delivered a series of readings from his works to over 200 guests. He arrived an hour late to the strains of 'God Save the Queen' and had to be escorted in, with rumours circulating about gout delaying his visit.[69] Mark Twain went as far as celebrating his 70th birthday at Delmonico's in 1905, albeit several years after Ranhofer's departure, which was attended by 170 celebrities, almost half of whom were women, including many authors. Each guest went away with a commemorative plaster of Paris bust of Twain, which could be viewed as either egotistical or ironic. Each table was photographed, and the number of speeches and tributes recorded meant there was probably more talking than eating. Amongst these speeches were forty cablegrams from English authors. The menu that evening was a bright illustrated homage to Twain, with sketches highlighting aspects of his life framing the order of service, including:

> Oysters – Consommé Souveraine, Green Turtle – Timbales Perigourdine – Filets of Kingfish Meunière, Cucumbers, Persillade Potatoes – Saddle of Lamb Colbert, Stuffed Tomatoes – Baltimore Terrapin, Mushrooms on Toast with Cream, Sherbet with Kirsch – Quail, Red Head Duck, Fried Hominy and Currant Jelly – Salad: Celery Mayonnaise – Fancy Ice Cream, Assorted Cakes, Bonbons, Coffee

> Served with Sherry, Sauterne, Champagne, Mineral Water, and Liqueurs.[70]

Sadly when Ranhofer died so too did Delmonico's. Despite its several twentieth century reincarnations, it never reclaimed its original glory. By 1905 it was widely advertising discount fifteen cent meals in the press.

In 1899, the year of Ranhofer's death, the following notice appeared:

> Delmonico's, the world-famous café and restaurant in twenty-sixth street, New York, has (says the correspondent of the *Morning Leader*) just closed its doors for the last time. Many of the old-timers were present for the occasion, but their spirit of jollity absent. The place was full and the cooking as excellent as ever, yet the wine did not seem to sparkle as of yore. A number of the habitués were entertained by Charles Delmonico. His guests were the last to leave, and as they went he said, 'This house shall be closed for a year. Nobody shall repeat the Delmonico record here'

> There were tears in many eyes. The reason for the discontinuance of Delmonico's at its present abode is that the general trend of society and wealth is every year going further up the Island of Manhattan. The present establishment, when it started, was in the very heart of the fashionable district.[71]

Some fifteen years prior to its closure, Charles Delmonico disappeared. He had been suffering from mental health issues, combined with a succession of failures on the stock market. One day he escaped his restraints and was found dead in the New Jersey mountains.[72]

Alongside the vast legacy of Delmonico's, Ranhofer has become a staple of American cultural history, a product of the first and second Industrial Revolutions. But he may not have become as globally renowned as he has without Delmonico's. Like so many chef/restaurant collaborations, it is often just as much about the location, image, reputation and patronage of the restaurant itself, as it is about the cooking. Charles Delmonico's great-uncles John and Peter, of Swiss origin, founded the Delmonico empire, together with their nephew Lorenzo. John's life was cut short, dying from a massive stroke at the age of forty-nine, during a hunting trip.[73]

In an interview with Lorenzo Delmonico who died in 1881 and took on sole ownership of Delmonico's restaurants in 1847, he revealed that Ranhofer was paid 4,000 dollars a year (incidentally, 2,000 dollars less than their previous chef), with the other cooks receiving between 15 and 30 dollars a week, almost four times less than the head chef. Interestingly, the head waiter received board and lodging in addition to a good salary, with table waiters being paid an average three dollars each month, which could be significantly increased with tips. One of the most written about meals at the flagship Delmonico's was the Grand Swan dinner. This featured a miniature lake embedded into the centre table, complete with swans and other birds swimming around for the entertainment of the seventy-four guests.[74]

The Meniers

Following on from the hugely successful Delmonico family fortunes it seemed only right to fleetingly mention another of those great nineteenth century entrepreneurial dynasties, that of Antoine Brutus Menier, who founded the Menier Chooclate Co in 1816. The story of the Cadbury and Rowntree families are inherent to the history of

British chocolatiers, whereas Menier's is a somewhat more glamorous success story.

Antoine Menier began his career grinding down cacao beans to sweeten his medicinal remedies, winning a medal for his efforts at the 1832 Paris Exposition. By the end of the nineteenth century Menier's was one of, if not the, largest manufacturer of chocolate in the world. Antoine's son, Émile-Justin, expanded and diversified the firm, acquiring large supplies of cocoa butter to make solid chocolate bars and covered bonbons.[75]

The Menier family of chocolatiers is one of the most interesting culinary dynastical stories. In 1895, Émile-Justin's first son, Henri, known in England as 'The man who would be king', acquired the island of Anticosti in Quebec, Canada, an island around 135 miles long, comparable to the size of Corsica, over 3,000 acres at a cost of 5 cents an acre. He came under fire for evicting the native Canadian fisherman who resided on the island and was often at odds with the Canadian authorities. He built himself a castle and established his own armed navy, with specific duties to fetch and carry supplies from the mainland, in addition to guarding the immediate waters around the island itself. Menier recruited an army of French workmen to build the infrastructure, from roads to houses, and acquired an elaborate steam boat to take him to and from France and Quebec.[76]

The French chocolate baron allegedly banned all Englishmen from the island and established a governing body with a number of departments, including forestry and agriculture, fisheries, roads and traffic, but devoid of any policing authorities. Born in 1853, he took over his father's chocolate manufacturing empire at the tender age of eighteen and by the time he reached twenty-five, he had doubled productivity. Being childless, after Henri's death, the estate was inherited by his brother Gaston, who failed to maintain the company.

After his death, Gaston's heirs, Hubert and Antoine Menier, found the pressure from their competitors overwhelming and were forced to sell the company as part of a merger with Cacao Berry. Following further commercial transactions, including that of Rowntree Mackintosh in the 1970s, the Menier name was finally absorbed under the Swiss umbrella of Nestlé.

In its heyday the Menier Chocolate Factory produced some of the world's finest cocoa-based treats. According to the *Hastings and St Leonards Observer* of November, 1900, the secret success of one of the United Kingdom's leading long-distance cyclists, Mr 'Tolley' March from Hastings, was down to peppermints and Menier chocolate.

The Gunters

'Everyone, but everyone has heard of Gunter's', was a common reaction to this most famous and enduring of late eighteenth century London-based confectioner's.[77] As well as a shop and a *maison du thé*, it was also one of the leading society caterers of its time, well into the twentieth century. They provided a catering service to large-scale events nationally, from the navy to elite wedding parties, as well as being patronized by the royal family. Gunter's was the number one caterer of choice for the cream of society for over 150 years. The menu below for the 1914 Rugby Hunt Ball, exemplifies some of their talents:

Chaud
Consommé garne
Poulet à la Marengo
Froid
Darioles d'Homard.
Filets des soles Princess
Zephyrs de volaille
Cotelettes à la zingari
Faison roti
Mousse à la westphalienne
Poulet braise
Sandwiches
Salade

Pâté de Gibier
Dinde à la Francaise
Jambon de York
Langue de Boeuf

Gelées au kirsch

Pain de pommes
Crèmes à la Chantilly
Pâtisserie.[78]

Born in 1731, James Gunter was the son of Walter Gunter, the last of the Gunter family to reside in Abergavenny, Wales. James left Wales to seek his fortune in London, going into partnership in 1777 with an Italian, Domenic Negri, to run the then already revered Pot and Pineapple confectionery shop in Berkeley Square.

When Gunter became sole proprietor he put his name to the shop and quickly turned it into one of the most fashionable venues in London. It was one of the only places ladies could visit unchaperoned, sitting in their carriages while waiters dashed to and fro serving the shop's acclaimed ices. On 24 August 1867, the satirical magazine *Punch* published a picture illustrating one such young lady languishing in her carriage, enjoying the trappings of modern Victorian middle class life, while several starving street urchins look on beseechingly. The poem that accompanied the picture reads:

> The weather is warm as I walk in the square,
> And observe her barouche standing tranquilly there,
> It is under the trees, it is out of the sun,
> In the corner where GUNTER retails a plum bun.
>
> How solemn she looks, I have seen a mute merrier –
> Plumes a sky-blue, and her pet a sky-terrier –
> The scene is majestic, and peaceful and shady,
> Miss Humble sits facing: I pity that lady.
> Her footman goes once, and her footman goes twice,
> Ay, and each time returning he brings her an ice:
> The patient Miss Humble receives, when he comes,
> A diminutive bun: let us hope it has plums![79]

The success of the shop, combined with its catering service, made James Gunter a very wealthy and respected man. He built a sixty-acre estate in Earl's Court, which was affectionately nicknamed 'Currant

Figure 37. William Gunter.

Jelly Hall' by his children.[80] James' son Robert was sent to Paris to train in the art of ice-cream making in 1815, as the inevitable successor to the Gunter empire,[81] which he maintained, together with his cousin John, until the 1850s, when the confectionery baton was passed to Robert's two sons, James and Robert junior, following his death.

I am unsure of his relationship within the Gunter clan, but there was a William Gunter who also worked on the premises and wrote a book called *Gunter's Confectioner's Oracle* in 1830. It has an introduction which is a strange personal ramble, and makes reference to the fact that his good friend William Kitchiner (who you can read more about in chapter four) persuaded him to write the book. He uses the Appendix to again digress about social gossip and seasonal foods, which leads into a diatribe about the digestive system, concluding with a strange

Eminent Gastronomes

A-Z of raw materials, partly written in French. If nothing else, it leads us to believe that William was indeed quite an eccentric. William Jeanes's experiences of working for William Gunter in Berkeley Square are recorded in his *Gunter's Modern Confectioner*. It is evident that he respected Gunter a great deal and he shares many of his employer's wisdoms with the reader:

> Mr. William Gunter used to recommend boiling, exactly opposite to what other confectioners advise.
>
> Mr. Gunter recommends to boil for *five* days.
>
> There are nine essential Points or Degrees in Boiling Sugar, and these were termed by Mr. Gunter, many years since, the *mystery of confectionery*. They are – Small Thread. Large Thread. Little Pearl. Large Pearl. The Blow. The Feather. The Ball. The Crack. The Caramel.[82]

There are also mentions of a Richard Gunter, a confectioner owning stores in Motcomb Street and Lowndes Street, London, during the mid-1800s. Whether he was also a direct relative remains unclear.[83]

In 1857 the 'Currant Jelly Hall' estate was put up to be let and the vast majority of its contents was sold off at auction.[84] Whether this indicates that Gunter's was no longer quite as successful as it was, or simply represents a lack of interest in any of the family members continuing to keep up the mansion and its grounds, remains unclear. Nonetheless, the records and positive references to the shop and its catering business, continue to appear with regularity right up until the 1930s.

James Gunter additionally owned a lease for the Hope and Anchor public house, purchased in 1810 and signed over to his son Robert on his death. The property was leased and then sublet, and a complicated court case raged for some years revolving around who should be in possession of the property and when.[85] Robert Gunter junior, the grandson of James Gunter, broke out of the confectioner's mould. He was a military man who settled in Yorkshire and became a Justice of the Peace and a popular Member of Parliament.

In its heyday, Gunter's provided many a talented confectioner with the opportunity to train and gain success in their own right, including William Jeanes, Samuel Hobbs and, most famously, William Jarrin, while Frederick Nutt was also employed at the original Pot and Pineapple as an apprentice to Domenico Negri. Nutt is an important contributor to the discourse of influential historical confectioners. He is now largely forgotten, but more on his life can be found in the next chapter. On the other hand, Jarrin is a name that has to a greater extent lived on in the culinary psyches of many an historic gastronomic researcher. Migration from France and Italy to escape war and persecution resulted in immigrants bringing about a British revolution in cooking and dining, from confectioners appearing on street corners, to a fashion for big country houses wanting to employ French cooks. German bakeries also began creeping into the major cities, along with a host of migrant street food sellers. There are some 7,000 trading pastry cooks and confectioners listed in the 1841 census for Great Britain. Although this figure just straddles the Victorian era, it's clear these businesses were established well before then, with nineteen confectioners trading in the city of Leeds alone as early as 1817.[86] I think you would be hard pushed to find one or two on the high street today.

William Jarrin

William Jarrin worked as an ornamental confectioner for James Gunter, but also had his own confectioner's shop in New Bond Street. He wrote the lovely and descriptive *Italian Confectioner* around 1822, which includes illustrations of some of his tools of the trade. Jarrin's store obviously wasn't as successful as Gunter's as he was declared insolvent just a year after writing his book. This coincided with him filing for a patent for a new apparatus he invented to cool liquids. He died at the age of sixty-four in 1848. A list of Jarrin's worldly goods, including much of the contents of his shop, which was put up for sale to cover the cost of his debts, was listed in the 27 May 1834 edition of the *Morning Advertiser* and makes for depressing reading. It also

Figure 38. William Jarrin.

provides us with a visual indication of what his confectioner's store would have looked like:

> ...preserved fruits, 70 dozen bottles of juice...wedding cakes and every other description of confectionery; a large assortment of china and glass...many dozens of show glasses and covers; trifle dishes, &c.; counters and pier tables, with marble top tables, on splendid bronze frames; nine elegant large-size brilliant-plate pier and chimney-glasses; plated waiters...lemonade cisterns, &c. Grecian lamps, eight-dozen of cane seat chairs, covered stools and tables, large eight-day dial, tea-trays and waiters...French bedsteads and bedding, two easy chairs, Brussels and Kidderminster carpets... The utensils, which are adapted for an establishment on a large-

scale, include superior copper stock and soup-kettles, French stewpans, moulds and shapes, strainers &c.; ice pails, freezing pots…The fixtures consist of register stoves, cooking apparatus, hot-plates, coppers, elegant gas-fittings, &c. Also, Jarrin's Patent for a refrigerator, with several copper and japanned refrigerators.

Marble, bronze, glass and cane, Grecian lamps, fancy carpets, all conjure up a sense of opulence and classic design. Jarrin's shop would have been engineered to cater to the wealthier classes and its tasteful furnishings and sparkling containers full of sweet delights are indicative of an establishment that he wanted to succeed, a place that suggests so much promise. Surely the saddest of all the items for sale are the rights to his patent refrigerator, a stark reminder perhaps of trying to achieve too much, too soon in a burgeoning, talented career.

Interestingly, William Jarrin, who boasted royal patronage, appeared to experience a slightly unusual catalogue of events that caused him both professional and financial issues. About ten years prior to his bankruptcy order, an assassination attempt was made upon his wife, who was shot at one evening while she was maintaining the shop and her husband was upstairs working. A man standing in the street had been seen watching the shop and proceeded to fire an air gun at the glass frontage, the bullet from which smashed the glass and just scraped past the leg of Mrs Jarrin. Despite the authorities' best efforts to catch the man, he was never found.[87] Following many discussions with the local magistrate it emerged that Jarrin had no known enemies and no previous grievances. However, five years later Jarrin found himself the victim of a large-scale swindling operation, in which he was commissioned to make up some 48 cases of jam, supposedly to be shipped to India for the benefit of expatriates living out there. He hired a huge team of staff in order to meet the deadline and deliver the goods, only to discover when he delivered the jam to the awaiting ship that the person who ordered it had just two hundred pounds available to pay the confectioner, against a total bill of £1,050. Thankfully Jarrin was able to remove the cases of jam before they passed through customs, and resell them, but he lost a considerable sum in the process.[88]

During the same year, one of Jarrin's former employees, an errand boy who he had dismissed due to 'some irregularity of conduct', was accused of breaking into Jarrin's premises in the early hours of a Sunday morning and stealing four dozen silver spoons and 200 sovereigns, amongst other items.[89] The year before this, the celebrated confectioner was taken to court and ordered to pay the sum of £1,671 and 4s to the Horticultural Society, for not providing enough food when catering for a society breakfast event.[90] Incidently, Robert Gunter of his former employer, Gunter's, acted as a witness in support of Jarrin in this case. Now, whether Jarrin was just a rather unlucky sort of chap, or was the type of character who simply provoked the worst in people, will remain conjecture. But his story is undoubtedly a fascinating one and he remains one of those culinary characters of the early nineteenth century who demands greater research.

Jarrin was as passionate about confectionery as if it were an art form, like sculpture. The *Italian Confectioner* is testament to this. He discusses all the forms of gum paste, from decorative flower moulding using softer pastes, to the hard plaster gum pastes that would have been used for pastillage – larger ornamental constructions. Jarrin goes into great detail about the various tools of his trade used to cut, shape, sculpt, varnish, paint and gild. This was confection at its most elaborate. Jarrin instructs the reader in a variety of shapes, from animals, birds and flowers, to modelling figures:

> On Modelling Figures in Gum Paste
>
> Model the limbs by hand, and fix on the head with a wire; and afterwards dress the figure, making every part of the drapery of its proper colour. To model the hand, you must divide the fingers with a pair of scissors and mark the nails and joints with a modelling tool: this method will be found much better than pushing the figures in wooden moulds, as is usually done.[91]

Yuan Mei

Born to a poor family in 1716, Yuan Mei was raised by his aunt to become one of the youngest and brightest of teachers to work at the prestigious Imperial Hanlin Academy, and one of China's best known gastronomes from the eighteenth century. Yuan Mei was a poet and scholar who wrote the *Sui yuan shi dan* ('Recipes of the Sui Yuan garden') in 1792. *Sui yuan shi dan* is both a critique of Chinese cuisine at the time, as well as a recipe book. It is a testament to his acerbic wit that Yuan has often been nicknamed the Chinese Brillat-Savarin. He was not really a cook himself, but rather he consulted with numerous cooks in order to acquire his knowledge and tested every recipe he included. He would notoriously only cook using produce that he could source from the market on the day. He was a perfectionist when working with other cooks, which earned him the reputation of something akin to Gordon Ramsay today, as confirmed by one of his employers:

> I once asked him why, when he could easily have got a job in some affluent household, he had preferred to stay all these years with me in the Sui Garden. 'To find an employer who appreciates one is not easy,' he said, 'but to find one who understands anything about cookery is harder still. So much imagination and hard thinking go into the making of every dish that one may well say I serve up along with it my whole mind and heart. The ordinary hard-drinking revelers at a fashionable dinner-party would be equally happy to gulp down any stinking mess. They may say what a wonderful cook I am, but in the service of such people my art can only decline. True appreciation consists as much in detecting faults as in discovering merits. You, on the contrary, continually criticize me, abuse me, fly into a rage with me, but on every such occasion make me aware of some real defect, so that I would a thousand times rather listen to your bitter admonitions than to the sweetest praise. In your service, my art progresses day by day. Say no more! I mean to stay on here!' ...But when he had continued with me not quite ten years, he died, and now I never sit down to a meal without thinking of him and shedding a tear.[92]

Yuan Mei's work represents the first definitive Chinese cookbook, reflecting a wealth of popular dishes of the time, divided into fourteen chapters:

Notice of Food and Drink (Directories of Food)
Warning of Food and Drink (Prohibited Food)
Seafood Dishes (Fresh Sea Food)
Fresh water Fish Dishes (Fresh River Food)

Pork Dishes (Special Animal Food)
Beef, Mutton and Venison Dishes (Miscellaneous Animal Food)
Fowl/Bird Dishes (Poultry)
Fish with and Without Scales (Aquatic and Scaled Food)
Vegetable Dishes (Vegetarian Food)
Side dishes (Side Dished)
Dim Sum (Pastries)
Rice and Congee (Rice and Porridge)
Tea (Tea)
Wine (Alcoholic Beverages)

Yuan Mei famously recommended that fresh tea leaves should never be exposed to heat, as this would strip the tea of all its original taste, thus making our system of dehydrating the leaves for everyday use rather a detrimental process. More on Yuan Mei's work can be found in *Slippery Noodles* by Hsiang Ju Lin.

Here is Yuan Mei's recipe for sea cucumber, taken from a translated copy of *Sui yuan shi dan* :

> Sea cucumber itself has no taste. It is hard to cook it well because it has much sand and can taste fishy. A kind with spikes is the best choice. First dip it in clean water in order to clear away sand. Use broth to stew it. Then cook it in chicken soup and broth until flaccid. Accessories are Chinese mushroom and black mo-er, because they are all a similar black color. Or prepare to stew the sea cucumber before the day of a dinner party so that it can be flaccid. I have seen a method for cooking it in observer Qian's home. This excellent method is to mix mustard and chicken soup with cold sea cucumber or first cut sea cucumber into dice then stew it with diced bamboo and diced Chinese mushrooms in chicken soup. The chef in minister Jiang's home uses thin sheets of bean curd, drumstick, and Chinese mushrooms stewed with sea cucumber which is a good practice.[93]

Nicolas Appert

Born in France in 1749, Nicolas Appert was a cook, confectioner and distiller, often credited with the invention of canning. His book, *L'Art de conserver les substances animales et végétales* (translated into English in 1811 as *The Art of Preserving All Kinds of Animal and Vegetable Substances for Several Years*), represents the findings of his long-term study into sealing, preserving and storing a multitude of food products. He went on to build one of the first commercial factories producing conserved foods in the world. His research sat in tandem with that of the British merchant, Peter Durand, who gained a patent in 1810 to develop sealable tin containers, rather than the glass bottles that Appert used. Durand sold his patent to Bryan Donkin and John Hall who wasted no time in exploiting it, opening the first canning factory in England. What is particularly interesting about this commercial race is that in the details of his patent, Durand talked about how his ideas for food preservation were actually acquired from a 'friend abroad'. Whether this was actually Appert, who should therefore be unconditionally credited with this invention, remains unclear.[94]

Appert's *The Art of Preserving*, must surely represent one of the most remarkably comprehensive accounts of preserving ever written. It describes the laborious processes that he must have had to go through, in order to establish an infallible method of preserving everything from asparagus to fish. Having read Appert's experiments, I will never again take for granted the fact that I can eat artichokes all year round, or rehydrate mushrooms from a packet, to bolster an emergency casserole. Here is Appert's description of how he finally managed to successfully preserve artichokes, no doubt following numerous experiments:

Artichokes
(*Artichauts*)

To preserve artichokes whole, I gather them of a middling size; after having taken off all the useless leaves and pared them, I plunge them into boiling water, and immediately afterwards into cold water. Having drained them, I put them into jars which are corked, &c. and they receive an hour's boiling.

To preserve cut artichokes (*en quartiers*), I divide them (taking fine specimens) into eight pieces. I take out the choke and leave very few of the leaves. I plunge them into boiling water, and afterwards into fresh water. Having been drained, they are then placed over the fire in a saucepan, with a piece of fresh butter, seasoning, and fine herbs. When half dressed, they are taken from the fire and set by to cool. They then are put in jars, which are corked, tied, luted, &c. and placed in the water-bath, in which they receive half an hour's boiling.[95]

Appert trained in Paris at one of the big eating houses of the time and before he was even thirty he was able to use his savings to invest in a confectioner's shop. It was while working in this capacity that he grew frustrated with the poor quality bottled fruits he purchased to use in his baking. Despite not knowing how food went bad – Pasteur having not yet published his ground-breaking research on bacteria – Appert simply found a way to counteract the process of deterioration, which secured him funding and notoriety.[96] As his work became more recognized, the French navy took foods packaged by the inventor on long voyages from 1806 onwards. His factory, *La Maison Appert,* was sadly destroyed in 1814 during the Napoleonic wars, but ever resourceful he managed to reinstate it a couple of years later. In addition to discovering new methods of preservation, we also have Appert to thank for indirectly inventing an autoclave that could be used to develop pressure cookers, and a type of gelatine from extracting marrow from animal bones more effectively, as well as crafting a concentrated broth that could be rehydrated: the stock cube.

Essentially, Nicolas Appert revolutionised the way in which we can store food, which had massive social and economic repercussions. The financial toll of costly and time-consuming experiments was a huge burden throughout Appert's life and he died in poverty aged ninety-one in a common grave.[97] This sad end is one of the reasons I think it is incredibly important that we recognize the life of this most renowned cook and inventor.

Chapter Four

The Overlooked and Uncredited

I have read much about numerous men and women throughout history who have achieved a huge number of amazing things, yet who remain sadly forgotten. Often those who receive credit are the ones lucky enough to have sought favour with the media, and who were acquainted with the right people, or by chance simply found themselves in the right place at the right time. As such, they are also the ones whose legacies survive. Goodness only knows what will become of those who are well-known today, through whatever latest fashion or tabloid trend they have aligned themselves with in order to reach that status. There are of course the genuine heroes and the not so genuine zeros, and many will no doubt be remembered both online and in books, for whatever reason, in years to come.

In terms of the culinary world, there is still a great deal of research out there to be undertaken, so there remains a chance of stumbling across a real gem of a gourmand or avant-garde writer, even a breakthrough cook, baker, distiller or confectioner who was the real intelligence behind a well-known recipe or brand. As well as master cooks, and food and recipe writers, there were many well-known and respected tavern, cook and coffee shop keepers of the past, who became known because of their popularity and reputation. This chapter pays homage to a few of these characters, but there are so very many more to be discovered. I am particularly pleased to be able to include a Welsh culinarian, having found it extremely difficult to source either Welsh or Irish notable cooks of old during my research for this book. Many of the best cooks in Ireland during the eighteenth and nineteenth centuries were immigrants and the Irish Tourist Association was not established until 1893, making it a largely inaccessible visitor destination until then. One English-born, Parisian-trained chef in particular, G. Frederick Marco, made a significant impression in both Belfast and Cork as head chef to some of Ireland's most distinguished hotels.¹ There is very little information available about Marco, suggesting the nature of native Irish cooks generally offers a much bigger research project for culinary historians.

Thomas Davey

Once heralded 'London's most famous cook', Thomas Davey's name is now all but a shadow on gastronomic history's wall.

For forty-seven years he presided over the kitchens of the illustrious Simpson's in the Strand. He famously chose to use only English meat and produce, refusing to cook anything imported or incorporate any French dishes into his menus. In fact, he refused to even use the word menu, preferring to retain the old English 'Bill of Fare'. He favoured traditional methods of cooking and would only use an open fire and spit.

When it came to his team of staff however, he was completely indifferent to recruiting foreign labour.

Despite working in a city that was rapidly changing and evolving with the times, one where experimentation and continental fusion was developing alongside modern technology and innovation in the kitchen, Davey must have cut a striking contrast. It is also important to consider that there was a traditionalist food movement in England at this time, and a divide between those who craved the new delights of haute cuisine and high-end cooking, alongside the conventional, less complicated old English styles.

Born in 1851, Davey, like many others before him, began his career as an apprentice, working in a tavern in Fleet Street, before acquiring the lowly position of assistant 'roast' cook at Simpson's in 1867 and then working his way up through the kitchen ranks. Overseeing a team of one hundred staff, Davey regularly cooked for all the great cultural icons of the Victorian era: Dickens, Thackeray, Sala, and Irving to name a few. He even cooked for Edward VII, just prior to the restaurant's large-scale redevelopment in 1903. It is said that the vast round mahogany table the king and his guests sat round was so large and heavy that all the new building work had to be completed around it.[2]

In his lifetime, Davey was head-hunted with frequency, particularly by American restaurants, who offered him all manner of incentives to come and join them.

Twice married, Thomas Davey had three children. He died at the age of seventy-two in 1914 at his home in Wimbledon. Physically all we know about Davey is that he was short, stout, wore a velvet cap and white apron and was always happy to talk to customers.[3] There was a photograph of him published in the *Illustrated London News* in 1906 in which he adorns one of those most Victorian of long handlebar moustaches. Aside from that, he is quite unremarkable, but very approachable and friendly looking.

We need to remember Thomas Davey, because for almost half a century, he *was* Simpson's-in-the-Strand. Unlike so many of the great restaurateurs of the age, Davey went against the grain and enshrined English cooking and cooking practices, a stance which commanded the highest level of respect and popularity.

Henry Jones

There are many inventors of key culinary products from the past that remain anonymous. Having recently completed a book exploring the bygone lives of the people behind the greatest inventions of the kitchen, I have begun to appreciate the need to tell more of these stories. Henry Jones definitely fits into that category.

Born in Monmouth, Wales, in 1812, Jones relocated to Bristol and opened his bakery there. During his formative years he focused on inventing a process of adding raising agents to plain flour to increase its longevity. He eventually achieved what he set out to do, and being a shrewd businessman and socialite Jones managed to persuade William Turnham, then cook to the Duke of Beaufort, to endorse it. From this point onwards, Jones's flour was in demand across all the great houses, with even the royal household taking an interest. By 1845 the flour was officially named as 'Self-Raising' and a patent was granted, after which Jones retailed it in his trademark yellow bags which were patronised by Queen Victoria.[4]

Despite gaining a highly lucrative patent in the United States in 1852, Henry Jones's innovation had still not become a groundbreaking

The Overlooked and Uncredited

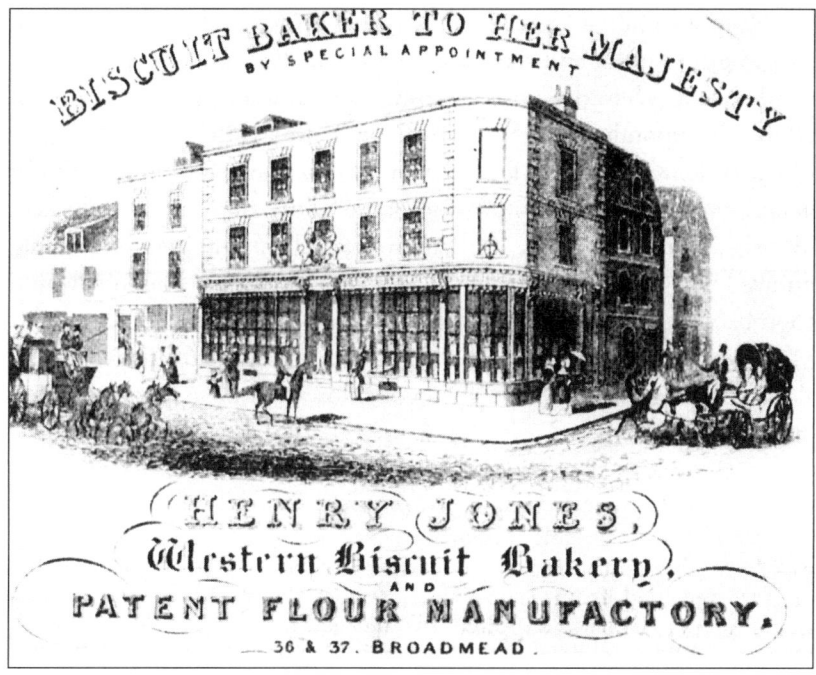

Figure 39. Henry Jones's Western Biscuit Bakery.

success. In the meantime, with war raging in the Crimea, the availability of food rations during conflict, in particular the quality of the bread, remained a critical ongoing issue. A description by a nurse out in the field at Scutari at this time, testifies to this:

> I suppose all English people can imagine the sour bread, which is all that is to be had here, and the bad butter too, which is moreover too scarce for the poor soldiers to be allowed, and a stolen scrape of even this is the greatest luxury to a dying man. For those who are not so bad, I am sure it is wholesome, and for want of it many reject the bread entirely, and sink. We have seen this often, nor is it to be wondered at; nothing but hunger induces us, in health to eat the food, and their appetites ought to be tempted to the utmost, but the materials are not to be had.[5]

In response to similar issues as this, Jones had already approached the Navy Victualling Office some ten years earlier, back in 1845. He sent them both samples and machinery with which to mill the flour itself, but had not received a positive reply. In frustration, he sent copies of all the correspondence he had provided the navy with to every Member of Parliament, in order to lobby them. This was the first public political action on behalf of an individual issue of its time, and it worked. Within a month, supplies of Henry Jones's self-raising flour were being enjoyed by every ship in the navy.[6] Weevil infested ship's biscuits would soon become a tooth breaking thing of the past.

American firms were also buying up significant quantities of Jones's flour, revealing part of its secret composition in a newspaper article that appeared in 1853:

> …during its manufacture, super-carbonate of soda and tartaric acid [are added] in suitable proportions.[7]

The British press during the mid-nineteenth century reveals a great deal of support alongside positive endorsements from the medical profession generally. Jones even found himself praised in the prestigious medical journal *The Lancet*:

> IMPORTANT INVENTION
> Approved of by the Lords of the Admiralty and eminent Medical Naval Authorities – By Royal Letters Patent.
> PREPARED FLOUR for making bread at Sea &c, by addition of water only. Manufactured by the patentee HENRY JONES 36 and 37 Broadmead, Bristol. By the use of this flour, captains, passengers to India &c, may have fresh bread daily through longest voyage; it is made in two or three minutes, and will be far superior to that by the ordinary mode. Sold in cases, (containing 14lb) 4s 6d; (20lb) 6s 6d; sample cases, 1s 6d each, forwarded to part, on receipt of a post office order. (Copy of a Letter from the Board of Admiralty London):
>
> Admiralty, July 5 1845. Sir – With reference to your letter of the 27th July, relative to Patent Prepared Flour, from the use of which nautical men may have fresh bread, daily during long voyages. I have to acquaint you that their Lordships have tried the flour

made into bread, which they find to be perfectly good, and wish to know whether your patent can be applied to flour manufactured in the victualling establishments. I am sir obedient servant William Letburn. For Comptroller of Victualling, Mr H. Jones, Broadmead, Bristol.[8]

Henry Jones's strap-line for his self-raising flour was 'Towers Above Them All'.[9] An appropriate phrase that in many ways should be attributed to this pioneering man himself, in terms of his clever flour, tenacity and political lobbying skills.

Jones was able to return to his beloved Wales a very wealthy and fulfilled man, living until the age of seventy-eight. Perhaps you will now all spare him a quick thought, each time a recipe you are preparing requires self-raising flour.

William Verrall

William Verrall was the landlord of the White Hart Inn, Lewes, in Sussex (now a swanky hotel and leisure club), between the years 1737 and 1760, He was also the writer of the classic *A Complete System of Cookery* (1759), a terrific contribution to the social history narrative of the Georgian period. He served an apprenticeship under the great Pierre Clouet, chef to the Duke of Newcastle.

There is a reference in the *Sussex Agricultural Express* of 25 January 1890 to a William Verrall owning a large estate – Southover Manor House in Lewes – and dying there in 1890. If William Verrall the cook had a grandson of the same name (and we know from the records, that he had a son, William Verrall the younger), which was quite typical of that period, then it suggests the family must have made a substantial amount of money somewhere along the line.[10] The Verralls of Lewes were, by the nineteenth century, an established family of brewers. The property, albeit now divided into apartments, still remains and the pictures that I have seen show a beautiful and quite enormous Georgian pile near the centre of the town. Despite this rather romanticized assumption, the press of 1761 records a notice of bankruptcy against Verrall – and this time, we know it's our man, as it describes him as an 'Inn holder'.[11] This was a year after he left the Inn and prior to this he experienced an unfortunate financial loss, when a large barn he owned, full of wheat, burnt down to the ground having been struck by lightning, together with two waggons, one of them brand new, also loaded up with wheat.[12] The local Lewes press of the period also makes reference to Verrall's antics as a racehorse owner and subsequent gambler. My hunch relating to Verrall's wealth however does begin to ring true around 1848, when the local Sussex Council purchased a plot of land from William Verrall (undoubtedly the grandson by this time), for the princely sum of £1,000, probably in the region of around £100,000 today.

William Verrall the younger died in 1837 aged seventy-eight, meaning he was born the same year that his father published *A Complete System of Cookery*. If all these Verralls are indeed William's direct descendants, his son would only have known him for two years as our inn-keeper, as William died in 1761. The White Hart Inn – also the political nerve centre of Lewes – had been floundering under his ownership and he was being forced out of his home and business by his creditors. The Duke of Newcastle, to whom William was formerly a kitchen servant, had managed to secure him a new job as keeper of the house of correction, but it came too late. As soon as the bankruptcy order was made, Verrall was no longer eligible for the job. He must have died a broken and disappointed man. His brother George took over his debts as his widow was unable to do so. There is very little else we can glean about William Verrall, other than what he wrote in his one and only book where he quite humbly describes himself as 'no more than what is vulgarly called a poor publican'.[13] He was clearly bad with money and in a letter from Monsieur Michell to the Duke of Newcastle we learn that he was 'a very odd man'. Make of that what you will, but it appears Verrall's life was cut quite short and had he lived longer and continued in his chosen career path, perhaps he may have become more renowned in his field.[14]

Below is a recipe from *A Complete System of Cookery* for loaf of beef collops. I chose this simply because it reminded me of old, early medieval trenchers and I like the way recipe books of the seventeenth and eighteenth centuries often move between the old methods of cooking and the new more sophisticated continental styles. It also made me think about the recent revival in popularity of serving food in large crusty cobs. Some things really never do change that much.

Un pain des escalopes de bœuf
Loaf of beef collops

Order a loaf of French bread the size of your dish roll'd flattish, take out the inside, and fry the crust in butter; take as much of the fillet of a sirloin or the tender part of a rump of beef as will do for your loaf, hash it raw very thin, oil a bit of butter, and fry it quick, season with only a morsel of onion and parsley minced; for the sauce take a large ladle or two of cullis, season with pepper, salt and nutmeg, a mushroom or two and shallots minced very fine; stew this a few minutes, and put in the hash; but don't let it boil a minute after, sprinkle in a little minced, squeeze the juice of a lemon or orange, pour it in and over your loaf, and serve it up.[15]

Pierre Clouet

Verrall's one-time mentor – and the man whose recipes he demonstrates throughout his book *A Complete System of Cookery* – was Pierre Clouet, master of the kitchens to the Duke of Newcastle from 1742, and then to Maréchal de Richelieu. He was rather put on a pedestal by Verrall, who noted that he was:

> of a temper so affable and agreeable as to make everybody happy around him. He would converse about indifferent matters with me or his kitchen boy, and the next moment, by a sweet turn in his discourse, give pleasure by his good behaviour and genteel deportment, to the first steward in the family. His conversation is always modest enough, and having read a little, he never wanted something to say, let the topick be what it would.[16]

Clouet specialized in the nouvelle cuisine of the age, but is perhaps more famous for his ongoing rift with the Duke of Newcastle, who was in agony at losing his best and trusted cook. The Duke wrote to Clouet after he'd left his service, criticizing and bemoaning Clouet's second replacement, Hervé, after raising similar arguments with his original replacement Jean Jorre. The translated version went something like this:

> It may be that the new cuisine does not please us here, but I cannot believe that he has mastered the art. His soups are usually too strong and his entrées and entremets are so disguised and so mixed-up that nobody can tell what they are made of. He never serves small hors d'oeuvres or light entrées, and he has no idea of the simple, unified dishes that you used to make for me and which are so much in fashion here, such as veal tendons, rabbit fillets, pigs' and calves' ears, and several other little dishes of the same kind…In other words, he has no resemblance to your ways and your cuisine, and to what I require.

Clouet responded with solidarity for his fellow colleagues – and with a forceful eloquence. It was this disparaging retort which no doubt brought the overdramatized termination of their professional relationship to an end:

> As regards his mixed-up entrées and entremets, French cuisine has never been anything but mixtures. This is what gives it that great variety which places it above all the other cuisines of Europe. Masters who do not like these mixtures should be so good as to inform the cook of this, and to let him know how they wish to be served, so that the cook can show his skill by conforming to their desires. It is also most unfortunate for a cook that his master should be incapable of judging his performance for himself, so that he is often judged by critics who are totally ignorant.[17]

There is a wonderful satirical print in the archives of the British Museum titled *The Duke of Newcastle and his Cook*. It illustrates both the Duke and Clouet speaking their thoughts aloud in the grand surrounds of Newcastle's kitchen: 'O! Cloe if you leave me. I shall be starv'd…' and 'Begar me can no relish dis dam English …'

Despite undoubtedly feeling chastised by Clouet's response to his letter, the Duke continued to argue with Hervé, replacing him as soon as he could.

Clouet had originally planned to move directly from the Duke's employment into the service of the Earl of Albemarle (William Keppel) who, to add insult to injury, also happened to be a very good friend of the Duke. No sooner had he signed his contract, than the earl died, leaving Clouet responsible for tens of thousands of his debts. It is after this that he went to work as maître d'hôtel for Maréchal de Richlieu in Paris, a famous military man who successfully captured Minorca from the British in 1756. In hard times, following the scarcities brought about by conflict, Richelieu had the ability to develop the most imaginative menus making use of a whole beast – usually an ox – its tail, tongue, kidneys, brains, every part of it to make numerous dishes, from consommés to aspics. In many ways, he understood the role of maître d'hôtel better than the ones he employed, which may or may not have been a challenge for Clouet.[18]

Elizabeth David acknowledged Clouet as 'an intelligent, enlightened and most meticulous cook'.[19]

Charles Carter

Charles Carter was cook to the Duke of Argyll, the Earl of Pontefract and Lord Cornwallis, amongst other nobility. He is also a featured paragon of Heston Blumenthal. Charles Carter penned several books:

> *The Compleat Practical Cook, or, a New System of the Whole Art and Mystery of Cookery* (1730)
> *The Compleat City and Country Cook, or, Accomplish'd Housewife* (1732)
> *The Compleat City and Country Cook, or, Accomplish'd Housewife* (1736) (updated version)
> *The London and Country Cook, or, Accomplish'd Housewife* (1749)

Despite good sales and a level of fame, a review of *The Compleat Practical Cook* was printed in *The London Magazine* in 1779, which described Carter as pompous and 'elevated with his own importance'.[20]

Much of Carter's dialogue does have a slightly self-righteous tone to it. In *The Compleat City and Country Cook*, he explains to his readers that he heralds from a long line of generations of accomplished cooks and lists his employers as mentioned above, including General Wood who he served in Flanders, Lord Whitworth in Berlin, General Wade in Spain and Portugal and others, boasting a wealth of well-travelled European experience. He is rather disparaging about the British obsession with recruiting foreign cooks and notes that English palettes are just as refined as French ones. He also claims that he is one of only a handful of cookery writers of his generation who included their own recipes and practices in their books. Much is written about the plagiarism of food writers during the eighteenth and nineteenth centuries. Yet many recipes were passed down from cooks to their apprentices, and from fathers and mothers to sons or daughters. Through borrowing and copying all the time, as Carter admits himself, much of what he learnt initially came from his father and father's fathers.[21]

As with many books of the period, women were often invited to contribute, and some manuals and guides were compiled by women, but then men put their names to them; happily nearly all of these women were acknowledged and credited accordingly. Carter's third edition of the *The London and Country Cook* (1749) is no exception. The title page informs us that the book is 'Revised and much improved by a gentlewoman; Many years Housekeeper to an eminent Merchant in the City of London'. As the reader continues with the preface it is clear that whoever put this edition together was not Carter himself. Rather, it is more likely to have been the said gentlewomen, in the style of Carter, who we are told has died. The editor is also critical of recipe book writers of the age, who she considers to be more concerned with the quantity of recipes included in a book, opposed to their value and quality, somewhat echoing Carter's own sentiments.

I am rather taken by Carter's recipe for carrot pudding, in his *The Compleat City and Country Cook*, which to me is very reminiscent of today's flourless carrot cakes, using melted butter and cream instead of oil.

Carrot Pudding

You must grate two Carrots very fine, put in a Pint of Cream, eight Eggs some Sugar, a little Sack, Salt and Nutmeg and four Ounces of melted Butter: Mix this well and cut a little candy'd Orange and Lemon-peel and put in, so bake it or boil it.[22]

Patrick Lamb

Patrick Lamb, born in 1650, was cook for an illustrious band of nobility including Charles II, James II, William and Mary, and Queen Anne. His recipes were published about a year after his death in 1710, under the title of *Royal Cookery; Or, the Complete Court-Cook* and can be found in the archives of the Royal Collection Trust. Like Carter, Lamb's father and grandfather had both served in the kitchens of the nobility. So, it is unsurprising to learn that he started his career in the royal kitchens at a very young age indeed, in 1662.

Francis Sandford's first-hand account of Charles II coronation in 1685 makes reference to Lamb and details all of the dishes that were served that day:

> Then 32 Dishes of Hot Meat, brought up by Gentlemen Pensioners, Bareheaded; which service should have been performed by the Knights of the Bath, had any been created at this CORONATION: After which, there were brought up a Supply of 14 Dishes more of Hot Meat by Private Gentlemen. Then followed the Mess of Potage, or Gruel, called Dillegrout, prepared by Patrick Lamb Esq, the KINGS Master-Cook, and brought up to the table by John Leigh Esq; in pursuance of his Claim as Lord of the Mannor of Adington in Surrey.[23]

Of course this was only a very small sample of the Coronation feast, totalling thousands of dishes. Sandford's illustrations show rows and rows of huge dining tables, with dishes of food filling every available space, women seated one side, men the other, while observers in the upper gallery look on. Perhaps the dining was done in rotation, or maybe only the most noble of guests got to share in the dinner itself.

Old Slaughter's was a well-known coffee house on St Martin's Lane that was patronized for almost two hundred years by a number of eminent visitors, including its regular resident famous author, Henry Fielding. The memoirs of one William Henry Pyne recall a number of incidents, events and conversations that took place there. The cook at Slaughter's was nicknamed the Grecian. He appears to have been a very

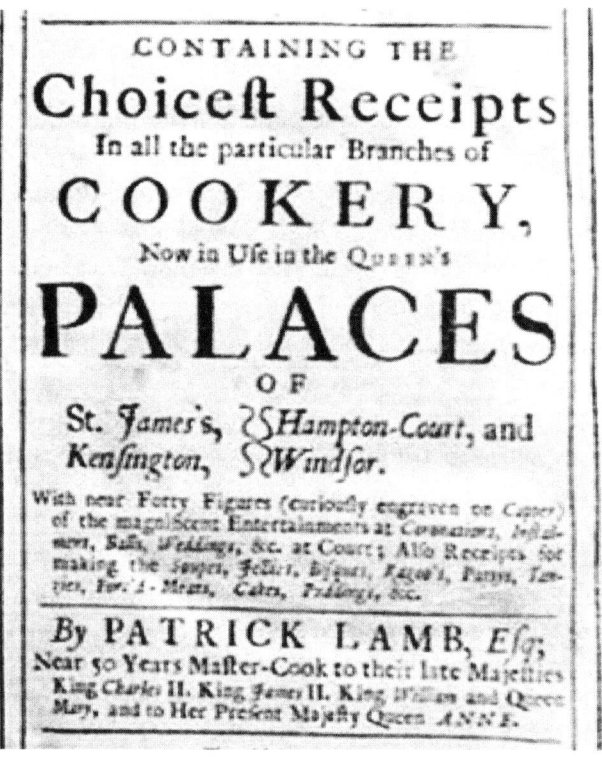

Figure 40. Title page of Patrick Lamb's *Royal Cookery*.

jovial, entertaining and eccentric character, who used to brag about working in Queen Anne's kitchens, although possibly in a menial role. He got very defensive about the coffee house and his own abilities as a cook, disliking the public praise of other similar businesses or steak houses. One place in particular which was popular at the time, Dolly's, received a lot of positive attention from punters who frequented Old Slaughter's. One of Old Slaughter's customers (Mr Lambert) joked one evening that the Grecian might want to visit Dolly's to receive lessons on broiling. This was the tipping point for the old cook, who launched into a tirade:

> Why, Mr Lambert…do you take me for a turn-broach – a scullion – a water-wagtail – a goose-grease-grubber – a pot-wolloper – an

ass – a fool!

He then basically says that hell would freeze over before he found himself in a position of having to learn from the likes of the staff at Dolly's, exclaiming:

> I, that sucked the culinary art with my mother's milk – Ask master, there…ask mistress there…wasn't I a child of the queen's privy kitchen – godson of Centlivre, yeoman of the mouth to the queen, and favourite disciple of Patrick Lamb, her majesty's first master cook?[24]

In addition to reiterating the reputation of Lamb, I also discovered from this memoir the existence of another named cook from Queen Anne's team, Centlivre, who was actually Joseph Centlivre, married to the very famous writer and actress of the age, Susanna Centlivre (née Freeman). He was 'Yeoman of the Mouth' to both Queen Anne and George I, and lived at court. He may also have been the son of Edward Centlivre, who was 'child of the [Royal] kitchen', between 1708-14.[25]

Below – for no other reason than it sounds so pretty – is Patrick Lamb's recipe for cowslip tart reproduced by Charles Dickens:

> Take the blossoms of a gallon of cowslips, mince them exceedingly small, and beat them in a mortar; put to them a handful or two of grated Naples biscuit and about a pint and a half of cream; boil them a little over the fire, then take them off and beat them in eight eggs with a little cream; if it does not thicken, put it over again till it doth; take heed that it doth not curdle. Season with sugar, rose water, and a little salt; bake it in a dish or little open tartlet. It is best to let your cream be cold before you stir in the eggs.[26]

It is also yet another example of one of those infuriating recipes that makes a crucial recommendation, required halfway through, but isn't included until the end of the instructions.

Alexandre Dumas

Dumas was famous in his own right, not least of all for writing *The Three Musketeers, The Count of Monte Cristo, The Man in the Iron Mask* and numerous other romantic classic works. I have included him in this chapter because he is to a much lesser extent known as both a travel writer and an expert cook and writer on food. His *Grand Dictionnaire de cuisine* and abridged *Petit Dictionnaire de cuisine*, were both published after his death in the later 1800s. He often combined his travel writing with anecdotes about a particular country's cuisine. In *Adventures in Czarist Russia,* Dumas was for some reason quite scathing about their obsession for tea, noting that, 'no home is so poor that it has no Samovar' – a costly item used to boil water. He also bemoans the overrated nature and availability of Russia's most coveted fish of the time, the starlet (a type of sturgeon), sarcastically exclaiming:

> Russia prides herself on her national *cuisine,* particularly on those dishes that no other country can offer, depending as they do upon ingredients found within her mighty empire and nowhere else in the world – starlet soup, for instance. Russians are passionately fond of it, but the only remarkable thing about it, to mind, is its cost – fifty or sixty francs in summer, three or four hundred in winter. Yet the simple bouillabaisse one gets in Marseilles is much more to my liking. What makes starlet soup so expensive? The transport charges![27]

In his *Impressions of Travel, in Egypt and Arabia Petraea,* Dumas described the 'bazaar of eatables' in Cairo:

> Its principal commodity was rice, which is…in fact, the most common food of the people. There was, also, a prepared paste of apricots, made in large, thin sheets, and rolled up like a carpet; measuring sometimes twenty-five or thirty feet in length and three or four in breadth. Another article was a compounded mass, in solid cubes of a hundred pounds of weight, made of dates ripe, dates too ripe, and dates too green. This is furnished at a low price, and forms the regular dessert, as rice does the regular dinner, of the lower classes.[28]

The Overlooked and Uncredited

Figure 41. Alexandre Dumas.

He was no doubt referring to the traditional 'date candy', which I have seen consumed in many a Middle Eastern country, extending as far as Cyprus. However, the apricot paste may have been used in the making of 'amardeen', sheets of concentrated apricots, another staple Middle Eastern sweet treat.

Dumas' travel memoirs represent a goldmine of early insightful records relating to the nineteenth century diets of far reaching countries such as Africa, and to numerous European accounts of culinary cultural dishes consumed across broad societies.

Dumas was of mixed French and African parentage. He was an old-fashioned cook, which is reflected both in his traditional recipes and in his cooking techniques, using basic methods like an open fire, despite the widespread use of gas. By this time, Dumas utilized a spit and dripping pan, a Dutch oven, heated directly by the hot ashes and a hastener to reflect the heat, all essentially equipment of the previous century. He introduces his *Grand Dictionnaire de cuisine* by outlining the three elements of appetite:

> Appetite that comes from hunger. It makes no fuss over the food that satisfies it. If it is great enough, a piece of raw meat will appease it as easily as a roasted pheasant or woodcock.
>
> Appetite aroused, hunger or no hunger, by a succulent dish appearing at the right moment, illustrating the proverb that hunger comes with eating.
>
> The third type of appetite is that roused by the main courses, and the guest is truly ready to rise without regret, a delicious dish holds him to the table with a final tempting of his sensuality.[29]

Delmonico's of New York named a number of their signatory dishes after him, as they did with many other acclaimed celebrities of the nineteenth century, including *Oysters à la Alexandre Dumas* and *Lamb en Brochette à la Dumas*.

Mary Eales

Alleged confectioner to Queen Anne and King William, her *Book of Receipts* was first published in 1718, then again in 1733 under the new title of *The Compleat Confectioner*, and more recently reprinted in 1985 by Prospect Books. Although many cooks were writing about ices by this time, Eales's 1733 edition is sometimes quoted as the first culinary book in England to include a recipe for iced cream, as opposed to a flavoured ice dessert:

> To make Ice Cream.
>
> Take Tin Ice-Pots, fill them with any Sort of Cream you like, either plain or sweeten'd, or Fruit in it; shut your Pots very close; to six Pots you must allow eighteen or twenty Pound of Ice, breaking the Ice very small; there will be some great Pieces, which lay at the

Bottom and Top: You must have a Pail, and lay some Straw at the Bottom; then lay in your Ice, and put in amongst it a Pound of Bay-Salt; set in your Pots of Cream, and lay Ice and Salt between every Pot, that they may not touch; but the Ice must lie round them on every Side; lay a good deal of Ice on the Top, cover the Pail with Straw, set it in a Cellar where no Sun or Light comes, it will be froze in four Hours, but it may stand longer; than take it out just as you use it; hold it in your Hand and it will slip out. When you wou'd freeze any Sort of Fruit, either Cherries, Rasberries, Currants, or Strawberries, fill your Tin-Pots with the Fruit, but as hollow as you can; put to them Lemmonade, made with Spring-Water and Lemmon-Juice sweeten'd; put enough in the Pots to make the Fruit hang together, and put them in Ice as you do Cream.[30]

Eales omits to regularly stir the ice cream, which would have resulted in a very coarse, unpleasant final dish, full of ice crystals.

No records identify Mary as the Queen's confectioner, although the first confectioner to Queen Anne on her accession to the throne in 1702 was indeed a woman, one Elizabeth Stephens. This had altered by 1712, as a man took over the role. We know this because he was accused of starting a fire in the palace that year whilst toasting almonds for a dessert to please Prince George.[31] Very little is known about Eales, although her namesake was buried in Covent Garden in 1718, bequeathing all of her worldly possessions to her daughter, interestingly called Elizabeth. This would mean that further editions of her book were posthumous and compiled by someone else.[32]

Given that so many recipe books were written anonymously, or pseudonymously, in the seventeenth and eighteenth centuries and that children were often named after their parents or other close family relatives, it wouldn't be unusual for Mary Eales to have either been someone else entirely, or actually, Elizabeth Stephens. Mary also claims that she worked under King William III and Mary. Sir Richard Blackmore's book recalling the activities of the failed assassination attempt on William in 1696, notes that one of the King's Confectioners was called Mr. Brown,[33] and a Mr Mortimer is confirmed as being the King's [master] Confectioner, as revealed in a letter from Mr Vernon to the Duke of Shrewsbury dated that same year.[34]

There would undoubtedly have been more than one confectioner in the king's service, but it is hard to find any mention of a Mary Eales anywhere, who we can establish was most definitely not the king's chief employer in this area. By the time George I came to the throne in 1714, the confectionery office was staffed by two yeoman and a groom. It is unlikely that arrangements in this area would have changed that radically. However, the pastry office during the reign of King William responsible for making pies, tarts and sauces, had a slightly larger team of two yeoman, two grooms, a member of staff to carry out all the heavy work, and a 'salsaryman' specifically tasked with preparing and making the sauces. Whether Mary was a part of this team is something to consider, although she does specifically express that she is a confectioner and the pastry staff were by suggestion, almost certainly all male.[35] An alternative is that Mary was a local trader, a sort of freelance independent confectioner, who carried out some work for the royal court. Either way, it is incredibly interesting to think that before the onset of mass media and modern communication individuals could remain mysterious, anonymous even, or to the other extent be given license to indulge in fraudulent practices. Whatever her motives and whoever she was, Mary Eales' work became a bestseller.

We know that initially Eales circulated manuscript copies of her compiled recipes, only to specific audiences, at a cost of five guineas, prior to the recipes being printed for wider distribution.[36] Five guineas was quite a sum then, so she may have been targeting the wealthy nobility. One theory is that once she had died, an opportunity was grasped by someone else who realized the potential for broadening her market, although there is no rock-solid proof to verify her death in 1718, other than someone with the same name being recorded as such in Covent Garden that year.

Pierre de Lune

Aside from Pierre de Lune being the name of both a rather well-known racehorse in the 1950s and a Royal yacht in the 1920s, he is within the context of this book a rather splendid cook of the seventeenth century, with little in the way of a remembered life, other than the legacy of his *Le Cuisinier* (1656), a book whose title would be borrowed by many other French cooks over the centuries. Whilst the first half is dedicated to seasonal cooking, the second includes the typical compilation of pastry-making, preserving and baking. His second book, *Le Nouveau et Parfait cuisinier* was published a few years later. He boasts the modern invention of bouquet garni, a small muslin bag stuffed with bay leaves, parsley, thyme etc. to flavour stews and stocks. *Le Cuisinier* is one of the earliest examples of how fresh, complimentary flavours were used to produce uncomplicated dishes that reflected the new era of Renaissance cooking. De Lune's recipe for crayfish soup epitomizes that new trend:

Crayfish soup

Wash the crayfish well, cook them in water with a bundle of herbs, a bit of salt and butter. Then draw out the tails and the legs, and pound the shells which you strain with the crayfish bouillon and place in a pot. Then you put the tail and leg meat in a pan with a bit of butter and fine herbs well chopped, and you place them in a pot or plate with the bouillon, the reddest you can strain. After, simmer bread crusts with the bouillon, three or four finely chopped mushrooms, arrange your crayfish and garnish the soup with roe and mushrooms, lemon juice and mushroom juice.[37]

A Parisian trained and well-travelled cook, de Lune's main employer was the military nobleman Henri, Duke of Rohan, who he served for many years, until his master's death in 1638. He then turned to cookery writing, with the specific desire to educate his readers for the purposes of seeking employment, either as cooks or in domestic service.[38]

John Nott

John Nott was cook to the Dukes of Bolton and Somerset, amongst others, and the author of *The Cooks and Confectioners Dictionary* (1723). It is in an A-Z format, like a dictionary, quite a unique novelty for an eighteenth-century cookery book. The only thing similar in its time is Massialot's dictionary of terms and dishes, which appears at the front of his *Le Cuisinier royale et bourgeois* in 1691.

He is perhaps not quite as forgotten as some of the other cooks in this section, as he is remembered by both Marcus Wareing and Heston

Blumenthal, at one time or other on their menus.

Nott's introduction to his dictionary is more than a little obsequious in its tone. He also plays it well to please both loyal advocates of British food, and those demanding the fashionable European imports of the period:

> I have taken upon me to collect a great Variety of Receipts, or Directions, for ordering these things with which Nature has furnishd us, according to the Practice of the most celebrated Artists; and also the nicest and most curious Dames and Housewives our Country has produced; as also, for the Entertainment of the more Curious, have inserted many Receipts, according to the Practice of the best Masters in the Arts of Cookery and Confectionary of France, Italy, Spain, Germany, and other Countries.

Nott is also quite witty, noting as he does that he has been coerced into writing an introduction to his book, simply on the basis that everyone else of his era has done the same thing. He compares not writing an introduction to 'a man to appear at church without a neckcloth, or a lady without a hoop-petticoat. Heaven forbid!'[39]

The increase in French migration to England led to French cuisine, their methods and ingredients, being embraced and revered by the nobility and middle classes, who aspired to employ the finest French cooks in their kitchens. It was also criticised quite widely and there was a definite force wishing to retain British food and British styles of cooking. Although French and continental recipes dominated elite bills of fare, it was important to maintain elements of traditional national dishes which would complement or be integrated into the order of service. The British media was flooded with critiques relating to French cuisine, with the French both satirized and admired in equal measure. Not all recipe writers of the time aspired to French and continental cooking either. Hannah Glasse's iconic *The Art of Cookery Made Plain and Easy*, openly criticized the trend for French influences in England during the eighteenth century. Despite this, she also included a number of French recipes in her work, not wanting to alienate a whole potential market of readers who craved French recipes. The writer known simply as L.S.R. also spoke very disparagingly of the trend for rich, heavy

French dishes as early as 1674 with *L'Art de bien traiter* ('The art of entertaining well'). He (or she) went so far as describing it in terms of its 'antique and disgusting manner of preparing things' and ridiculing the renowned François Pierre de La Varenne, challenging his/her readers with 'Are you not already quaking at the thought of a soup of teals in mulled wine, of tenderloin in sweet sauce? Can you gaze without horror on this beef shank soup…does it not make you laugh, or rather weep out of compassion?'[40]

Frederick Nutt

As noted in the previous chapter, Nutt was instrumental to the story of the success and popularity of early Georgian confectioners.

There are several early references to a John Frederick Nutt who was the proprietor of the Turk coffee house, Hyde Park Corner, London, and was filed with bankruptcy in 1797. Whether this is the same Nutt employed by the Pot and Pineapple and writer of several inspirational confectionery recipe books – most notably *The Complete Confectioner* (1790) – is debatable, but the dates would match up. He was trained by Domenico Negri and Peter Wetten, about neither of whom much is known, except that they were business partners under the sign of the notorious Pot and Pineapple of Berkeley Square, prior to Negri and James Gunter joining forces. Many newspapers at the time heralded Wetten and Negri as the 'most celebrated confectioners in the world'.[41]

In 1809 Frederick Nutt followed on from the success of *The Complete Confectioner*, already printed in five editions, with his book *The Imperial and Royal Cook*. We can assume that when he wrote *The Complete Confectioner* and its subsequent re-editions, that Nutt was not new to his job: the title page states that the book was the result of 'many years of experience', and the preface adds:

> As the Author had the honour to occupy a distinguished situation in this particular department, he has availed himself of several years' experience and application in compiling this performance, which he again submits to the indulgence and candour of his readers.[42]

Later editions of *The Complete Confectioner* are endorsed by the renowned Parisian pastry chef and distiller Jean-Jacques Machet.

Machet wrote a book in 1803, titled *Le Confiseur moderne, ou, L'Art du confiseur et du distillateur,* which informs us that:

> *Depuis plus de vingt ans que j'exerce l'état de confiseur et de distillateur chez l'étranger et dans les villes de France les plus adonnées à ces professions.*

Roughly translated, this is:

> For more than twenty years that I have been a confectioner and a distiller in foreign countries and in the towns of France most devoted to these professions.[43]

How Nutt and Machet came to know one another remains a mystery. Perhaps, being such a well-travelled man, Machet became acquainted with Nutt in London. It was quite typical for cooks and confectioners to travel widely in the eighteenth and nineteenth centuries, gaining greater understanding and experience of their art. Many cooks also migrated across Europe and sometimes America, establishing themselves either independently or in the households of foreign nobility. This earned them a reputation and the opportunity to enhance their careers. Machet himself noted that many of the Italian chocolatiers who based themselves in France had excellent reputations.[44]

Below is Nutt's recipe for Sweetmeat Biscuits, which reminded me a bit of Florentines:

Sweetmeat Biscuits

> Take some Naples biscuits that have been baked, and cut them in small pieces, about an inch and a half square, and about one inch thick, and lay them on your wire, and put them in the oven just to crisp them, then make some iceing with whites of eggs, and sugar, and orange flower water, and dip one side of the biscuit in it; then cut some sweetmeats in small pieces, such as lemon and orange peel and angelico, and just throw over the top of them put them, put them on your wire: you need no paper under them, then put them in the oven to harden the iceing, and they are done.[45]

Sir Kenelm Digby

A central Jacobean figure once integral to British political affairs, a courtier, and the son of an executed gunpowder plot conspirator, Sir Kenelm Digby, Oxford graduate turned privateer and explorer, wrote a series of memoirs, philosophical treatises and romantic tales. After he returned from sea, he became caught up in a strange accusatory investigation into the death of his beloved wife. Although he employed several cooks, he spent a lot of time testing recipes and combining new flavours in his well-stocked London kitchen. This kitchen contained an array of pie plates, syllabub dishes, kettles, graters, colanders and much more. He would work between there and his laboratory, mixing, trialling, experimenting and fusing culinary arts with chemistry. He is said to have invented the modern wine bottle from both an interest in the production of glass and distilling.[46] Digby experimented with

Figure 42. Sir Kenelm Digby.

corking and leaving alcohol to mature, a process that would have been impossible using the traditional style of bottle then in use. This led to him becoming one of the pioneers of sparkling cider. He used Redstreak apples and went to great lengths to explain how to store the corked bottles, keeping them cool to prevent explosion. He suggests wrapping the bottles in hay during cold weather to minimize freezing and in sand in hot weather to stop accelerated fermentation.[47]

His recipe for mead (or metheglin), published in *The Closet of Sir Kenelm Digby Knight Opened* (1669), is extremely detailed and instructional for the time. Just when you think the recipe has finally come to an end, it starts up again and imparts a little more advice, ensuring that you follow every rule in order to achieve a successful outcome:

> Take one measure of honey, and three measures of water, and let it boil till one measure be boiled away, so that there be left three measures in all; as for example, take to one pot of honey, three pots of water, and let it boil so long, till it come to three pots. During which time you must skim it very well as soon as any scum riseth; which you are to continue till there rise no scum more. You may, if you please, put to it some spice, to wit, Cloves and Ginger; the quantity of which is to be proportioned according as you will have your Meath, strong or weak. But this you do before it begin to boil. There are some that put either Yeast or Beer, or Leaven of bread into it, to make it work. But this is not necessary at all; and much less to set into the sun…Afterwards for to Tun it, you must let it grow luke-warm, for to advance it. And if you do intend to keep your meathe a long time, you may put into it some hopps on this fashion. Take to every barrel of meathe a pound of hops withouth leaves, that is, of ordinary hops used for beer, but well cleansed, taking only the flowers, without the green-leaves and stalks. Boil this pound of hops in a pot and half of fair water, till it come to one pot, and this quantity is sufficient for a barrel of Meathe… When you tun your meathe, you must not fill your barrel by half a foot, that so it may have room to work. Then let it stand six weeks slightly stopped; which being expired, if the meathe do not work, stop it up very close. Yet must you not fill up the Barrel to the very brim. After six months you draw off the clear into another barrel, or strong bottles, leaving the dregs, and filling up your new barrel,

or bottles, and stopping it or them very close.

The meath that is made this way (viz. In the spring, in the month of April or May, which is the proper time for making of it), will keep many a year'.[48]

Charles Herman Senn

Swiss cook and writer Charles Herman Senn was born in 1862 and died working at his desk at 110 Victoria Street, London, in 1934. He is perhaps one of the most bafflingly forgotten heroes of the culinary world, who wrote over thirty books and was one of the founders of the Universal Cookery and Food Association, linked with the famous *L'Art culinaire* in France.

Senn worked in collaboration with Brown and Polson to create a range of special sauces, with their patented corn flour formula, including caper, anchovy, shrimp, mustard and Hollandaise sauce, amongst others. Senn's *The Book of Sauces*, published in 1915, was heralded at the time as the largest and most complete volume of sauce recipes in the world.

This is a delightful book, of which I have a copy myself, and traces the origins of sauce, whilst deconstructing the ways in which their components come together in the cooking process. Senn advises on the reasons why sauces can fail, their characteristics and the processes involved with heating and cooking, seasoning and flavouring each one appropriately. I don't believe there is any other book like it in terms of the thorough way in which Senn documents the evolution and variety of sauces, exclaiming:

> Until the beginning of the nineteenth century, the art of sauce making was hardly known in England. The charge made at that time against the English nation by a celebrated epigrammist, who said that we had many religions but only one sauce, would hardly hold good now, for it is reckoned that there are at least 650 different sauces and gravies known at this moment. An ingenious cook will have as little trouble to form that number of sauces in different varieties, as a musician with his seven notes, or a painter with his pallet and colours; nor is it too much to assert that there is no other

branch in cookery which offers better opportunities to display the ability of a cook than this.⁴⁹

Here is Senn's recipe for a basic Veloutée, or Velvet Sauce, which has had a popular resurgence in recent years:

1oz flour, 2oz butter, 1 pint of veal stock, ¼ gill mushroom liquor, ½ gill of cream, 1 small bouquet garni, 6 peppercorns, salt, nutmeg, lemon juice.

Cook the flour with an ounce of butter together without browning, stir in the stock and mushroom liquor, add the bouquet and crushed peppercorns, boil slowly for twenty minutes, stir frequently and skim. Pass through a sieve or tammy keep on the side of the stove, put a few tiny pieces of butter on top to keep from forming a skin. Just before using it add the cream. Stir well and let it get thoroughly hot without boiling, season with salt if necessary, a pinch of nutmeg, and about a teaspoonful of lemon juice. The sauce is now ready for use, and will serve as a foundation for any white sauce or as a veloutee by itself. The cream may be omitted if used as a foundation sauce.⁵⁰

In 1894, the *Dundee Evening Telegraph* christened Senn, 'The British Soyer' (despite the fact that he was Swiss). It recalled how he started his career working as an apprentice cook in Basel, Switzerland, before finding employment at a well-respected confectioners in Neuchâtel, then returning to Basel to work in a leading restaurant as head chef. Following a two-year stint, he moved to England and found a position at the Westcliffe Hotel, Folkestone, moving into the role of second chef at the prestigious Reform Club, London. He then secured head chef positions at the Members' Mansion and then Tivoli restaurant in the Strand, where he remained some seven years, before acquiring premises for the new Universal Cookery and Food Association (UCFA) at 329 Vauxhall Bridge Road. He was appointed Secretary of the London Annual Cookery and Food Exhibitions and was recruited by the government to look into the state of cookery in the navy.⁵¹ The UCFA grew in popularity at a steep rate, from a membership of 186 in 1892 to 917 in 1897, and over 1200 by 1902. The Association's main objectives were to build awareness, and new networks and partnerships, as well

The Overlooked and Uncredited

as conducting charitable and educational work. Their annual cookery exhibitions took place from 1885 into the 1930s, with the intention of showcasing:

> various branches of the culinary art…and the manufacturers of food specialities and various accessories exhibit their productions and introduce novelties. At these exhibitions, may be seen school children busy at work preparing simple menus, and teachers demonstrating household and artisan cookery, to show how dinners for the working classes may be prepared at a small cost. Hospital and invalid dietary also finds a place in the display of tempting and palatable dishes for the sick and suffering. Naval and marine cooks may be seen demonstrating the preparation of wholesome food for our sailors, in contrast to the 'salt junk' and ship's biscuits so frequently provided for them, while the Army cooking in barrack or camp kitchen for the preparation of our soldiers' rations is always interesting to visitors to the Association's exhibitions.

The UCFA also offered free lectures for the poor and middle class families living in overcrowded districts, alongside courses in 'sick-room cookery' and 'nautical cookery'. They provided welfare opportunities for professional cooks, including a lucrative insurance scheme for members, an employment bureau and a benevolent fund. As a direct consequence of his position with the UCFA, Senn became a consultative committee member for the London County Council Cookery Technical School for Boys, considered the forerunner of the Westminster Hotel School (now the School of Hospitality at Westminster Kingsway College), pioneered by Escoffier, amongst others. The list of illustrious patrons for UCFA ranged from Queen Alexandra to the Lord Mayor of London.[52]

Senn acquired British citizenship in 1906.[53]

William Kitchiner

I think it's safe to say that William Kitchiner was a bit of a polymath. He was an optician, musician, scientist, inventor and, of course, a cook. On the death of his father, William inherited a vast sum of money, which enabled him to focus on his interests, as opposed to having to sustain paid work in one area. He was recognised by the Royal Society for his scientific achievements with telescopes amongst other things. A trained doctor, with the title M.D., Kitchiner probably never practised medicine formally. Instead his musical talents led to him to publish *The Loyal, National and Sea Songs of England*, which was dedicated to King George IV,[54] and he wrote and composed the music for a musical drama in 1820, entitled *Ivanhoe or the Knight Templar*. He established a weekly 'committee of taste' at his home, which was by invitation only, to

Figure 43. William Kitchiner.

The Overlooked and Uncredited 199

sample his gastronomic creations, often simple dishes, but surrounded by a great deal of pomp and etiquette. His dinners were served promptly at five o'clock, his suppers at half-past nine. The minutes of his committee reflect Kitchiner's quirkiness and no-nonsense attitude:

> At the last general meeting, it was unanimously resolved, that:
>
> 1st An invitation to ETA BETA PI must be answered in writing as soon as possible after it is received – within twenty-four hours at latest, reckoning from that on which it is dated; – otherwise the secretary will have the profound regret to feel that the invitation has been definitely declined.
>
> 2nd. The secretary having represented that the perfection of several of the preparations is so exquisitely evanescent, that the delay of *one minute,* after their arrival at the meridian of concoction, will render them no longer worthy of men of taste;
>
> Therefore, to ensure the punctual attendance of those illustrious gastrophilists, who on grand occasions are invited to join this high tribunal of taste for their own pleasure and the benefit of their country, it is irrevocably resolved, 'That the janitor be ordered not to admit any visitor, of whatever eminence of appetite, after the hour at which the secretary shall have announced that the specimens are ready. By order of the Committee
> WILLIAM KITCHINER, Secretary.

So intolerant was he of poor time-keeping that he erected a large placard which hung over the chimney stating: 'Come at Seven, go at Eleven.'[55]

While Americans uphold George Speck as the inventor of the potato chip in the 1850s, several decades earlier Kitchiner had included a recipe in his book *The Cook's Oracle* (1817) which is very reminiscent of what we recognise today as a British salted crisp.

Potatoes Fried in Slices or Shavings No 104

> Peel large potatoes; slice them about a quarter of an inch thick, or cut them in shavings round and round, as you would peel a lemon; dry them well in a clean cloth, and fry them in lard or dripping. Take care that your fat and frying pan are quite clean; put it on a

quick fire, watch it and as soon as the lard boils, and is still, put in the slices of potato, and keep moving them till they are crisp. Take them up and lay them to drain on a sieve: send them up with a very little salt sprinkled over them.

He was only 51 when he died suddenly from a heart attack at his home in Camden, London, following a dinner spent out with friends, so little remains today about this extraordinary man. However, Terry Pratchett's *Discworld* anthology pays homage to Kitchiner, with its references to wow-wow sauce, a sauce created by Kitchiner, the recipe for which was published in *The Cook's Oracle*:

Wow-wow Sauce for Stewed or Boiled Beef

Chop some parsley-leaves very finely, quarter two or three pickled cucumbers, or walnuts, and divide them into small squares, and set them by ready; put into a sauce-pan a bit of butter as big as an egg; when it is melted, stir to it a table-spoonful of fine flour, and about half a pint of the broth in which the beef was boiled; add a tablespoonful of vinegar, the like quantity of mushroom catch-up, or port wine, or both, and a teaspoonful of made mustard; let it simmer together till it is as thick as you wish it, put in the parsley and pickles to get warm, and pour it over the beef, or rather send it up in a sauce-tureen.[56]

John Farley and Collingwood & Woollams The London Tavern

Farley, along with William Verrall, arguably wrote one of the very first restaurant cookbooks, *The London Art of Cookery* (1783), which was based on his time spent as principal cook at the London Tavern. A renowned tavern and eating house, demolished and rebuilt several times, it had a central dining room that could seat some 355 people. Made popular in the eighteenth and nineteenth centuries due to its reputation for business, public and political meetings, it was supposedly frequented by Charles Dickens and even cited in his novel *Nicholas Nickleby*:

The Overlooked and Uncredited

Figure 44. John Farley.

'I am going to the London Tavern this morning,' said Mr Nickleby.

'Public meeting?' inquired Noggs.

Mr Nickleby nodded. 'I expect a letter from the solicitor respecting that mortgage of Ruddle's. If it comes at all, it will be here by the two o'clock delivery. I shall leave the city about that time and walk to Charing Cross on the left-hand side of the way, if there are any letters, come and meet me, and bring them with you.'[57]

It has been noted that Farley lifted many of Hannah Glasse's recipes without crediting her, which, despite this being very commonplace, it puts a bit of a dampener on his character for me. This is also ironic, considering Farley's preface which, like so many other cookery books of its time, seeks to demote other recipe writers and previous publications:

The Generality of books of this kind are so grouped together, without Method, or order, as to render them exceedingly intricate and bewildering; and the receipts written with so much carefulness and Inaccuracy, as not only to render them exceedingly perplexing, but frequently totally unintelligible.[58]

Francis Collingwood and John Woollams also both worked at the London Tavern, before moving on to The Crown and Anchor. The fourth edition of their 1792 book, *The Universal Cook,* which was published in 1806, pays homage – unlike Farley's slightly ungrateful preface – to some of the great culinary names past and present. Interestingly, it notes that Farley also took inspiration from his peers:

> we flatter ourselves, that the alterations we have made in the different receipts, the new ones we have added, and the methodical manner in which we have arranged the whole, will in some degree entitle us to the patronage of the Public. Glasse, Mason, Raffald and Farley are like us equally indebted to the labours of our predecessors.

The Universal Cook was translated into French and probably German (due to the fact that it was reviewed in a number of German periodicals), during the eighteenth century. This was quite unusual for the time and is testament its popularity, as well as indicating an overriding European respect for English cooking. The *Allgemeine Literatur-Zeitung* of 1794 summed up *The Universal Cook* as:

> ...*einem für jede gute Hauswirthschaft unentbehrlichen Handbuche Der Preis beyder.* ('An indispensable handbook for every good housekeeper').[59]

Figures 45 & 46. Francis Collingwood and John Woollams.

The French translation was embraced a little less wholeheartedly, which was unsurprising considering the political situation between the two countries at the time. The introduction to *Le Cuisinier anglais universel, ou, Le Nec plus ultra de la gourmandise*, which was accompanied by two portraits of Collingwood and Woollams looking rather smug, reads:

> The English must eat well, look at their 'embonpoint'! If occasional recipes seem odd, they will at least, 'cher lecteur', broaden your experience, acquainting you with 'le catchup' and 'le browning', which are unknown even to our best chefs.'[60]

Here is Collingwood and Woollams' recipe for stewed hare, complete with catchup and browning:

To Stew a Hare

Paunch and case your hare, cut it as for eating, and put it into a large saucepan, with three pints of beef gravy, a pint of red wine, a large onion stuck with cloves, a bundle of winter savory, a slice of horse radish, two blades of beaten mace, an anchovy, a spoonful of walnut catchup, one of browning, half a lemon, and chyan and salt to your taste. Put on a close cover, set it over a gentle fire, and stew it for two hours. Then take it up into a soup dish, and thicken your gravy with a lump of butter rolled in flour. Boil it a little, and strain it over your hare. Garnish with lemon cut like straws.[61]

Mary Tillinghast

Mary Tillinghast was an early cook and recipe book writer of works including *Rare and Excellent Receipts*, published in 1678. This was followed by *The Young Cook's Monitor; or Directions for Cookery and Distilling*. It is also suspected that Tillinghast was the anonymous author of *The True Way of Preserving and Candying* (1681), as it addresses the readers in almost exactly the same way as *The Young Cook's Monitor*, confusingly penned simply by someone called M.H. One theory for all this confusion over names and provenance is that Mary got married, which changed her initials.

Her books were addressed to her scholars, so she was clearly a teacher in the art of cookery and she obviously valued the practical elements of cooking above the theoretical, noting 'no person can do that with a pen, that your seeing and observing shall do'. She adds that seven years under apprenticeship would also be pointless if all you were to do was refer to recipes in a book, suggesting that perhaps she herself spent this amount of time training, before becoming an accomplished cook and trainer.[62] The 1690 edition of *The True Way of Preserving and Candying* was printed at the author's house in Lime Street, London, which in the late seventeenth century was a fairly affluent district of London. It was also a district synonymous with the growing scientific community and scholars of early scientific research, so it is possible that Mary went on to marry an eminent scientist of the Renaissance age. Who indeed was the H, in Mary's signatory M.H? We will probably never know. Few technical books of this calibre were written and published by women, *for* women, in the sixteenth century. It is a travesty that Mary's legacy has not been maintained and that we know so very little about her. Clearly respected by the later culinary fraternity, Tillinghast was quoted by Kitchiner in *The Cook's Oracle*. It has been suggested, due to the knowledgable content of *The True Way of Preserving and Candying*, that Tillinghast was possibly a trained confectioner, particularly as this was a popular new career choice for women during the latter part of the seventeenth century.[63] Here is her recipe for making marmalade, taken from *The True Way*:

To make Marmalad of Orenges

Take the Peels of fair Sevil Orenges, and boyl them in *three* several Waters, till they are very tender; then put them into fair cold Water, and let them stand Three dayes; shifting the Water twice a day; then drain them from the Water, and beat them in a wooden Mortar: Then take some Pippins, and pare them, and core them, and weigh a Pound of Pippins and boyl it in fair Water, till it is so soft that you can force it through a Cullendar; which being done, put half a Pound of the Orenges to it, and boyl it a little together: Then take one Pound and a Quarter of Sugar beaten, and cearsed and put to it and set it on the Fire, keeping of it stirring till you perceive it is enough; which you may understand by droping a little upon a Plate. When it is enough, put it into flat Pots or Glasses; and when it is cold, paper it up and set it in your Closset. You may make Cakes of the same to dry, by putting a Pound and Ten Ounces of the Sugar to a Pound of Pippin, and half a Pound of the Orenge and lay it out upon Plates to dry, and put it in a Stove. And to make it dry crisp you must shake a little fine Sugar over it, put into a piece of fine Linnen, and when one side is dry then turn them upon Papers, put in a dry Sieve; and dust the other side too and set them in the Stove again: And when it is dry, pack it up in a Box, with Papers between one another.[64]

Menon

Very little is known about Menon. He was allegedly the founding father of 'nouvelle cuisine' and a prolific cookery writer of the eighteenth century. He pushed the boundaries of cooking practises, moving away from the complicated processes of French haute cuisine, towards a lighter, more elegant and even healthier approach to both cooking and the presentation of food. His work acknowledged the science of food and its relation to health. He was an advocate for raising the status of cooks and his writing has an air of intellectual and academic authority, using footnotes, quoting from art history and using broad literary references. His 1746 book *La Cuisinière bourgeoise* is thought to represent the foundations of all future cook's and cookery writer's guides to seasonal cooking, and the first that did not rely on religious dates in the calendar to make decisions on what to eat and when. His section on spring, for example, covering the months of March, April and May, mentions nothing about Lent, but simply acknowledges it as the worst season for accessing poultry, game vegetables and fruit. It was a brave move away from the strict religious dietary laws which had previously governed people's approaches and attitudes towards food.

Menon's *La Cuisinière bourgeoise* is in fact a book of monumental importance, with universal appeal. It sold thousands and is sometimes referred to as the first bestseller in the cookery book category, with over sixty-five editions printed over a seventy-year period.[65] It is also a book that outlines the importance of good manners and table etiquette, recommending amongst other things not to bring your dog with you if you are invited to dinner, to never turn your sleeves up at the table prior to eating, to avoid treading on anyone's feet under the table, and never to call a servant 'waiter', as if you were dining out in a tavern. He also advises that you should never hold your plate up to indicate you want to be served (a favourite faux pas of mine), or take salt from a salt cellar using one's fingers, never gnaw on a meat bone and never compare a dish to another you have eaten elsewhere. My particular favourite recommendations of Menon's for adhering to good manners at dinner, are not to sing during dessert unless asked to, and not to pelt other guests with pieces of bread during the meal. As if these things would generally occur at eighteenth century dinner parties? Menon not only makes recommendations for his primarily French audience of readers, but for the English too. Noting that the English practice of wiping one's fingers and knives on a piece of bread to clean them wasn't customary in France, he stipulated that everyone should comply with not wiping their fingers on a tablecloth.[66]

It is the mystery of the writer that appeals the most about Menon, as devoid of even a Christian name even the gender is contentious. Was Menon a female writer? This would perhaps account for the absence of any proper identity. Menon is also a very common Indian surname, as well as being an honorary Indian title, bestowed on the wealthier classes by kings, although we are always given to understand that Menon is clearly of French origin. Whoever Menon was, he or she did in many ways contribute to the revolutionary way in which people started viewing food and the value that should be placed upon those that know how to cook it.

Dartoise Laguipierre

Aside from being Antoine Carême's beloved mentor, from whom Carême owed much of his culinary knowledge, Dartoise Laguipierre was Napoleon's chief cook. Known for his incredible aptitude and good nature, he accompanied Napoleon on all his campaigns, which meant he had to learn to improvise and experiment outside the comfort zone of the royal kitchens. It was said he could create the most complicated of coulis, under an army tent in a military camp, better than many of his peers could produce one in a fully kitted-out kitchen.

Physically, Laguipierre was said to have favoured vintage styles, continuing to wear the fashions of Louis XVI's time, even applying hair-powder, when everyone else had stopped wearing it in this way.[67]

Carême described Laguipierre as 'the most remarkable chef of our time.'[68] which makes it seem even more distressing that he got left behind in the archives of culinary excellence. Like Charles Senn, Laguipierre was particularly well known for his sauces. His legend lives on with Laguipierre sauce, which is a fish fumet, with butter and glaze, seasoned with lemon juice.[69] The French cook Charles Ranhofer, famous for his many years in service at the illustrious Delmonico's restaurant in New York, also paid tribute to Laguipierre in his hugely popular treatise of 1894, *The Epicurean*, with numerous recipes, including the following:

Consommé à la Laguipierre

For Garnishing. – Butter some small molds, shaped like small half pigeon's eggs: fill these with a game mousse, made of any seasonable game; set them on tin sheets; poach in a slack oven, unmold, and serve them in a separate vegetable dish, adding some oval shaped chicken quenelles, laid on a buttered tin through a bag, and poached in a little boiling water in a slow oven. Serve separately small one-quarter inch square crusts made of twelve turns of puff paste or trimmings and aked white in a very slow oven.[70]

Laguipierre died at the age of sixty-two, in the most unusual and tragic way in 1812, found frozen to death in his carriage, following Napoleon's failed attempts at invading Russia.

John Mollard

John Mollard wrote *The Art of Cookery Made Easy and Refined* (1802). He was another head cook of the notorious London Tavern, of which he was also part owner. In 1790, he went into partnership with Michael Richold and John Allen, amongst others, to purchase the lease of the Freemasons' Tavern.[71]

There are numerous accounts of Richold, who was a wine merchant, going bankrupt in 1802. This presumably must have had an impact on the finances of the Freemasons' Tavern, as an auction of its contents was advertised that same year.[72]

The following extract from Nathaniel Newnham-Davis's *Dinners and Diners: Where and How to Dine in London* (1899) provides a wonderfully visual description of the Tavern. Albeit a century later, it is doubtful that much of the style and glory of this particular dining emporium would have changed significantly.

> At the entrance to the Tavern stand two great janitors. Facing the doorway, at the end of a wide hall, is a long flight of stairs broken by a broad landing and decorated with statues. Up and down this ladies and gentlemen are passing, and I ask one of the janitors what is going on in the ballroom. 'German Liederkranz. Private entertainment. What dinner, sir? Victory Chapter. Drawing-room,' is the condensed information given by the big man, and he points a white-gloved hand to a passage branching off to the right. On one side of the passage is a door leading into a bar where three ladies in black are kept very busy in attending to the wants of thirsty Freemasons. On the other side is a wide shallow alcove in the wall fitted with shelves and glazed over, and in this is a curious collection of plate, great salvers, candelabra, and centrepieces. Beside the alcove is a glass door, and outside it is hung a placard with 'Gavel Club. Private' upon it. At the end of the passage a little Staircase leads up to higher regions, and on the wall, is an old-fashioned clock with a round face and very plain figures, and some oil paintings dark with age.
>
> On the first landing there is a placard outside a door with 'Victory Chapter' on it, and higher up outside another door another placard with 'Perfection Chapter' on it. From the stream of guests and waiters which is setting up the stairs it is evident that there are many banquets to be held to-night.
>
> The drawing-room is white-and-gold in colour. Four Corinthian pillars, the lower halves of which are painted old-gold colour, with gold outlining the curves of their capitals, support a highly-

ornamented ceiling, the central panel of which is painted to represent clouds, with some little birds flitting before them. The paper is old-gold in colour with large flowers upon it. There is some handsome furniture in the room – a fine cabinet, a clock of elaborate workmanship, and some good china vases. The curtains to the windows are of red velvet. At the end of the room farthest from the door is a horseshoe table, with red and white shaded candles on it, ferns, chrysanthemums, and heather in china pots, pines, and hothouse fruits, and at close intervals bottles of champagne and Apollinaris. At the other end of the room, where stands a piano, with a screen in front of it, the gentlemen in evening clothes are chatting, having put their coats and hats on chairs and piano wherever room can be found. The waiters, in black with white gloves, are putting the last touches to the decorations.

Dinner is announced; a move is made to the table, and each man finds his place marked for him. There is a precedence in Freemasonry, as at Court, and this is adhered to in arranging the places at table.

The Victory is a Chapter which is very much in touch with the army and navy, and looking round the table, the company, but for the sombreness of their attire – for one or two Orders at the buttonhole, and here and there a decoration at the throat, are the only spots of colour – might be hosts and guests at some military mess dinner. The 'Most Wise,' who sits at the head of the table, does not belong to either of the services, but on one side of him is the heir to a dukedom, who led at one time a troop of the Household Cavalry, and on the other one of the most popular of our citizen soldiers, equally at home on parade as in his civic chair when Master of one of the City Companies. These are flanked again by a well- known brigade-surgeon and a cheery Admiralty official. The gentleman who has just said grace, in two Latin words, left very pleasant recollections behind him when as ex-Lord Mayor he left the Mansion-House. All round the table are faces with the sharp soldierly cut or naval bluffness.

The 'Grand Secretary' has ordered the dinner, and in the whole length and breadth of the world that hospitable Freemasonry covers, no man knows better how to construct a menu than he does.

Crevettes.
Tortue clair.

Filets de sole Meunière.
Vol-au-vent aux huîtres natives.
Faisan Souvaroff.
Selle de mouton.
Céleri braise Bordelaise.
Layer. Pommes Parisienne.
Poularde rôtie.
Lard grillé. Salade.
Bombe glacée Duchesse.
Os à la moëlle.
Dessert. Café.[73]

Mollard was signing himself as affiliated to the London Tavern in 1808 and the Crown and Sceptre Tavern, Greenwich, in 1827. By 1836 he was working at the Park Hotel, Norwood, and had republished his *Art of Cookery*.[74] John worked for at least one more establishment, Eel Brook, Pomona Place, Middlesex, before he died, somewhere between 1837 and 1839.[75] A coroner's inquest in response to the death of a John Mollard in 1838, reported that a man of this name died suddenly on a Fulham omnibus heading into London's West End. Although it isn't certain whether this was our man Mollard, reports confirmed that he had 'been the proprietor of a great number of first-rate hotels'.[76]

There are also articles from the early nineteenth century in which a John Mollard fitting the description of our famous cook, is mentioned as having invented a brand new type of fish sauce. Little is known of Mollard's personal life, other than that his wife Sarah was on her third husband when she married him. Her will, originally bequeathed to John before he died, referred to the grandchildren she had from her second marriage, suggesting that they had no children of their own.[77] Mollard's recipe for the unusual 'Solomongundy', doesn't seem to resemble traditional versions that I have seen during the nineteenth century. Both a fundamentally adulterated Jamaican and Canadian dish, the former undoubtedly influencing the latter, this was a popular Regency side speciality of pickled herring and chopped meats, mixed with hard-boiled egg and butter.[78] The Jamaican version is more of a salted fish pâté.

Here is John Mollard's interpretation from his *Art of Cookery*.

Solomongundy

Chop small and separately lean of boiled ham, breast of dressed fowl, picked anchovies, parsley omlets of eggs white and yellow (the same kind as for garnishing), eshallots, a small quantity of pickle cucumbers, capers and beet root. Then rub a saucer over with fresh butter, put it in the center of a dish, and make it secure from moving. Place round it in partitions the different articles separately till the saucer is covered, and put on the rim of the dish some slices of lemon.[79]

There are so many other wonderful unsung heroes of the culinary world who I would like to pay tribute to and some who deserve greater research. To add to those already included in this chapter, I would like to briefly add John Simpson, who was cook to the Marquis of Buckingham and Lord Berwick. John Simpson had three books to his name, two with the same title, updated just ten years apart: *A Complete System of Cookery* and then *Simpson's Cookery, Improved and Modernised* in 1834. His recipes appear to be a variation of the same theme – a list of menus and dishes all served up over a five-year period in service to the Marquis, including accounts of meals where various members of the royal court were present. His latter book, although under his name, was confusingly compiled by Henderson William Brand, cook in the kitchens of George IV.[80]

Peter Harvey, owner of the Black Dog Inn, Middlesex, invented a very popular sauce called Harvey's sauce for fish around 1760. He was a highly-esteemed cook who was patronised by Sir Henry Peyton. The sauce is quoted in Dickens' *The Mystery of Edwin Drood*. The Black Dog Inn remained open until 1850, and was a popular retreat for highwaymen.[81]

Harvey's sauce was later trademarked as Lazenby's, following a convoluted court battle and then family acquisition of the rights, widely documented in the press at the time. The Victoria & Albert Museum have a print of a poster circa 1910, advertising the new Lazenby brand which went on to modify the condiment as more of a Worcestershire sauce.

Dincă was a nineteenth-century black gypsy Romanian slave, a well-educated and highly skilled trained cook. He was denied his freedom to marry and as a consequence killed both his lover and himself. He was a slave to one Lady Profirița, who provided him with a good education and initially made him her footman during a visit to Paris, where he was also provided with his own light and spacious rooms. Whilst in France his mistress arranged for him to be trained in the art of cooking and to have French lessons. Dincă learnt a great deal about the culture of the city and was exposed to a variety of intellectual influences. While training, he was introduced to Clementina, a French cook herself, who was oblivious to Dincă's social status and moved on with him as he travelled back to Moldavia with Lady Profirița, now as her cook, rather than as her footman. Clementina put pressure on Dincă to marry her and when he requested his freedom from Lady Profirița she refused, slapped him across the face and humiliated him by denouncing him as an 'impertinent gypsy'. Distraught at being denied his liberty, he took a pistol and fatally shot both himself and Clementina. Lady Profirița was said to be mortified by the consequences of her actions and it is reputed that this case was fundamental to the case for finally abolishing slavery in Romania.[82]

History reminds us that there were cooks all over the world inventing, creating and enriching the lives of others, throughout some of the most turbulent and changeable periods. It needs reiterating that there is still a great deal of research to be undertaken in order to reveal the identities and achievements of those cooks and cookery writers that time has neglected. There is also a need generally to legitimise and honour this great art form academically. It is ironic that the profession struggled for so many centuries to gain greater acknowledgement and professional acceptance. Yet, despite the hugely popular media it attracts, culinary historical discourse remains a largely obscure subject of study. If this book has inspired you to read more, may I suggest starting with Auguste Escoffier's *Memories of My Life,* which is so valuable an account of a dedicated life spent in service, from one so humbled and talented, that it is hard not to become addicted to this most exciting of vocations.

Notes

Introduction

1. Chris Rojek, 'Celebrity' in *Wiley Blackwell Encyclopedia of Consumption and Consumer Studies,* eds., Daniel Thomas Cook and J. Michael Ryan (London: Wiley and Sons, 2015).
2. John Feather, *A History of British Publishing* (London: Routledge, 2005).
3. David Charles Douglas and George William English, eds., *Historical Documents, 1042-1189* (London and New York: Routledge, 1996), p.1198.
4. Earl D. Lyon, 'Roger de Ware, Cook', *Modern Language Notes*, Vol. 52 (1937), pp.491-94.
5. Jean-Louis Flandrin and Massimo Montanari, eds., *Food: A Culinary History* (New York and UK: Columbia University Press, 2013), p.392.

Chapter One

1. Peter Brears, *Cooking and Dining in Medieval England* (London: Prospect Books, 2012), p.13.
2. Betty Travitsky and Anne Prescott, *Seventeenth-Century English Recipe Books* (Hants: Ashgate Publishing, 2008), p.16.
3. Thomas J. Craughwell, *Thomas Jefferson's Crème Brûlee* (Quirk Books, 2012), p.4.
4. Helen McKearin, 'Notes On Stopping, Bottling And Binning', *Journal of Glass Studies*, 13 (1971), p.124.
5. 'Efficacy of Soap', *Sunderland Daily Echo and Shipping Gazette,* 11 January 1935, p.8.
6. John Murrell, *A New Booke of Cookerie,* (London: 1615).
7. Elise Fleming (pseud. Dame Alys Katharine), *Sugar Paste: A Cook's 'play dough'* (http://damealys.medievalcookery.com/CooksPlayDough.html).
8. Ibid.
9. Rebecca Ann Bach and Gwynne Kennedy, eds., *Feminisms and Early Modern Texts: Essays for Phyllis Rackin* (New Jersey: Susquehanna University Press, 2010), p.26.
10. Gervase Markham, *The English Housewife,* ed., Michael R. Best (Canada: McGill-Queen's Press, 1994).
11. *Notes and Queries* 5 (1864), p.488.
12. 'Gervase Markham', *Ballymena Observer*, 16 July 1948, pp.4-5.
13. Gervase Markham, *The English Housewife*, ed., Countess Constance De La Warr (London: Grovesnor Library, 1908), p.56.
14. Mary Tolford Wilson, 'Amelia Simmons Fills a Need: American Cookery, 1796', *The William and Mary Quarterly* 14 (1957), p.17-19.
15. Michael R. Best, p.xiii.
16. Ibid., p.72.
17. Tom Jaine, *Oxford Dictionary of National Biography* (Oxford: Oxford University Press, 2004).
18. Robert May, *The Accomplist Cook* (1660), p.238.

19. Sussex Archaeological Society, *Sussex Archaeological Collections Relating to the History and Antiquities of the County* (Sussex, 1857).
20. 'Pastry Making in Olden Times', *Sussex Advertiser*, 1 June 1867.
21. John Timbs *Nooks and Corners of English Life, Past and Present* (London: Griffith and Farran, 1867) pp.194-95.
22. Ibid., p.199.
23. William Poole *Milton and the Idea of the Fall* (Cambridge: Cambridge University Press, 2005), p.71.
24. William Rabisha, *The Whole Body of Cookery Dissected* (London: Calvert, 1673), p.14.
25. Ibid., p.208.
26. Terry Breverton, *The Tudor Kitchen* (Stroud: Amberley Publishing Limited, 2015).
27. Marjorie Keniston McIntosh, *Working Women in English Society, 1300-1620* (Cambridge: Cambridge University Press, 2005), p.200.
28. William Weaver, *America's First Book of Botanic Healing, 1762-1778* (London and NY: Routledge, 2001), p.19.
29. Howard Coutts, *The Art of Ceramics: European Ceramic Design, 1500-1830* (New Haven: Yale University Press, 2001), p.86.
30. Albrecht Classen, *The Power of a Woman's Voice in Medieval and Early Modern Literatures* (Berlin: Walter de Gruyter, 2007), p.339.
31. Ibid., pp.360-63.
32. Cathy Hartley, *A Historical Dictionary of British Women* (London: Europa Publications, 2003), p.465.
33. Alan Davidson and Tom Jaine, eds., *The Oxford Companion to Food* (Oxford: Oxford University Press, 2014), p.877.
34. Pae-yong Yi, *Women in Korean History* (Seoul: Ewha Woman's University Press, 2008), p.180-81
35. Choi Yearn-hong, 'Jang Gye-hyang: Joseon's poetess, first cookbook author and philanthropist', *Korea Times*, 19 December 2014.
36. National Folk Museum of Korea, *Encyclopedia of Korean Seasonal Customs*, Vol. 1 (Korea, 2014), p.191.
37. Terence Scully, *The Opera of Bartolomeo Scappi (1570): L'arte et prudenza d'un maestro cuoco, 'The Art and Craft of a Master Cook'* (Canada: University of Toronto Press, 2011).
38. Bartolomeo Scappi, *Opera dell'arte del cucinare,* facsimile edition in two volumes (Italy: Arnaldo Forni, 2002).
39. Terence Scully, *The Opera of Bartolomeo Scappi (1570): L'arte et prudenza d'un maestro cuoco, 'The Art and Craft of a Master Cook'* (Canada: University of Toronto Press, 2008).
40. Joan DeJean, *The Essence of Style: How the French Invented High Fashion, Fine Food, Chic Cafés, Style, Sophistication and Glamour* (New York: Simon and Schuster, 2007), pp.136-39.
41. Noel Riley Fitch, *The Grand Literary Cafés of Europe* (London: New Holland Publishers, 2006), p.43.
42. Michael Krondi, *Sweet Invention; A History of Dessert* (Chicago Review Press, 2011), p.197.
43. François Massialot, *The Court and the Country Cook* (London: A & J Churchill, M.Gillyflower, 1702), p.95.

44. Alan Davidson and Tom Jaine, eds., *The Oxford Companion to Food* (Oxford: Oxford University Press, 2014), p.459.
45. Mary Ellen Snodgrass, *Encyclopedia of Kitchen History* (New York and London: Routledge, 2004), p.565.
46. Richard Hosking, ed., *Food and Language: Proceedings of the Oxford Symposium on Food and Cooking* (Totnes: Prospect Books, 2010), p.163.
47. Malcolm Walsby and Natasha Constantinidou, *Documenting the Early Modern Book World* (BRILL, 2013), p.265.
48. H. Leeming, 'A 17th-Century Polish Cookery Book and its Russian Manuscript Translation', *Slavonic and East European Review*, 52 (1974), pp.500-513.
49. Zygmunt Gloger, *Encyklopedia wiedzy o książce, Krakow-Warsaw* (Poland: Hieronim, 1971), p.110. Czerniecki was also very particular about the specific qualities a cook should aspire to. Here is Czerniecki's version, roughly translated into English
50. Stanisław Czerniecki, *Compendium ferculorum albo zebranie potraw*, eds., Jaroslaw Dumanowski and Magdalena Spychaj (Warszawa: Muzeum Pałac w Wilanowie, 2012), p.44.
51. Ibid.
52. Ken Albala, *The Banquet: Dining in the Great Courts of Late Renaissance Europe* (USA: University of Illinois Press, 2007), p.98.
53. Anne Willan and Mark Cherniavsky, *The Cookbook Library* (California: University of California Press, 2012), p.103.
54. Lancelot de Casteau, *Ouverture de Cuisine* ('Opening the Kitchen'), translated by Daniel Myers. [http://www.medievalcookery.com/notes/ouverture.html]
55. Ibid.
56. Ibid.
57. Stuart B. Schwartz, *Tropical Babylons: Sugar and the Making of the Atlantic World, 1450-1680* (California: University of North Carolina Press, 2004), p.244.
58. R. A. Stirling, *Philip IV and the Government of Spain, 1621-1665* (Cambridge: Cambridge University Press, 2002), p.331.
59. Manuel Fernández y González, *El cocinero de su majestad: Memorias del tiempo de Felipe III* (Madrid, 1907).
60. Ken Albala, *Cooking in Europe, 1250-1650* (Greenwood Press, 2006), p.115.
61. Carolyn A. Nadeau, 'Spanish Culinary History in Cervantes, Bodas de Camacho and Revista Canadiense de Estudios Hispánicos' 29, *Invierno* (2005), p.348).
62. Miguel de Cervantes, *Don Quixote* (London: Wordsworth Editions, 1998), p.538.
63. Carolyn A, Nadeau, *Food Matters: Alonso Quijano's Diet and the Discourse of Food in Early Modern Spain* (Canada: University of Toronto Press, 2016), p.27.
64. Carroll-Mann, Robin (pseud. Lady Brighid ni Chiarain), *An English translation of Ruperto de Nola's Libre del Coch*, (2017) http://www.florilegium.org/files/FOOD-MANUSCRIPTS/Guisados1-art.html [accessed 31 December 2016].
65. William Bradford and Charles Deane, eds., *History of Plymouth Plantation*, (Boston: Massachusettes Historical Society, 1856), p.125.
66. Dwight Heath, ed., *Mourt's Relation: A Journal of the Pilgrims of Plymouth* (Bedford, Massachusetts: Applewood Books, 1986), p.62.
67. Bradford and Deane, p.94.
68. F. M. Townscend, Milton Grigg, and A. Lawrence Kocher, *Coke-Garrett House Architectural Report, Block 27 Building I Lot 279-280, Originally entitled: "Architectural*

Report The Coke-Garrett House and Outbuildings Block 27", (Williamsburg, Virginia: Colonial Williamsburg Foundation Library Research Report Series, 1990).
69. *The Prairie Farmer* (Chicago: Prairie Farmer Publishing Company, 1867), p.58,
70. Historic Genealogical Society, *The New England Historical and Genealogical Register: Volume 33* (1879, New England: Heritage Books, 1995).
71. Alonzo Lewis and James Newhall, *History of Lynn, Essex County, Massachusetts, 1629-1864* (Massachusetts: George C. Herbert, 1890). pp.209-11.

Chapter Two

1. Alan Davidson, '*Food: The Natural History of British Cookery Books*', 52 (1983), pp. 98-106.
2. Charmaine O'Brien, *The Colonial Kitchen: Australia 1788-1901* (Lanham: Maryland: Rowman and Littlefield, 2016), p.140.
3. Michael Symons, *One Continuous Picnic: A Gastronomic History of Australia* (Australia: Melbourne University, 2007), p.75.
4. Sofia Eriksson, Madelaine Hastie and Tom Roberts, eds., *Eat History: Food and Drink in Australia and Beyond* (Newcastle: Cambridge Scholars Publishing, 2014), p.172.
5. *Bendigo Advertiser*, 17 September, 1892, p.6.
6. Ibid.
7. Andrew F. Smith, ed., *The Oxford Companion to American Food and Drink* (New York: Oxford University Press, 2007), p.461.
8. Janet Zilkia, *Latino Food Culture* (Connecticut: Greenwood Press, 2008), p.9.
9. Encarnación Pinedo, *Reminiscences of Life in Alta California* (1901), Santa Clara University Library, Archives & Special Collections. http://content.scu.edu/cdm/ref/collection/pinedo/id/1092
10. Dan Strehl, ed., *Encarnación's Kitchen: Mexican Recipes from Nineteenth Century California* (California: University of California Press, 2005), p.126-27.
11. Advertisement for Elizabeth Raffald's shop, *Manchester Mercury*, 7 October 1766, p.3.
12. Elizabeth Raffald, *The Experienced English Housekeeper* (London, 1786).
13. Hannah Barker, *The Business of Women: Female Enterprise and Urban Development in Northern England, 1760-1830* (Oxford: Oxford University Press, 2006), p.132.
14. *The London Gazette*, 27 November, 1779, p.3.
15. *The Mt. Sterling Advocate,* Mt. Sterling, Ky., 18 August 1909.
16. Barker, p.49.
17. Emma Kay, *Dining with the Georgians* (Gloucestershire: Amberley Publishing, 2014), p.176.
18. Elizabeth Raffald, *The Experienced English Housekeeper* (York: T. Wilson and R. Spence, 1806), p.160.
19. Richard Hosking, *Food and Language: Proceedings of the Oxford Symposium on Food and Cooking 2009* (Oxford: Oxford Symposium, 2010), p.314.
20. Lorna Sage, Germaine Greer and Elaine Showalter, eds., *The Cambridge Guide to Women's Writing in English* (Cambridge: Cambridge University Press, 1999).
21. Sir Leslie Stephen, *Dictionary of National Biography* (London: Smith, Elder, 1897), p.403.

Notes

22. Mary Hamilton Papers, Correspondence from Elizabeth Maria Rundell, Letter 30 April, 1787. Ref: GB 133 HAM/1/8/6/1, in the University of Manchester Archives [online] 20 December, 2016. Available from : http://www.library.manchester.ac.uk/search-resources/guide-to-special-collections/uomarchives/
23. Emma Kay, *Dining with the Georgians*, p.94
24. Maria Eliza Rundell, *Mrs Rundell's Domestic Cookery* (London: Routledge, Warnes and Routledge, 1859), p.113.
25. Mary Tolford Wilson, 'Amelia Simmons Fills a Need: *American Cookery*, 1796', *The William and Mary Quarterly* 14 (1957), pp.16-30.
26. Michael Ayers Trotti, *The Body in the Reservoir: Murder & Sensationalism in the South* (USA: University of North Carolina Press, 2008).
27. Tolford Wilson, 'Amelia Simmons Fills a Need: *American Cookery*, 1796', pp.16-30.
28. Dorothy A. Mays, *Women in Early America: Struggle, Survival, and Freedom in a New World* (California ABC-CLIO, 2004), p.70.
29. James Gilreath, ed., *Federal Copyright Records 1790-1800* (USA: Library of Congress, 1987), p.141
30. H. Baldwin, ed., *The Plays and Poems of William Shakspeare* (1790), p.520.
31. John Harland and Thomas Turner Wilkinson, *Lancashire Folklore, 1867* (Kessinger Publishing, 2003).
32. Mary Tolford Wilson, ed., *The First American Cookbook: A Facsimile of 'American Cookery', 1796* (New York: Dover Publications, 1958), p.16.
33. Karen Hess, ed., *American Cookery, Amelia Simmons* (Massachusetts: Applewood Books, 1996), p.46.
34. Katherine E. Harbury, *Colonial Virginia's Cooking Dynasty* (South Carolina: University of South Carolina Press, 2004).
35. Cynthia Bertelsen, *The American Boarding House, a Brief Introduction: The Case of Mary Randolph* (USA, 2016) https://gherkinstomatoes.com/2016/02/11/36008/ [accessed 20 November 2016]
36. Mary Randolph, *The Virginia Housewife* (Baltimore: John Plaskitt, 1836), p.19.
37. Leslie Alexander, ed., *Encyclopedia of African American History* (ABC-CLIO, 2010), p.114.
38. Harry Haff, *The Founders of American Cuisine* (North Carolina: McFarland & Co, 2011), p.70.
39. Mrs Fisher, *What Mrs Fisher Knows About Old Southern Cooking,* ed., Karen Hess (Bedford USA: Applewood Books, 1995), p.58.
40. Laura Shapiro, *Perfection Salad: Women and Cooking at the Turn of the Century* University of California Press, 2008, California), p.104-5.
41. Fannie Merritt Farmer, *The Boston Cooking-School Cook Book* (1896, Boston :Little Brown and Company), p.176.
42. Advertisement for Marshall's School of Cookery, *Yorkshire Post and Leeds Intelligence*, 4 October, 1886.
43. Advertisement for Marshall's School of Cookery, *Bath Chronicle and Weekly Gazette*, 16 October 1884.
44. Agnes B. Marshall, *The Book of Ices* (London: Marshall's School of Cookery, 1857), p.40.
45. John Deith, Harlan Walker, eds., *Cooks and Other People: Proceedings of the Oxford Symposium on Food and Cookery, 1995* (Oxford: Oxford Symposium, 1996).

46. *Exeter and Plymouth Gazette*, 9 December, 1887.
47. *Bury Free Press*, 2 October 1886.
48. *Pall Mall Gazette*, 30 March 1886.
49. Kathryn Hughes, *The Short Life and Long Times of Mrs Beeton* (London: Harper Collins, 2013), p.7.
50. *Mrs Beeton's Book of Household Management* (London: S. O. Beeton, 1861), p.563.
51. Regular feature celebrating famous women's birthdays. Highlights Eliza's life and work, *Washington Herald*, 18 November 1914, p.6.
52. Eliza Leslie, *Miss Leslie's Behaviour Book* (Philadelphia: T. B. Peterson & Bros, 1839), p.291.
53. Ibid., p.128.
54. Ibid., p.291.
55. Elizabeth Goodfellow, *Mrs Goodfellows Cookery as it Should Be* (Philadelphia: T. B. Peterson & Bros, 1865).
56. Andrew F. Smith, ed., *The Oxford Companion to American Food and Drink*, (Oxford: Oxford University Press, 2007).
57. Becky Diamond, *Mrs Goodfellow: The Story of America's First Cooking School* (USA: Westholme Publishing, 2012).
58. Eliza Leslie, *Seventy-Five Receipts for Pastry, Cakes and Sweetmeats* (Boston: Munroe and Francis, 1836).
59. Emma Kay, *Dining with the Georgians,* pp.148-9.
60. Stephanie R. Maroney, *To Make a Curry the India Way: Tracking the Meaning of Curry Across Eighteenth-Century Communities,* in 'Food and Foodways. Explorations in the History and Culture of Human Nourishment' *Food Globality and Foodways Localities* 19 (2011).
61. Mary Randolph, *The Virginia House-Wife* (Carolina: University of South Carolina Press, 1824).
62. Hannah Glasse, *The Art of Cookery Made Plain and Easy* (London: J. Rivington and Sons, 1788), p.63.
63. *The Black Hills Union and Western Stock Review*, 5 November 1909.
64. Maria Parloa, *Appledore Cook Book* (Massachusetts: Applewood Books, 2008), p.3.
65. Richard James Hooker, *The Book of Chowder* (Boston: Harvard Common Press, 1978), p.75.
66. Elizabeth Driver, *Culinary Landmarks: A Bibliography of Canadian Cookbooks, 1825-1949* (Toronto: University of Toronto Press, 2008), p.116.
67. *The Pickens Sentinel,* 5 July 1883.
68. Maria Parloa, *Camp Cookery: How to Live in Camp* (Boston: Estes and Lauriat, 1878), p.29-30.
69. *Falkirk Herald*, 11 February 1928, p.7.
70. Emma Seifrit Weigley, 'It Might Have Been Euthenics: The Lake Placid Conferences and the Home Economics Movement', *American Quarterly* 26, (1974), pp. 79-96.
71. Andrew F. Smith, p.155.
72. Mrs S. T. Rorer, *Mrs Rorer's Philadelphia Cook Book* (Philadelphia: Arnold and Company, 1886), pp. 251-252.
73. Elizabeth David, *Is There a Nutmeg in the House?* (London: Penguin,2001), pp.152-53
74. Advertisment and article about the fifth edition of *The Cook and Housewife's Manual, The Scotsman,* 5 December, 1835, p.1.

Notes

75. Margaret Dods (pseud. Christian Isobel Johnstone), *The Cook and Housewife's Manual* (Edinburgh, 1828), pp.51-2.
76. *Caledonian Mercury*, 16 June 1759.
77. Susanna MacIver, *Cookery and Pastry as Taught and Practised by Mrs MacIver* (London: C. Eliot and T. Kay, 1789), p.61.
78. Public announcement of births and deaths, *Morning Advertiser*, 18 February 1841.
79. *Kentish Weekly Post or Canterbury Journal*, 17 June 1800.
80. Advertisement, *Derby Mercury*, 26 June 1800.

Chapter Three

1. Jean-Louis Flandrin and Massimo Montanari, p.431.
2. Amy B. Trubek, *Haute Cuisine: How the French Invented the Culinary Profession* (Philadelphia: University of Pennsylvania Press, 2000), p.38-39.
3. *The Sphere*, 11 August 1956.
4. Theodore Zeldin, *A History of French Passions 1848-1945: Intellect, Taste and Anxiety* (Oxford: Clarendon Press, 1993), p.748.
5. Anne Willan, *The Country Cooking of France* (San Francisco: Chronicle Books, 2012), p.19.
6. Alan Davidson and Tom Jaine, *The Oxford Companion to Food* (Oxford: Oxford University Press, 2014), p.366.
7. Christian Coff, *The Taste for Ethics: An Ethic of Food Consumption* (The Netherlands: Springer, 2006), p.75.
8. Alan Davidson and Tom Jaine, *The Oxford Companion to Food*, p.367.
9. Denise Gigante, *Gusto: Essential writings in Nineteenth-Century Gastronomy* (New York and Oxford: Routledge, 2013).
10. Jean Anthelme Brillat-Savarin, *The Physiology of Taste* (USA: Dover Publications, 2012).
11. Janet Fletcher, *Cheese and Wine: A Guide to Selecting, Pairing and Enjoying* (San Francisco: Chronicle Books, 2011), p.41.
12. Article about people who have given up on life and gone to bed, *Falkirk Herald*, 7 March 1928.
13. Jean Anthelme Brillat-Savarin, *The Physiology of Taste*, (Philadelphia: Lindsay & Blakiston, 1854), p.334.
14. *Lower Sandusky Freeman*, 19 May 1849.
15. Patricia Brady, *Martha Washington: An American Life* (New York: Penguin, 2006).
16. Bruce Chadwick, *The General and Mrs Washington: The Untold Story of a Marriage and a Revolution* (Illinois: Sourcebooks Inc, 2007).
17. Fritz Hirschfeld, *George Washington and Slavery : A Documentary Portrayl* (Columbia and London: University of Missouri Press, 1997), p.70.
18. Linda Bauer, *Capitol Hill Cooks: Recipes from the Whitehouse, Congress and all of the Past Presidents* (USA and Plymouth, UK: Taylor Trade Publications, 2010), p.270.
19. Ibid., p.269.
20. Barry H. Landau, *The President's Table: Two Hundred Years of Dining and Diplomacy* (New York: Harper Collins, 2011), p.3.
21. Marie Kimball, *Thomas Jefferson's Cook Book* (Ohio: James Direct, 2007).
22. Thomas J. Craughwell, p.12.

23. Marjorie Charlot, *Did You Know? Over One Hundred Facts About Haiti and Her Children* (Bloomington: Universe, 2015).
24. Bruce Lancaster and John Harold Plumb, *The American Revolution* (Boston: Houghton Mifflin Harcourt, 2001), p.342.
25. B. Clermont, *The Professed Cook; or, The Modern Art of Cookery, Pastry and Confectionery* (London: C. Richards, 1812), p.189.
26. Frank E. Grizzard, *George Washington: A Biographical Companion* (Denver: ABC-CLIO, 2002), p.121.
27. Kim S. Collier, *George Washington and the American Revolution* (USA: Library of Congress, 2010), p.70.
28. *Gazette of the United States,* 13 October 1795.
29. Robert Walsh, Eliakim Littell and John Jay Smith, *The Museum of Foreign Literature, Science and Art,* Vol. 27 (Philadelphia: Adam Waldie, 1835), p.330.
30. *Nottingham Gazette, and Political, Literary, Agricultural & Commercial Register for the Midland Counties,* 24 June 1814.
31. James Salter and Kay Salter, *Life is Meals: A Food Lover's Book of Days* (USA: Pan Macmillan, 2014).
32. Antoine B. Beauvilliers, *The Art of French Cookery* (London: Longman, 1827), p.121.
33. Auguste Escoffier, *Memories of My Life,* (London: Wiley, 1996) p.4
34. Emma Kay, *Dining with the Victorians* (Gloucestershire: Amberley Publishing, 2015), p.213-14
35. Yannick Alléno and Vincent Brenot, *Sauces: Reflexions of a Chef* (Paris: Hachette, 2014).
36. Auguste Escoffier, *A Guide to Modern Cookery* (Cambridge: Cambridge University Press, 2013), p.31.
37. Nicole Kelby, *White Truffles in Winter* (Surrey: Alma Books, 2012).
38. Auguste Escoffier, *Memories of My Life,* pp.116-17.
39. Anna Marie Fisker and Tenna Doktor Olsen, *Jules Gouffé* (Denmark: Aalborg University, 2012).
40. Académie Culinaire, Jules Gouffé, http://www.academieculinairedefrance.com/index.php?option=com_content&view=article&id=78:jules-gouffe&Itemid=120&lang=fr _[accessed 22 January,2017].
41. Thevenot is mentioned as coming out of retirement to undertake the catering for an impending royal wedding, *North Devon Gazette,* 21 July 1896.
42. *Sporting Life,* 14 December 1870.
43. William Blanchard, ed., *The Epicure's Year Book and Table Companion of 1869* (London: Bradbury, Evans, and Co, 1869), pp. 118-19.
44. Jules Gouffé, *The Royal Cookery Book* (London: Sampson Low, Son, and Marston, 1869), p.155.
45. Peter Hayden, 'The Fabriques of Antonin Carême', *Garden History,* 24 (1996), pp.39-44.
46. Stephen Mennell, *All Manners of Food: Eating and Taste in England and France from the Middle Ages to the Present* (Urbana and Chicago: University of Illinois Press, 1996), p.147.
47. *Fraser's Magazine,* Vol. 29 (London: G. W. Nickisson, 1844,), p.613.
48. Paul Metzner, *Crescendo of the Virtuoso: Spectacle, Skill and Self-Promotion in Paris During the Age of Revolution* (California: University of California Press, 1998),

Notes

p.69-70.
49. Ian Kelly, *Cooking for Kings: The Life of the First Celebrity Chef Antonin Carême* (London: Short Books Ltd, 2004).
50. Ibid.
51. M. A. Carême, *The Royal Parisian Pastrycook and Confectioner* (London: F. J. Mason, 1834), p.66.
52. Emma Kay, *Dining with the Georgians*, p.139-40.
53. Helen Morris, *Portrait of a Chef: The Life of Alexis Soyer, Sometime Chef to the Reform Club* (Cambridge: Cambridge University Press), p.16.
54. Louis Eustache Ude, *The French Cook* (London: John Ebers, 1822), p.383.
55. Peter McClusky, *Ontario Garlic: The Story from Farm to Festival* (Charlston, USA: History Press, 2015), p.27.
56. Colin Smythe, 'Charles Elmé Francatelli, Crockford's and the Royal Connection', *Petits Propos Culinaires* 101 (2014), pp.19-20.
57. Detailed description of the dinner party. *Westmorland Gazette*, 28 December 1867.
58. Charles Elmé Francatelli, *The Modern Cook* (Massachusettes: Applewood Books, 2008), p.365.
59. Michael Garval, 'Alexis Soyer and the Rise of the Celebrity Chef' in *Romantic Circles* ed., Denise Gigante (North Carolina: North Carolina State University, 2007).
60. Helen Morris, p.25.
61. Alexis Benoit Soyer, *A Shilling Cookery for the People* (London: Routledge & Co, 1854), p.146-48.
62. *The Red Cloud Chief*, 2 November 1900.
63. *Manchester Courier and Lancashire General Advertiser*, 15 September 1900.
64. *The Evening Times*, 12 October 1899, p.6.
65. *The Red Cloud Chief*, 2 November 1900.
66. Charles Ranhofer, *The Epicurean, A Complete Treatise of Analytical and Practical Studies on the Culinary Art* (Chicago: The Hotel Monthly Press, 1920), p.4.
67. Mark McWilliams, *Food and the Novel in Nineteenth-Century America* (Maryland: Rowman AltaMira, 2012), p.149.
68. Oscar Wilde, *A Critic in Pall Mall: Being Extracts from Reviews and Miscellanies* (Start USA: Publsihing, 2012).
69. Una Pope-Hennessy, *Charles Dickens* (Edinburgh: R & R Clark, 1947).
70. Milton Meltzer, ed., *Mark Twain Himself: A Pictorial Biography* (Columbia and London: University of Missouri Press, 2002).
71. *St James's Gazette*, 1 May 1899.
72. *Western Times*, 18 January 1884.
73. *New York Daily Tribune*, 12 November 1842.
74. *Nottingham Evening Post*, 26 September 1881.
75. Michael Stephen Smith, *The Emergence of Modern Business Enterprise in France, 1800-1930* (USA: Harvard University Press, 2006), p.279.
76. *The Red Cloud Chief*, 2 November 1900.
77. Pamela Haines, *Tea at Gunter's* (London: Bloomsbury Reader, 2011).
78. *Northampton Mercury*, 16 January 1914, p.2.
79. *Punch*, Vol. 52 (London, 1867), p.76.
80. *Country Life*, Vol. 174 (1983), p.1320.
81. *Radcliffe Culinary Times*, Vol. 8 (Radcliffe Culinary friends of the Schlesinger

Library. 1999).
82. William Jeanes, *Gunter's Modern Confectioner* (London: Dean and Son, 1870).
83. Elizabeth David and Jill Norman, eds., *Harvest of the Cold Months: The Social History of Ice and Ices* (London: Faber and Faber, 2011).
84. Public auction announcement, *Morning Advertiser*, 20 May 1857.
85. 'Reports of Cases in Chancery, argued and determined' in *Rolls Court during the time of Lord Langdale, Master of the Rolls. [1838-1866]*, Vol. 23, (London: Saunders and Benning, 1858).
86. Emma Kay, *Dining with the Georgians*, p.89.
87. *Morning Advertiser*, 8 November 1824.
88. *Morning Chronicle*, 3 August 1829.
89. *Morning Post*, 28 July 1829.
90. *Globe,* 05 July 1828.
91. William Alexis Jarrin, *The Italian Confectioner* (London: William Ainsworth, London, 1827), p.224.
92. Joanna Waley-Cohen, 'Celebrated Cooks of China's Past', *Food In History*, 14 (2007), pp.14-24.
93. Jacqueline M. Newman, 'Yuan Mei: China's Greatest Gastronome', *Food in History,* 17 (2010), pp.27-29.
94. Emma Kay, *Dining with the Georgians*, p.140-41.
95. Nicolas Appert, *The Art of Preserving* (London: Black, Parry and Kingsbury, 1812), p.66.
96. *Gnowangerup Star and Tambellup-Onegerup Gazette*, 10 May, 1941.
97. Samuel Colt, *Inventors and Inventions, Volume 1* (New York: Marshall Cavendish, 2008), p.32.

Chapter Four

1. Mac Con Mairtın, Iomaire, *'Haute cuisine restaurants in nineteenth and twentieth century Ireland',* Proceedings of the Royal Irish Academy, Vol. 115C, (2015).
2. *Chronicle, Australia*, 20 June 1914, p.2.
3. *Ballymena Observer*, 10 April 1914.
4. 'Ambitious baker's self-raising success', *Bristol Post*, 9 July 2012.
5. *Hertford Mercury and Reformer*, 20 January 1855.
6. Neil Hanson, *The Custom of the Sea* (London: Random House, 2011).
7. *The Daily Union*, 2 January 1853, p.88.
8. *The Lancet*, Vol. 2 (London: John Churchill 1845).
9. *Western Daily Press*, 28 September 1922.
10. *Sussex Agricultural Express*, 29 March 1890.
11. *Leeds Intelligencer,* 10 March 1761.
12. *Sussex Advertiser*, 22 August 1757.
13. William Verrall, *A Complete System of Cookery* (London, 1759), p.1.
14. Naomi Tadmor, *Family and Friends in Eighteenth-Century England* (Cambridge: Cambridge University Press, 2001), p.229.
15. Verrall, p.109.
16. Ibid., p.33.

17. Romney Sedgwick, 'The Duke of Newcastle's Cook', *History Today*, 5 (1955), pp.308-16.
18. Michael Symons, *A History of Cooks and Cooking* (USA: University of Illinois Press, 2004), p.45.
19. Elizabeth David, p.134.
20. *The London Magazine, Or Gentleman's Monthly*, Vol. 48 (London: R. Baldwin, 1779).
21. Charles Carter, *The Compleat City and Country Cook* (London: Bettesworth and Hitch, 1736), pp.5-7.
22. Ibid, p.156.
23. Francis Sandford, *The History of the Coronation of James II, King of England, Scotland etc.* (London: Newcomb, 1687), p.119.
24. William Henry Pyne, *Wine and Walnuts* (London: Longman, Hurst, Rees, Orme and Brown, 1823), pp. 115-16.
25. R. O. Bucholz, *The Augustan Court: Queen Anne and the Decline of Court Culture* (California: Stanford University Press, 1993), p.308.
26. Charles Dickens, *All the Year Round*, Vol. 19 (London: Chapman and Hall, 1868).
27. Elena Molokhovets, *Classic Russian Cooking* (Bloomington and Indianapolis: Indiana University Press, 1998), p.59.
28. Alexandre Dumas, *Impressions of Travel, in Egypt and Arabia Petra* (London: J. S. Taylor, 1839), p.80.
29. Louise Colman, ed., *Alexander Dumas' Dictionary of Cuisine* (Oxford: Routledge, 2013).
30. Mary Eales, *Mrs Mary Eales's receipts* (London: J. Brindley, 1733), p.93.
31. J. Roberts, *The History of the Life and Reign of Queen Anne* (London: William Taylor, 1722).
32. S. M. Pennell, 'Mary Eales', *Oxford Dictionary of National Biography*, (Oxford: Oxford University Press, 2004).
33. Sir Richard Blackmore, *A True and Impartial History of the Conspiracy Against the Person and Government of King William III, of Glorious Memory, in the Year 1695* (London: J. Knapton), p.162.
34. James Vernon, ed., *Letters Illustrative of the Reign of William III, from 1696 to 1708, Volume I* (London: Henry Colburn, 1841), p3.
35. John, M.Beattie, *The English Court in the Reign of George I* (Cambridge: Cambridge University Press, 1967), p.88.
36. Janet Theophano, *Eat my words: Reading Women's Lives Through the Cookbooks They Wrote* (New York: Palgrave Macmillan, 2002), p.192.
37. Pierre de Lune, 'Le Cuisinier', in *L'Art de la cuisine française au XVII* (Paris: Payot and Rivages, 1995), p.293.
38. Anne Willan and Mark Cherniavsky, *The Cookbook Library: Four Centuries of the Cooks, Writers and Recipes that made the Modern Cookbook* (USA: University of California Press, 2012). p.168.
39. John Nott, *The Cooks and Confectioners Dictionary* (London: C. Rivington, 1723), p.2-3.
40. Sean Takats, *The Expert Cook in Enlightenment France* (Baltimore: JHU Press, 2011).
41. *Northampton Mercury*, 19 April 1806.
42. Frederick Nutt, *The Complete Confectioner: Or, The Whole Art of Confectionary Made Easy* (London, Richard Scott, 1807).

43. J. J. Machet, *Le confiseur moderne ou l'Art du confiseur et du distillateur* (Paris: Chez Maradan, 1821).
44. Michael Krondl, *Sweet Invention: A History of Dessert* (Chicago: Chicago Review Press, 2011), p.204.
45. Frederick Nutt, *The Complete Confectioner, Or, The Whole Art of Confectionery, Made Easy* (London: J Smeeton, 1809), p.12.
46. Joe Moshenska, *A Stain in the Blood, the Remarkable Voyage of Sir Kenelm Digby* (London: William Heinemann, 2016).
47. Henry Jeffreys, *Empire of Booze* (London: Random House, 2016).
48. Sir Kenelm Digby Knight, *The Closet of Sir Kenelm Digby Knight Opened* (Tredition, Germany, 2012), p.5.
49. Charles Senn, *The Book of Sauces* (Chicago: The Hotel Monthly Press, Chicago, 1915), p.6.
50. Ibid., p.87.
51. *Dundee Evening Telegraph*, 24 April 1894.
52. Stephen Mennell, *All Manners of Food: Eating and Taste in England and France from the Middle Ages to the Present* (Urbana and Chicago: University of Illinois, 1996,) pp.186-88.
53. *London Daily News*, 13 April 1906.
54. *Illustrated London News*, 21 April 1883.
55. Samuel Palmer, *St Pancras, Memoranda Relating to the Parish* (London: Field and Turr, 1870), p.291.
56. William Kitchiner, *The Cook's Oracle* (New York: Cosimo Inc, 2005), p.20.
57. Charles Dickens, *The Life and Adventures of Nicholas Nickleby* (London: Chapman and Hall, 1839), p.8.
58. John Farley, *The London Art of Cookery, and Housekeeper's Complete Assistant* (London: John Barker, 1800), p.4.
59. *Allgemeine Literatur-Zeitung* (Schwetschke: 1794), p.1047.
60. Jane Grigson, *Jane Grigson's Fruit Book* (London: Atheneum Publishers), p.37.
61. Francis Collingwood and John Woollams, *The Universal Cook, and City and Country Housekeeper* (London: J. Scatcherd, 1801), p.141.
62. Mary Tillinghast, *The True Way of Preserving and Candying and Making Several Sorts of Sweet Meats, etc.* (London: 1695).
63. Mary Ellen Snodgrass, *Encyclopaedia of Kitchen History* (New York: Fitzroy Dearborn, 2004), p.268.
64. Tillinghast, pp.17-19.
65. Jennifer J. Davis, *Defining Culinary Authority: The Transformation of Cooking in France, 1650-1830* (Louisiana: LSU Press 2013).
66. *Pall Mall Gazette*, 20 October 1866.
67. *Southern Reporter and Cork Commercial Courier*, 19 May 1842.
68. Prosper Montagne and Charlotte Snyder Turgeon, eds., *New Larousse Gastronomique* (Crown Publishers, 1977), p.533.
69. Rodney Dale, *Wordsworth Dictionary of Culinary and Menu Terms* (Hertfordshire: Wordsworth Editions, 2000), p.246.
70. Charles Ranhofer, p.252.
71. *Lloyds' Evening Post*, 1 March 1790.
72. The Library and Museum of Freemasonry, *Catalogue 1802-1883 BE 18CAT*, http://

freemasonry.london.museum/archives [accessed 25 January, 2017].
73. Lieut.-Col. Nathaniel Newnham-Davis, *Dinners and Diners: Where and How to Dinein London* (London: Grant Richards 1899).
74. Advertisement, *Globe, London,* 6 February 1837.
75. *Oxford University and City Herald*, 28 December 1839.
76. *Morning Chronicle*, 2 November 1838.
77. *Bell's Weekly Messenger*, 18 November 1838.
78. Kirstin Olsen, *Cooking with Jane Austen* (London and Connecticut: Greenwood Publishing group, 2005), p.172.
79. John Mollard, *The Art of Cookery Made Easy and Refined* (London: J. Nunn, 1802), pp.183-84.
80. Arnold Whitaker, *English Cookery Books* (Germany: DOGMA, 2012), p.135.
81. Carole J. Skelly, *Dictionary of Herbs, Spices, Seasonings and Natural Flavorings* (New York: Routledge, 2013).
82. Sorina Georgescu, '(Ex) Slave Identities Shaped By Journeys Abroad: African-American Frederick Douglass In His Autobiographies and Romanian Roma Slavedincă' in Gheorghe Sion's Emanciparea Țiganilor', *University of Bucharest Review*, 10 (2008).

Notes on the Illustrations

Chapter One

Figure 1. Design for a 'boulting hutch'. Illustration from the 1653 edition of Hugh Plat's *The Jewell House of Art and Nature*.
Figure 2. Title page from Gervase Markham's *The English Huswife* (1623).
Figure 3. Frontispiece and title page from the 1671 edition of Robert May's *The Accomplisht Cook*.
Figure 4. Extract from Edward Kidder's *Receipts of Pastry and Cooking*.
Figure 5. Illustration of a 'Lamb Pastey' from Edward Kidder's *Receipts of Pastry and Cooking*.
Figure 6. Extract from William Rabisha's *The Whole Body of Cooking Dissected* (1682).
Figure 7. Extract from Anna Wecker's *Ein Köstlich new Kochbuch* (1598).
Figure 8. Frontispiece from Hannah Woolley's *The Queen-like Closet* (1675).
Figure 9. Portrait of Bartolomeo Scappi, from *Opera di Bartolomeo Scappi* (1605).
Figure 10. Francesco Procopio dei Coltelli.
Figure 11. A gravure of Le Café Procope, rue de l'Ancienne-Comédie, Paris, 1900.
Figure 12. Frontispiece to an edition of François Pierre de La Varenne's *Le Cuisinier françois*, published in Amsterdam c. 1700.
Figure 13. 'Squanto teaching Plymouth colonists' from *The Teaching of Agriculture in the High School* (1911).

Chapter Two

Figure 14. Cookery Class at the Working Men's College, Melbourne, from *The Illustrated Australian News*, 1 May 1891.
Figure 15. Cover of Margaret Pearson's *Australian Cookery* (1889).
Figure 16. Frontispiece of Elizabeth Raffald's *The Experienced English Housekeeper* (1782).
Figure 17. Fannie Farmer, Memorial in Medford, Massachusetts, USA (2016).
Figure 18. Portrait of Agnes Bertha Marshall, used as the frontispiece of *Mrs A. B. Marshall's Larger Cookery Book of Extra Recipes* (1891).
Figure 19. Marshall's Patent Freezer in Agnes B. Marshall's *The Book of Ices* (1857).
Figure 20. Frontispiece of *Mrs Beeton's Book of Household Management* (1861).
Figure 21. Eliza Leslie, Sally Thomas (artist), from Library of Congress, https://www.loc.gov/item/det1994022252/PP/ [accessed 29 November, 2016].
Figure 22. Frontispiece and title page from a later edition of Hannah Glasse's *The Art of Cookery Made Plain and Easy*, c. 1777.
Figure 23. Portrait and clipping about Sarah Tyson Rorer, from New York Public Library, http://digitalcollections.nypl.org/items/9cf721ac-9d64-35d7-e040-e00a18063251 [accessed 5 January, 2017].

Notes on the Illustrations

Chapter Three

Figure 24. Portrait of Alexandre Balthazar Laurent Grimod de La Reynière, from a 1904 edition of *Almanach des gourmands*.
Figure 25. Jean Anthelme Brillat-Savarin, an eighteenth century portrait.
Figure 26. Thomas Jefferson (1801), from Library of Congress, https://www.loc.gov/item/96522974/ [accessed 15 October, 2016].
Figure 27. Samuel Fraunces (circa 1770-85), Fraunces Tavern Museum, New York City.
Figure 28. Fraunces Tavern, New York, 1900, from Library of Congress, https://www.loc.gov/item/det1994021942/PP/ [accessed 5 January, 2017].
Figure 29. Auguste Escoffier, in Nathaniel Newnham-Davis's *The Gourmet's Guide to London* (1914).
Figure 30. Portrait of Jules Gouffé, from the 1873 edition of Jules Gouffé's *Le Livre de pâtisserie*.
Figure 31. Portrait of M.A. Carême, from M.A. Carême's *Le Pâtissier royal parisien* (1815).
Figure 32. Portrait of Louis Eustache Ude, frontispiece of the 1829 edition of Louis Eustache Ude's *The French Cook*.
Figure 33. Charles Elmé Francatelli in Charles Elmé Francatelli's *The Cook's Guide* (1861).
Figure 34. Portrait of Alexis Benoit Soyer, frontispiece of the 1849 edition of Alexis Benoit Soyer's *The Modern Housewife, or Ménagère*.
Figure 35. Portrait of Charles Ranhofer, from *The Epicurian* (1894).
Figure 36. Delmonico's, New York, 1906, from Library of Congress, https://www.loc.gov/item/2007663966/ [accessed 16 October, 2016].
Figure 37. Portrait of William Gunter, frontispiece of the 1830 edition of *Gunter's Confectioner's Oracle*.
Figure 38. Portrait of William Jarrin, frontispiece of the 1827 edition of William Jarrin's *The Italian Confectioner*.

Chapter Four

Figure 39. Henry Jones' Western Biscuit Bakery, circa 1845.
Figure 40. Title page of Patrick Lamb's *Royal Cookery* (1710).
Figure 41. Alexandre Dumas, engraving by Maurin (1842).
Figure 42. Sir Kenelm Digby, from Yale Center for British Art, Paul Mellon Collection, http://collections.britishart.yale.edu/vufind/Record/3633108 [accessed 07 December, 2016].
Figure 43. William Kitchiner, engraving after a portrait by Charles Turner, 1827.
Figure 44. *Mr. John Farley Cook at the London Tavern*, from Yale Center for British Art, Paul Mellon Collection, http://collections.britishart.yale.edu/vufind/Record/3638736 [accessed 18 December, 2016].
Figure 45 & 46. Frontispiece from Francis Collingwood and John Woollams's *The Universal Cook* (1797).

List of Illustrations

Chapter One

1. Design for a 'boulting hutch'. Illustration from Hugh Plat's *The Jewell House of Art and Nature*.
2. Title page from Gervase Markham's *The English Huswife*.
3. Frontispiece from Robert May's *The Accomplisht Cook*.
4. Extract from Edward Kidder's *Receipts of Pastry and Cooking*.
5. Illustration of a 'Lamb Pastey' from Edward Kidder's *Receipts of Pastry and Cooking*.
6. William Rabisha's *The Whole Body of Cooking Dissected*.
7. Anna Wecker's *Ein Köstlich new Kochbuch*.
8. Frontispiece from Hannah Woolley's *The Queen-like Closet*.
9. Portrait of Bartolomeo Scappi, from *Opera di Bartolomeo Scappi*.
10. Francesco Procopio dei Coltelli.
11. Café Procope, Paris, 1900.
12. Frontispiece to an edition of François Pierre de La Varenne's *Le Cuisinier françois*.
13. Squanto teaching Plymouth colonists.

Chapter Two

14. Cookery class at the Working Men's College, Melbourne.
15. Cover of Margaret Pearson's *Australian Cookery*.
16. Frontispiece of Elizabeth Raffald's *The Experienced English Housekeeper*.
17. Fannie Farmer, Memorial in Medford, Massachusetts, USA.
18. Agnes Bertha Marshall.
19. Marshall's Patent Freezer.
20. Frontispiece of *Mrs Beeton's Book of Household Management*.
21. Eliza Leslie.
22. Frontispiece and title page of Hannah Glasse's *The Art of Cookery Made Plain and Easy*.
23. Sarah Tyson Rorer.

Chapter Three

24. Alexandre Balthazar Laurent Grimod de La Reynière.
25. Jean Anthelme Brillat-Savarin.
26. Thomas Jefferson.
27. Samuel Fraunces.
28. Fraunces Tavern, New York, 1900.
29. Auguste Escoffier.
30. Jules Gouffé.

List of Illustrations

31. M.A. Carême.
32. Louis Eustache Ude.
33. Charles Elmé Francatelli.
34. Alexis Benoit Soyer.
35. Charles Ranhofer.
36. Delmonico's, New York, 1906.
37. William Gunter.
38. William Jarrin.

Chapter Four

39. Henry Jones' Western Biscuit Bakery.
40. Title page of Patrick Lamb's *Royal Cookery*.
41. Alexandre Dumas.
42. Sir Kenelm Digby.
43. William Kitchiner.
44. John Farley.
45 & 46. Francis Collingwood and John Woollams.

Bibliography

Academie Culinaire: Jules Gouffe, http://www.academieculinairedefrance.com/index.php?option=com_content&view=article&id=78:jules-gouffe&Itemid=120&lang=fr [accessed 22 January 2017].

Albala, Ken, *Cooking in Europe, 1250-1650* (Greenwood Press, 2006).

Albala, Ken, *The Banquet: Dining in the Great Courts of late Renaissance Europe* (USA: University of Illinois Press, 2007).

Alexander, Leslie and Rucker, Walter, eds., *Encyclopedia of African American History* (ABC-CLIO, 2010).

Alléno, Yannick and Brenot, Vincent, *Sauces: Reflexions of a Chef* (Paris: Hachette, 2014).

Allgemeine Literatur-Zeitung (Schwetschke: 1794).

Annual Biography and Obituary for the Year 1828, Vol 12 (London: Longman, Hurst, Rees, Orme and Brown, 1828).

Appert, Nicolas, *The Art of Preserving* (London: Black, Parry and Kingsbury, 1812).

Arber's Stationers' Registers 'Murrell's Works' *Quarterly Review* 3, 1894.

Bach, Rebecca Ann and Kennedy, Gwynne, eds., *Feminisms and Early Modern Texts: Essays for Phyllis Rackin* (New Jersey: Susquehanna University Press, 2010).

Baldwin, H., ed., *The Plays and Poems of William Shakspeare* (1790).

Barker, Hannah, *The Business of Women: Female Enterprise and Urban Development in Northern England, 1760-1830* (Oxford: Oxford University Press, 2006).

Bauer, Linda, *Capitol Hill Cooks: Recipes from the White House, Congress and all of the Past Presidents* (USA and Plymouth, UK: Taylor Trade Publications, 2010).

Beattie, John M., *The English Court in the Reign of George I* (Cambridge: Cambridge University Press, 1967).

Beauvilliers, Antoine B., *The Art of French Cookery* (London: Longman, 1827).

Bertelsen, Cynthia, *The American Boarding House, a Brief Introduction: The Case of Mary Randolph* (USA, 2016) https://gherkinstomatoes.com/2016/02/11/36008/ [accessed 20 November 2016].

Bibliography

Beeton, Isabella, *Mrs. Beeton's Book of Household Management* (London: Beeton, 1861).

Blackmore, Sir Richard, *A True and Impartial History of the Conspiracy Against the Person and Government of King William III, of Glorious Memory, in the Year 1695* (London: J. Knapton, 1723).

Blanchard, William, ed., *The Epicure's Year Book and Table Companion of 1869* (London: Bradbury, Evans, and Co, 1869).

Bradford, William and Deane, Charles, eds., *History of Plymouth Plantation* (Boston: Massachusettes Historical Society, 1856).

Brady, Patricia, *Martha Washington: An American Life* (New York: Penguin, 2006).

Brears, P., *Cooking and Dining in Medieval England* (London: Prospect Books, 2012).

Breverton, Terry, *The Tudor Kitchen* (Stroud: Amberley Publishing Limited, 2015).

Brillat-Savarin, Jean Anthelme, *The Physiology of Taste* (USA: Dover Publications, 2012).

Bucholz, R.O., *The Augustan Court: Queen Anne and the Decline of Court Culture* (California: Stanford University Press, 1993).

Carême, M. A., *The Royal Parisian Pastrycook and Confectioner* (London: Mason, 1834).

Carroll-Mann, Robin (pseud. Lady Brighid ni Chiarain), *An English translation of Ruperto de Nola's Libre del Coch*, http://www.florilegium.org/files/FOOD-MANUSCRIPTS/Guisados1-art.html [accessed 31 December 2016].

Carter, Charles, *The Compleat City and Country Cook* (London: Bettesworth & Hitch 1736).

Chadwick, Bruce, *The General and Mrs. Washington: The Untold Story of a Marriage and a Revolution* (Illinois: Sourcebooks Inc, 2007).

Charlot, Marjorie, *Did You Know?: Over One Hundred Facts About Haiti and Her Children* (Bloomington: iUniverse, 2015).

Casteau, Lancelot de, *Ouverture de Cuisine* (Liège: Leonard Streel, Licensed Printer, 1604).

Classen, Albrecht, *The Power of a Woman's Voice in Medieval and Early Modern Literatures* (Berlin: Walter de Gruyter, 2007).

Clermont, B., *The Professed Cook; or, The Modern Art of Cookery, Pastry and Confectionery* (London: C. Richards, 1812).

Coff, Christopher, *The Taste for Ethics: An Ethic of Food Consumption* (The Netherlands: Springer, 2006).

Collier, Kim S., *George Washington and the American Revolution* (USA: Library of Congress, 2010).

Collingwood, Francis and Woollams, John, *The Universal Cook, and City and Country Housekeeper* (London: J. Scatcherd, 1801).

Colt, Samuel, *Inventors and Inventions, Volume 1* (New York: Marshall Cavendish, 2008).

Country Life, Volume 174 (Country Life Ltd, 1983).

Coutts, Howard, *The Art of Ceramics: European ceramic design*, 1500-1830 (New Haven: Yale University Press, 2001).

Craughwell, Thomas J., *Thomas Jefferson's Crème Brûlée* (Quirk Books, 2012).

Czerniecki, Stanisław, *Compendium ferculorum albo zebranie potraw*, eds., Jaroslaw Dumanowski and Magdalena Spychaj (Warsaw: Muzeum Pałac w Wilanowie, 2012).

Dale, Rodney, *The Wordsworth Dictionary of Culinary and Menu Terms* (Hertfordshire: Wordsworth Editions Ltd, 2000).

David, Elizabeth, *Is There a Nutmeg in the House?* (London: Penguin, 2001).

David, Elizabeth and Norman, Jill, eds., *Harvest of the Cold Months: The Social History of Ice and Ices* (London: Faber and Faber, 2011).

Davidson, Alan 'Food: The Natural History of British Cookery Books', *The American Scholar* 52 (1983).

Davidson, Alan and Jaine, Tom, eds., *The Oxford Companion to Food* (Oxford: Oxford University Press, 2014).

Davis, Jennifer J., *Defining Culinary Authority: The Transformation of Cooking in France, 1650-1830* (Louisiana: LSU Press, 2013).

Deith, John and Walker, Harlan, eds., *Cooks and Other People: Proceedings of the Oxford Symposium on Food and Cookery, 1995* (Oxford: Oxford Symposium, 1996).

DeJean, Joan, *The Essence of Style: How the French Invented High Fashion, Fine Food, Chic Cafés, Style, Sophistication and Glamour* (Simon & Schuster, New York, 2007).

Diamond, Becky, *Mrs. Goodfellow: The Story of America's First Cooking School* (USA: Westholme Publishing, 2012).

Dickens, Charles, *All the Year Round*, Vol. 19 (London: Chapman & Hall, 1868).

Dickens, Charles, *The Life and Adventures of Nicholas Nickleby* (London: Chapman & Hall, 1839).

Dircks, Henry, *Inventors and Inventions* (London: E. and F. N. Spon, 1867).

Dods, Margaret [pseud. Christian Isobel Johnstone], *The Cook and Housewife's Manual* (Edinburgh, 1828).

Douglas, David Charles and English, George William, eds., *Historical Documents, 1042-1189* (London and New York: Routledge, 1996).

Driver, Elizabeth, *Culinary Landmarks: A Bibliography of Canadian Cookbooks, 1825-1949* (Toronto: University of Toronto Press, 2008).

Dumas, Alexandre, *Dictionary of Cuisine,* ed., Louise Colman (Oxford: Routledge, 2013).

Dumas, Alexandre, *Impressions of Travel, in Egypt and Arabia Petra* (London: J. S. Taylor, 1839).

Eales, Mary, *Mrs. Mary Eales's receipts* (London: J. Brindley, 1733).

Eriksson, Sofia and Hastie, Madelaine and Roberts, Tom, eds., *Eat History: Food and Drink in Australia and Beyond* (Newcastle: Cambridge Scholars Publishing, 2014).

Escoffier, Auguste, *A Guide to Modern Cookery* (Cambridge: Cambridge University Press, 2013).

Escoffier, Auguste, *Memories of My Life* (London: Wiley, 1996).

Farley, John, *The London Art of Cookery, and Housekeeper's Complete Assistant* (London: John Barker, 1800).

Feather, John, *A History of British Publishing* (London: Routledge, 2005).

Fernández y González, Manuel, *El cocinero de su majestad: Memorias del tiempo de Felipe III* (Madrid, 1907).

Fisker, Anna Marie and Olsen, Tenna Doktor, *Jules Gouffé* (Denmark: Aalborg University, 2012).

Fisher, Abby, *What Mrs. Fisher Knows About Old Southern Cooking,* ed., Karen Hess (Bedford USA: Applewood Books, 1995).

Fitch, Noel Riley, *The Grand Literary Cafés of Europe* (London: New Holland Publishers, 2006).

Flandrin, Jean-Louis and Montanari, Massimo, eds., *Food: A Culinary History* (New York and UK: Columbia University Press, 2013).

Fleming, Elise (pseud. Katharine, Dame Alys), *Sugar Paste: A Cook's 'Play Dough'*, http://damealys.medievalcookery.com/CooksPlayDough.html

Fletcher, Janet, *Cheese and Wine: A Guide to Selecting, Pairing and Enjoying* (San Francisco: Chronicle Books, 2011).

Francatelli, Charles Elmé, *The Modern Cook* (Massachusettes: Applewood Books, 2008).

Fraser's Magazine, Vol. 29 (London: G. W. Nickisson, 1844).

Garval, Michael, 'Alexis Soyer and the Rise of the Celebrity Chef', in *Romantic Circles* ed., Denise Gigante (North Carolina: North Carolina State University, 2007).

Georgescu, Sorina, '(Ex) Slave Identities Shaped by Journeys Abroad: African-American Frederick Douglass in his Autobiographies and Romanian Roma Slavedincă in Gheorghe Sion's Emanciparea Țiganilor', *University of Bucharest Review*, 10 (2008).

Gigante, Denise, *Gusto: Essential Writings in Nineteenth-Century Gastronomy* (New York and Oxford: Routledge, 2013).

Gilreath, James, ed., *Federal Copyright Records 1790-1800* (USA: Library of Congress, 1987).

Glasse, Hannah, *The Art of Cookery made Plain and Easy* (London: J. Rivington, 1788).

Gloger, Zygmunt, *Encyklopedia wiedzy o książce, Krakow-Warsaw* (Poland: Hieronim, 1971).

Goodfellow, Mrs, *Mrs. Goodfellow's Cookery as it Should Be* (Philadelphia: T. B. Peterson & Brothers, 1865).

Gouffé, Jules, *The Royal Cookery Book* (London: Sampson Low, Son, and Marston, 1869).

Grigson, Jane, *Jane Grigson's Fruit Book* (London: Atheneum Publishers, 1982).

Grizzard, Frank, *George Washington: A Biographical Companion* (Denver: ABC-CLIO, 2002).

Haff, Harry, *The Founders of American Cuisine* (North Carolina: McFarland & Co, 2011).

Bibliography

Haines, Pamela, *Tea at Gunter's* (London: Bloomsbury Reader, 2011).

Hanson, Neil, *The Custom of the Sea* (London: Random House, 2011).

Harbury, Katherine E., *Colonial Virginia's Cooking Dynasty* (South Carolina: University of South Carolina Press, 2004).

Harland, John and Turner Wilkinson, Thomas, *Lancashire Folklore, 1867* (Kessinger Publishing, 2003).

Hartley, Cathy, *A Historical Dictionary of British Women* (London: Europa Publications, 2003).

Hayden, Peter, 'The Fabriques of Antonin Carême', *Garden History*, 24 (1996).

Heath, Dwight, ed., *Mourt's Relation: A Journal of the Pilgrims of Plymouth* (Bedford, Massachusetts: Applewood Books, 1986).

Hess, Karen, ed., *American Cookery, Amelia Simmons* (Massachusetts: Applewood Books, 1996).

Hirschfeld, Fritz, *George Washington and Slavery: A Documentary Portrayal* (Columbia and London: University of Missouri Press, 1997).

Historic Genealogical Society, *The New England Historical and Genealogical Register*, Vol. 33 (1879, New England: Heritage Books, 1995).

Hooker, Richard James, *The Book of Chowder* (Boston: Harvard Common Press, 1978) .

Hosking, Richard, ed., *Food and Language: Proceedings of the Oxford Symposium on Food and Cooking* (Totnes: Prospect Books, 2010).

Hughes, Kathryn, *The Short Life and Long Times of Mrs Beeton* (London: Harper Collins, 2013).

Jaine, Tom, ed., *Oxford Dictionary of National Biography* (Oxford: Oxford University Press, 2004).

Janer, Zilkia, *Latino Food Culture* (Connecticut: Greenwood Press, 2008).

Jarrin, William Alexis, *The Italian Confectioner* (London: William Ainsworth, London 1827).

Jeanes, William, *Gunter's Modern Confectioner* (London: Dean and Son, 1870).

Jeffreys, Henry, *Empire of Booze* (London: Random House, 2016).

Ju Lin, Hsiang, Richard, *Slippery Noodles* (London: Prospect Books, 2015).

Kay, Emma, *Dining with the Georgians* (Gloucestershire: Amberley Publishing, 2014).

Kay, Emma, *Dining with the Victorians* (Gloucestershire: Amberley Publishing, 2015).

Kelby, Nicole, *White Truffles in Winter* (Surrey: Alma Books, 2012).

Kelly, Ian, *Cooking for Kings: The Life of the First Celebrity Chef Antonin Carême* (London: Short Books Ltd, 2004).

Kidder, Edward, *Receipts of Pastry and Cookery* (London: c1740)

Kimball, Marie, *Thomas Jefferson's Cook Book* (Ohio: James Direct, Inc, 2007).

Kitchiner, William, *The Cook's Oracle* (New York: Cosimo Inc, 2005).

Knight, Sir Kenelm Digby, *The Closet of Sir Kenelm Digby Knight Opened* (Tredition, Germany 2012).

Krondl, Michael, *Sweet Invention: A History of Dessert* (Chicago: Chicago Review Press, 2011).

Lamb, Patrick, *Royal Cookery; or, The Complete Court-Cook* (London: printed for Maurice Atkins, 1710).

Lancet, The, Vol. 2 (London: John Churchill 1845).

Landau, Barry H., *The President's Table: Two Hundred Years of Dining and Diplomacy* (New York: Harper Collins, 2011).

Lancaster, Bruce and Plumb, John Harold, *The American Revolution* (Boston: Houghton Mifflin Harcourt, 2001).

Leeming, H., 'A 17th-Century Polish Cookery Book and Its Russian Manuscript Translation', *The Slavonic and East European Review*, 52 (1974).

Leslie, Eliza, *Miss Leslie's Behaviour Book* (Philadelphia: T. B. Peterson and Bros, 1839).

Leslie, Eliza, *Seventy-Five Receipts for Pastry, Cakes and Sweetmeats* (Boston: Munroe and Francis, 1836).

Lewis, Alonzo and Newhall, James, *History of Lynn, Essex County, Massachusetts, 1629-1864* (Massachusetts: George C Herbert, 1890).

Library and Museum of Freemasonry, *catalogue 1802-1883 BE 18CAT*, http://freemasonry.london.museum/archives [accessed 25 January, 2017].

London Magazine, Or Gentleman's Monthly, Vol. 48 (London: R. Baldwin, 1779).

Lune, Pierre de, *Le Cuisinier*, in *L'Art de la cuisine française au XVII* (Paris: Payot and Rivages, 1995).

Lyon, Earl, 'Roger De Ware, Cook', *Modern Language Notes*, Vol. 52 (1937), pp.491-94.

Mac Con Mairtın, Iomaire, 'Haute cuisine restaurants in nineteenth and twentieth century Ireland', *Proceedings of the Royal Irish Academy*, Vol. 115C, (2015).

Machet, J. J., *Le confiseur moderne ou l'Art du confiseur et du distillateur* (Paris: Chez Maradan, 1821).

MacIver, Susanna, *Cookery and Pastry As Taught and Practised by Mrs. MacIver* (London: C. Eliot and T. Kay, 1789).

Maroney, Stephanie R., *To Make a Curry the India Way: Tracking the Meaning of Curry Across Eighteenth-Century Communities* in 'Food and Foodways. Explorations in the History and Culture of Human Nourishment,' *Food Globality and Foodways Localities* 19 (2011).

Markham, Gervase, *Countrey Contentments, or The English Housewife*, ed., Michael R. Best (London: By John Beale, for R. Jackson, and are to be sold at his shop neere Fleet-streete Conduit, 1623).

Marshall, Agnes B., *The Book of Ices* (London: Marshall's School of Cookery, 1857).

Mary Hamilton Papers, Correspondence from Elizabeth Maria Rundell, Letter 30 April, 1787. Ref: GB 133 HAM/1/8/6/1. In University of Manchester Archives [online]. 20 December, 2016. Available from: http://www.library.manchester.ac.uk/search-resources/guide-to-special-collections/uomarchives/

Massialot, François, *The Court and the Country Cook* (London: A. & J. Churchill, M. Gillyflower, 1702).

May, Robert, *The Accomplisht Cook* (London: 1660).

Mays, Dorothy A., *Women in early America: Struggle, Survival, and Freedom in a New World* (California ABC-CLIO, 2004).

McClusky, Peter, *Ontario Garlic: The Story from Farm to Festival* (Charlston, USA: History Press, 2015).

McIntosh, Marjorie Keniston, *Working Women in English Society*, 1300-1620 (Cambridge: Cambridge University Press, 2005).

McKearin, Helen, 'Notes On Stopping, Bottling and Binning', *Journal of Glass Studies*, 13 (1971).

McWilliams, Mark, *Food and the Novel in Nineteenth-Century America* (Maryland: Rowman AltaMira, 2012).

Mennell, Stephen, *All Manners of Food: Eating and Taste in England and France from the Middle Ages to the Present* (Urbana and Chicago: University of Illinois Press, 1996).

Meltzer, Milton, ed., *Mark Twain Himself: A Pictorial Biography* (Columbia and London: University of Missouri Press, 2002).

Metzner, Paul, *Crescendo of the Virtuoso: Spectacle, Skill and Self-Promotion in Paris During the Age of Revolution* (California: University of California Press, 1998).

Mollard, John, *The Art of Cookery Made Easy and Refined* (London: J. Nunn, 1802).

Molokhovets, Elena, *Classic Russian Cooking* (Bloomington and Indianapolis: Indiana University Press 1998).

Montagne, Prosper and Snyder Turgeon, Charlotte *The New Larousse Gastronomique* (London: Crown Publishers, 1977).

Montiño, Francisco Martínez, *Arte de cocina, pasteleria, vizcocheria, y conserveria* (Imprenta de Pantaleon Aznar, 1778).

Morris, Helen Soutar, *Portrait of a Chef: The Life of Alexis Soyer, Sometime Chef to the Reform Club* (Cambridge: Cambridge University Press, 2013).

Moshenska, Joe, *A Stain in the Blood, the Remarkable Voyage of Sir Kenelm Digby* (London: William Heinemann, 2016).

Murrell, John, *A New Booke of Cookerie* (London: 1615).

Nadeau, Carolyn A., 'Spanish Culinary History in "Cervantes", "Bodas de Camacho" and Revista Canadiense de Estudios Hispánicos' 29, *Invierno* (2005).

National Folk Museum of Korea, 'Encyclopedia of Korean Seasonal Customs', Vol. 1 (Korea, 2014).

Newman, Jacqueline M., 'Yuan Mei: China's Greatest Gastronome' *Food in History,* 17, (2010).

Newnham-Davis, Lieut.-Col. Nathaniel, *Dinners and Diners: Where and How to Dine in London* (London: Grant Richards, 1899).

Nott, John, *The Cooks and Confectioners Dictionary* (London: C. Rivington, 1723).

Nutt, Frederick, *The Complete Confectioner: Or, The Whole Art of Confectionary Made Easy* (London, Richard Scott, 1807).

O'Brien, Charmaine, *The Colonial Kitchen: Australia 1788-1901* (Lanham: Maryland: Rowman and Littlefield, 2016).

Olsen, Kirstin, *Cooking with Jane Austen* (London and Connecticut: Greenwood Publishing group, 2005).

Pae-yong Yi, *Women in Korean History* (Seoul: Ewha Woman's University Press, 2008).

Palmer, Samuel, *St Pancras, Memoranda Relating to the Parish* (London: Field and Turr, 1870).

Parloa Maria, *Appledore Cook Book* (Massachusetts: Applewood Books, 2008).

Parloa, Maria, *Camp Cookery: How to Live in Camp* (Boston: Estes and Lauriat, 1878).

Pennell, S. M., 'Mary Eales', in *Oxford Dictionary of National Biography* (Oxford: Oxford University Press, 2004).

Encarnación Pinedo, *Reminiscences of Life in Alta California* (1901), Santa Clara University Library, Archives & Special Collections. http://content.scu.edu/cdm/ref/collection/pinedo/id/1092

Pae-Yong Yi, *Women in Korean History*, 한국 역사 속의 여성들 by Ewha (Korea: Womans University Press, 2008).

Poole, William, *Milton and the Idea of the Fall* (Cambridge: Cambridge University Press, 2005).

Pope-Hennessy, Una, *Charles Dickens* (Edinburgh: R & R Clark, 1947).

Prairie Farmer, The, (Chicago: Prairie Farmer Publishing Company, 1867).

Punch, Vol. 52 (London, 1867).

Pyne, William Henry, *Wine and Walnuts* (London: Longman, Hurst, Rees, Orme and Brown, 1823).

Rabisha, William, *The Whole Body of Cookery Dissected, Taught and Fully Manifested* (London: E. Calvert, 1673).

Radcliffe Culinary Times, Vol. 8 (Radcliffe Culinary friends of the Schlesinger Library, 1999).

Raffald, Elizabeth, *The Experienced English Housekeeper* (London: R. Baldwin, 1786).

Randolph, Mary, *The Virginia Housewife* (Baltimore: John Plaskitt, 1836).

Ranhofer, Charles, *The Epicurean, A Complete Treatise of Analytical and Practical Studies on the Culinary Art* (Chicago: Hotel Monthly Press, 1920).

'Reports of Cases in Chancery, argued and determined' in *Rolls Court during the time of Lord Langdale, Master of the Rolls [1838-1866], Volume 23* (London: Saunders and Benning, 1858).

Roberts, J., *The History of the Life and Reign of Queen Anne* (London: William Taylor, 1722).

Rojek, Chris, 'Celebrity', in *Wiley Blackwell Encyclopedia of Consumption and Consumer Studies,* eds., Daniel Thomas Cook and J. Michael Ryan (London: Wiley and Sons, 2015).

Rorer, Mrs S. T., *Mrs. Rorer's Philadelphia Cook Book* (Philadelphia: Arnold and Company, 1886).

Rundell, Maria Eliza, *Mrs. Rundell's Domestic Cookery* (London: Routledge, Warnes and Routledge, 1859).

Salter, James and Salter, Kay, *Life is Meals: A Food Lover's Book of Days* (USA: Pan Macmillan, 2014).

Sandford, Francis, *The History of the Coronation of James II, King of England, Scotland etc.* (London: Newcomb, 1687).

Sage, Lorna and Greer, Germaine and Showalter, Elaine, *The Cambridge Guide to Women's Writing in English* (Cambridge: Cambridge University Press, 1999).

Schwartz, Stuart B., *Tropical Babylons: Sugar and the Making of the Atlantic World, 1450-1680,* (California: University of North Carolina Press, 2004).

Scully, Terence, *The Opera of Bartolomeo Scappi (1570): L'arte et prudenza d'un maestro cuoco, 'The Art and Craft of a Master Cook'* (Canada: University of Toronto Press 2011).

Sedgwick, Romney, 'The Duke of Newcastle's Cook', *History Today,* 5: (1955).

Senn, Charles, *The Book of Sauces* (Chicago: The Hotel Monthly Press, Chicago, 1915).

Shapiro, Laura, *Perfection Salad: Women and Cooking at the Turn of the Century* (California: University of California Press, 2008).

Skelly, Carole J., *Dictionary of Herbs, Spices, Seasonings, and Natural Flavorings* (New York: Routledge, 2013).

Smith, Andrew, F., ed., *The Oxford Companion to American Food and Drink* (New York: Oxford University Press, 2007).

Smith, Michael Stephen, *The Emergence of Modern Business Enterprise in France, 1800-1930*, (USA: Harvard Uni Press, 2006).

Smythe, Colin, 'Charles Elmé Francatelli, Crockford's and the Royal Connection', *Petits Propos Culinaires* 101, 2014.

Snodgrass, Mary Ellen, *Encyclopaedia of Kitchen History* (New York and London: Routledge, 2004).

Soyer Alexis Bénoit, *A Shilling Cookery for the People* (London: Routlede & Co, 1854).

Stephen, Leslie Sir, *Dictionary of National Biography* (London: Smith, Elder & Company, 1897).

Stirling, R.A., *Philip IV and the Government of Spain, 1621-1665*, (Cambridge: Cambridge University Press, 2002).

Strehl, Dan, ed., *Encarnación's Kitchen: Mexican Recipes from Nineteenth Century California* (California: University of California Press, 2005).

Sussex Archaeological Society, *Sussex Archaeological Collections Relating to the History and Antiquities of the County* (Sussex, 1857).

Symons, Michael, *One Continuous Picnic: A Gastronomic History of Australia* (Australia: Melbourne University, 2007).

Symons, Michael, *A History of Cooks and Cooking* (USA: University of Illinois Press, 2004).

Tadmor, Naomi, *Family and Friends in Eighteenth-Century England* (Cambridge: Cambridge University Press, 2001).

Takats, Sean, *The Expert Cook in Enlightenment France* (Baltimore: JHU Press, 2011).

Theophano, Janet, *Eat my words: Reading Women's lives through the cookbooks they wrote* (New York: Palgrave Macmillan, 2002).

Thick, Malcolm, *Sir Hugh Plat: The Search for Useful Knowledge in Early Modern London* (London: Prospect Books, 2010).

Tillinghast, Mary, *The True Way of Preserving and Candying* (London, 1695).

Timbs, John, *Nooks and Corners of English Life, Past and Present*, (London: Griffith and

Farran, 1867).

Townscend, F. M. and Grigg, Milton and Kocher, Lawrence, *Coke-Garrett House Architectural Report, Block 27 Building I Lot 279-280,* Colonial Williamsburg Foundation Library Research Report Series, 1510 (Williamsburg, Virginia, 1990).

Travitsky, Betty and Prescott, Anne, *Seventeenth-Century English Recipe Books* (Hants: Ashgate Publishing Ltd, 2008).

Trotti, Michael, *The Body in the Reservoir: Murder & Sensationalism in the South* (USA: University of North Carolina Press, 2008).

Trubek, Amy B., *Haute Cuisine: How the French Invented the Culinary Profession* (Philadelphia: University of Pennsylvania Press, 2000).

Ude, Louis Eustache, *The French Cook* (London: John Ebers, 1822).

Verrall, William, *A Complete System of Cookery* (London, 1759).

Vernon, James, ed., *Letters Illustrative of the Reign of William III, from 1696 to 1708, Volume I* (London: Henry Colburn, 1841)

Waley-Cohen, Joanna, 'Celebrated Cooks of China's past', *Food In History*, 14 (2007).

Walsby, Malcolm and Constantinidou, Natasha, eds., *Documenting the Early Modern Book World* (BRILL, 2013).

Walsh, Robert and Littell, Eliakim and Smith, John Jay, eds., *The Museum of Foreign Literature, Science and Art,* Vol. 27 (Philadelphia: Adam Waldie, 1835).

Weaver, William, *America's First Book of Botanic Healing*, 1762-1778 (London and NY: Routledge, 2001).

Weigley, Emma Seifrit, 'It Might Have Been Euthenics: The Lake Placid Conferences and the Home Economics Movement', *American Quarterly,* 26 (1974).

Whitaker, Arnold, *English Cookery Books* (Germany: DOGMA, Germany, 2012).

Wilde, Oscar, *A Critic in Pall Mall: Being Extracts from Reviews and Miscellanies* (Start USA: Publishing, 2012).

Willan, Anne, *The Country Cooking of France* (San Francisco: Chronicle Books, 2012),

Willan, Anne and Cherniavsky, Mark, *The Cookbook Library* (California: University of California Press, 2012).

Wilson, Mary Tolford, 'Amelia Simmons Fills a Need: American Cookery, 1796', *The*

Bibliography

William and Mary Quarterly 14 (1957).

Wilson, Mary Tolford, ed., *The First American Cookbook: A Facsimile of 'American Cookery', 1796* (New York: Dover Publications, 1958).

Yearn-hong, Choi 'Jang Gye-hyang: Joseon's poetess, first cookbook author and philanthropist', *Korea Times*, 19 December 2014.

Zeldin, Theodore, *A History of French Passions 1848-1945: Intellect, Taste and Anxiety* (Oxford: Clarendon Press, 1993).

Web Resources

British Newspaper Archive http://www.britishnewspaperarchive.co.uk/

Library of Congress, Historic American Newspapers http://chroniclingamerica.loc.gov

Trove, National Library of Australia http://trove.nla.gov.au/newspaper

Yale Center for British Art http://britishart.yale.edu/collections/search

Library of Congress https://www.loc.gov

Index

Accomplisht Cook, The 29, 30, 109
Africa, 12, 21, 123, 185
Almanach des Gourmands, 116
America, 19-21, 27, 64-66, 81-83, 85-87, 92, 100-102, 106, 125, 153, 174, 199
American Cookery, 63, 79, 81, 82-83, 85, 87, 100, 102-104, 110
Appert, Nicolas, 14, 167-169
Armitages, The, 66
Art of Cookery, 65, 102-103
Arte de Cozina, Pasteleria Vizcocheria y Conserveria, 59-61
Art of Preserving all kinds of animal and vegetable substances for several years, 168
Ascott Park, 29
Asia, 43, 165-167
Australia, 69-73, 105

Bacon, Nathaniel, 21
Balzac, 49, 126
Beauvilliers, Antoine, 14, 113, 125-126
Béchamel, 18, 52
Beeton, Isabella, 10, 14, 68, 95-97
Bibendum, 114
Book of Household Management, 96,
Boston Cooking School, 87
Bradford, William, 63
Brillat-Savarin, Jean Anthelme 117-118

Café Procope, 48
Carter, Charles, 179-180
Centlivre, 183
Charles II, 35, 181
Chaucer, Geoffrey, 12
Chinese, 43, 165-167
Chinese food, 113, 165-167
Cleland, Elizabeth, 109
Clouet, Pierre, 175, 177
Collingwood, Francis, 202
Colonists, 21, 62, 64
Compendium ferculorum, 53
Complete Confectioner, 191
Complete System of Cookery, A, 175-177, 211
Cooks and Confectioners Dictionary, 189
Cook's Oracle, 199, 200
crème brulee, 50
Crockford's Club, 140, 141
Cuisinier françois, Le 49-51, 52
Czerniecki, Stanisław, 53-54

Index

Davey, Thomas, 171-172
Dawson, Thomas, 19, 36
de Casteau, Lancelot, 54-55
de la Varenne, François Pierre, 49-52, 191
de Lune, Pierre, 188-189
de Nola, Ruperto, 61
Delmonico's. 152-156, 186, 207
Denis, Diderot, 49
Dewe, Thomas, 25
Dickens, Charles, 147, 154, 183, 200
Digby, Sir Kenelm, 193-194
Dincă, 212
Dods, Margaret, 108-111
Don Quixote, 60
Donkin, Bryan, 168
Dormer family, 29
Dumas, Alexandre, 185
Dundee School of Cookery, 69
Durand, Peter, 167-168

Eales, Mary, 186-188
Eccles cake, 77
El Cocinero Español, 73-74
Escoffier, Auguste, 14, 127-132, 197

Farley, John, 201, 202
Farmer, Fannie, 86-90, 91
Fisher, Abby, 85-86
Fitz-Stephen, William, 11
Francatelli, Charles Elmé, 143-146
France Gastronomique, La 114

Fraunces, Samuel, 122-125
Freemasons' Tavern, 208
French Cook, The, 142

George Pudding, 80
Georgian, 7, 14, 27, 69, 80, 149, 153, 175, 191
Germany, 37, 39, 95, 113, 130, 190,
Glasse, Hannah, 14, 63, 65, 100, 102-104, 190
Gonzalez, Manuel, 59
Goodfellow, Elizabeth, 99-101,
Gouffé, Jules, 132-135
Gourmandism, 117
Granado, Diego, 61
Grande Taverne de Londres, 125-126
Grimod de La Reynière, Alexandre Balthazar Laurent, 14, 113, 115-117
Guide Culinaire, 128-130
Gunter's, 158-162
Gunter, William, 158-162
Gunter's Confectioner's Oracle, 160
Gye-hyang, Jang, 43-44

Hall, John, 168
Harvey, Peter, 211
Haute Cuisine, 88, 112, 114, 171,
Hemmings, James, 119, 121-123
Hercules, 119-123

International Exposition, 134
Ireland, 17, 35, 62, 73, 148-149,

Index

170,
Italian Confectioner, 162, 165
Italians, 36, 44, 48, 49, 55, 112, 143-146

Jarrin, William, 162-165
Jean, le Rond d'Alembert, 49
Jeanes, William, 161
Jefferson, Thomas, 97, 121-122
Johnstone, Christina J, 108-111
Johnson, Samuel, 102
Jones, Henry, 172-175
Jumberlie, 86

Karim, Abdul, 145
Kidder, Edward, 30-35
King William, 181
Kitchiner, William, 191
Korean, 43
Kuchmistrzostwo, 53

Laguipierre, Dartoise, 137, 138, 206-207
Lamb, Patrick, 181-183,
Lancet, The, 174
Leslie, Eliza, 97-99
Libre del coch, 61-62
Libro del arte de cozina, 61
Livre de cuisine, 135
London Tavern, The, 128, 201-202, 207, 210
Louis XIV, 49

Machet, Jean Jacques, 191-192
MacIver, Susanna, 109
Manchester, 75-76, 78

March-Pane, 33
Marco G. Frederick, 170
Marie-Antoine or Antonin Carême, 136-140
Marin, François, 139
Markham, Gervase, 22, 25, 26-27
Marquis d'Uxelles, 52
Marshall, Agnes Bertha, 90-95
Marshall's School of Cookery, 90, 94
Massialot, François, 49-50
May, Robert, 20, 28-30, 109
Mei, Yuan, 165-167
Melbourne Working Men's College, 70
Memories of My Life, 128, 212
Menier, 156-158
Menon, 205-206
Michelin Guide, 114
Middle East, 21, 55, 185
Modern Cook, 146
Mollard, John, 207-210
Montino, Francisco Martinez, 59-60
Murrell, John, 22-25

Napoleon, 135, 138, 141, 154, 169, 206, 207
National Portrait Gallery, 96
National School for Cookery, 69
Native Americans, 21, 63-64
New York, 105, 123, 124, 152-153,
Nott, John, 189-191
Nouvelle Cuisine, 177, 205

Index

Nouveau cuisinier, Le 189
Nutt, Frederick, 191-192

Opera dell'arte del cucinare, 44, 46
Ouverture de cuisine, 54, 56

Parks, William, 80-81
Paris, 48-49, 92, 94, 117, 126, 132-134, 136, 138, 139, 157, 159, 170, 179, 189, 212
Paris Jockey Club, 133-134
Parloa, Maria, 104-106
Pâtissier royal parisien, Le 139, 227
Partridge, John, 36
Pearson, Margaret, 68-72
Pêche Melba, 130-132
Pepys, Samuel, 30
Physiologie du goût, 118
Pinedo, Encarnación, 73-75
Plagiarism, 26, 180
Plat, Hugh, 11, 20, 21, 22-23,
Poland, 54
Potatoes Fried in Slices or Shavings, 199
Prince Curnonsky, 113
Procopio dei Coltelli, Francesco, 48-49
Punch, 159

Queen Anne, 182-183
Queen Victoria, 14, 132, 144, 145, 172

Rabisha, William, 34, 35-36

Raffald, Elizabeth, 75-77, 90, 100
Randolph, Mary, 83-85
Ranhofer, Charles, 151-156
Reform Club, 144, 151, 196
Renaissance, 13, 20, 21, 22, 26, 55, 189, 204
Revolutionary War, 123
Ritz, César, 128-130
Rosół, 54
Rundell, Maria, 78-79

Sailland, Maurice, 113
Savoy Hotel, 128, 130, 132
Scappi, Bartolomeo, 44-45
Schellhammer, Maria Sophia, 37-40
Scotland, 69, 71-73
Self-Raising Flour, 172-175
Senn, Charles Herman, 195-197
Sherman, William, 65-66
Shilling Cookery for the People, 148-149
Simmons, Amelia, 63, 65, 80-83, 110
Simpson, John, 211
Simpson's, 171-172
Slavery, 85, 119-120, 212
Solomongundy, 210, 211-212
Soyer, Alexis Benoist, 146-151
Spanish, 55, 59, 60-62,
Speck, George, 199
Squanto, 63-64
Suiyuan, Shidan, 165, 167

Thanksgiving, 64
Tillinghast, Mary, 203-204,

Timbs, John, 33
Trifle, 36, 163
Twain, Mark, 154
Tyson, Rorer Sarah, 106-108

Ude, Louis Eustache, 14, 65,
  140-143
Unglerowa, Helen, 53
Universal Cook, 202
Universal Cookery and Food,
Association, 195, 196

Verrall, William, 175-177
Versailles, 49, 140
Victorian, 41, 68, 78, 90, 95, 147-148,
  159, 162, 171-172,
Virginia House-Wife, The, 83-84
Voltaire, 49

Wales, 17, 159, 172, 175
Warburton, 75, 76
Washington, George, 119-120
Weckerin, Anna, 39
Wellcome Library, 32, 79
Wetten, Peter, 191
*What Mrs Fisher Knows about Old
Southern Cooking,* 85-86
White Hart Inn, 175-176
Winslow, Edward, 63
Woollams, John, 202-203
Woolley, Hannah, 20, 41-43
Worshipful Company of Cooks, 11